Praise for *Reach All Readers*

"*Reach All Readers* is a gift for elementary teachers—and their students! Anna Geiger deftly packs the what, why, and how of the science of reading into one user-friendly, empowering book that you'll keep coming back to again and again."

—Kate Winn,
Teacher & Host of IDA Ontario's Reading Road Trip Podcast

"We've long needed *Reach All Readers*, a book on effective reading instruction written for teachers, by a teacher. Anna presents what she's learned about the science of reading and instruction in an accessible and useful text. You'll want to read it cover-to-cover, discuss chapters with colleagues, and hang on to it as a reference book."

—Margaret Goldberg,
Co-founder of The Right to Read Project

"Anna Geiger doesn't just present the science; she equips educators with practical strategies and resources, translating them into actionable knowledge that can be readily applied in the classroom. Whether you're a seasoned teacher or just starting out, this book empowers you to become a more informed and effective practitioner. Aptly named, *Reach All Readers* illustrates Geiger's knack for making the science of reading less "science-y.""

—Faith Borkowsky,
Founder of High Five Literacy, LLC, Author, and Co-host of The Literacy View Podcast

"Anna has been able to capture the complexities of implementing the science of reading and make it seem simple and tangible to any educator who wants to make a difference in the lives of their students. This will make a perfect book study text for schools and teachers across the country."

—Brent Conway,
Assistant Superintendent, Pentucket Regional School District

"My own science of reading journey is a lot like Anna's; I put a lot of hours into self-education. I wish this book was available when I started! It's established that students learn to read best when their teachers follow a strong scope and sequence and provide direct, systematic instruction. Teachers learning about the science of reading need the same. Every page and chapter of *Reach All Readers* equips teachers to best serve all students. As an SOR geek I couldn't put it down. As a dedicated practitioner, I will return to it often."

—Virginia Quinn-Mooney,
*Host of Science of Reading Happy Hour, Moderator and Group Expert for
"What I Should Have Learned in College"*

"Anna's clear and concise writing makes complex topics easy to understand. Packed with valuable info, her book is a go-to resource for elementary teachers and deserves a spot on your bookshelf."

—Lindsay Kemeny,
*Author of 7 Mighty Moves: Research-Backed, Classroom-Tested Strategies to Ensure K-to-3
Reading Success*

Reach All Readers

Reach All Readers

USING THE SCIENCE OF READING TO TRANSFORM
YOUR LITERACY INSTRUCTION

ANNA GEIGER

JB JOSSEY-BASS™
A Wiley Brand

Library of Congress Cataloging-in-Publication Data is Available

ISBN 9781394205653 (Paperback)
ISBN 9781394205660 (epdf)
ISBN 9781394205677 (epub)

Cover Design: Wiley

SKY10077385_061724

For Kate,
my sister and friend

Contents

Chapter 7   Vocabulary   **159**
            How to Decide Which Words to Teach: The Three Word Tiers   160
            Teaching Individual Tier Two Words   162
            Teaching Tier Three Words   165
            Teaching Word-Learning Strategies   168
            Key Things to Remember   172
            Free resources   172
            Learn More   172
            Notes   172

Chapter 8   Comprehension   **175**
            What Is Comprehension?   175
            Teaching Sentence Comprehension   180
            Reading Comprehension Strategies   185
            Putting It All Together   195
            Key Things to Remember   197
            Learn More   197
            Free Resources   197
            Notes   198

Chapter 9   Linking Reading and Writing   **201**
            Teach Handwriting   202
            Teach Spelling   203
            Teach Students to Write About What They Read   206
            Teach That Sentences Contain a "Who" and a "Do"   206
            Teach Students to Expand Simple Sentences   207
            Teach Students to Combine Sentences   210
            Teach Students to Connect Sentences   210
            Teach Students to Write Paragraphs   212
            Other Ways for Students to Respond to Text in Writing   214
            Key Things to Remember   214
            Free Resources   214
            Learn More   215
            Notes   215

Chapter 10   Dyslexia   **217**
            What Is Dyslexia?   217
            Help for Dyslexia   222

Foreword

Let me tell you a story. It begins with an elementary school teacher who is committed to supporting her students to become skilled readers and writers. She spends years perfecting what she learned in college, by creating a literacy-rich environment and sparking a love of reading. She trusts her intuition and lets her students lead the way.

Then one day, she reads something that calls into question everything she believes to be true about how children learn to read and how reading should be taught. At first, she smugly dismisses this new information as false. But in the back of her mind, she is haunted by the students she hasn't been able to reach. And so, the investigation begins.

The teacher discovers information about reading that is different from what she was previously taught. She uncovers research that causes her to realize that the craft she has been perfecting has flaws, and that there might be a more effective approach. The teacher experiences a range of emotions that include anger, regret, shame, and ultimately fierce motivation to learn as much as she can about the science of reading.

Does this story sound familiar to you? As a teacher-educator in the graduate reading science program at Mount St. Joseph University, this story is painfully familiar to me. It is the story I hear over and over and over again from countless passionate, committed, skilled, veteran teachers. Anna Geiger was one of those teachers. Over the years, I've watched Anna grapple with the reading research and learn to share her new understanding with me and with others in her coursework, her blog, her podcast, and now in her book, *Reach All Readers*.

So, how did we get here? Why is Anna's story of learning, unlearning, and relearning familiar to so many educators? By way of explanation, the book begins with a brief but captivating journey through the history of the reading wars. Information about reading instruction is contextualized within the science of learning. Practical applications to the classroom and direct contrasts between balanced literacy and structured literacy punctuate the key research findings about how children learn to read and the elements of effective instruction.

The central content of the book is structured into chapters on each of the essential early literacy skills—oral language, phonemic awareness, phonics, fluency, vocabulary, reading comprehension—with an additional chapter on the link between reading and writing. These chapters are full of brief, relevant research summaries and practical applications to the classroom. The information will empower educators to understand how research works, and how it can be used to improve reading outcomes. Teachers will appreciate the many step-by-step guides, sample lesson plans, and links to additional resources included in each chapter.

Throughout the book, explanations of how research-aligned instruction differs from the all-too-common balanced literacy approach clarify the actions teachers can take to get better results. But simply knowing the research isn't sufficient. To support implementation of research-aligned instruction in schools, the final two chapters on dyslexia and multi-tiered systems of support focus on building a system that meets the needs of all learners. The content on using assessment within a collaborative problem-solving model for building a tiered system of instruction and intervention is particularly useful. Teachers will appreciate the practical suggestions on topics such as flexible grouping, intentional scheduling, careful program selection, and differentiation of classroom instruction.

While reading *Reach All Readers,* teachers will recognize that Anna has been exactly where they are on this transformational journey, which makes her the perfect guide to illuminate the next steps. The book will be useful to everyone who wants a practical resource for digesting the research and putting it into practice in schools. I hope other teacher-educators will recognize the role the book can play in teacher preparation.

Whether you are just beginning your journey toward the reading research or are responsible for guiding others, you can rely on *Reach All Readers* to provide the right balance of knowledge and application. Anna and I share the goals of accelerating the learning trajectory of current educators and preventing future teachers from repeating her painful story. I am honored to elevate this book as part of the solution.

Dr. Stephanie Stollar
Part-time Assistant Professor, Mount St. Joseph University
Founder of the Reading Science Academy

Acknowledgments

I am forever grateful to my husband, Steve, for his never-ending patience and love, and to Eliana, Isaiah, Micah, Josiah, Mariah, and Elisha, who obligingly stopped playing the piano or bouncing a basketball in the kitchen so I could write without distractions. I am also thankful for my mom's generosity in caring for my children, so that I am able to attend out-of-town conferences to learn from the experts in person.

I am immensely grateful for Emily Hanford's reporting, which broke through my stubbornness and led me down a path I never foresaw; I'm never going back. I appreciate everyone who patiently spoke with me in the early days as I struggled to let go of practices that I'd held dear for decades: Mitchell Brookins, Emily Gibbons, Jocelyn Seamer, Deedee Wills, Jean Gunderson, Sue Brokmeier, and countless others.

Endless thanks goes to the many experts who have taken an hour out of their day to join me for a podcast interview; they are my teachers.

I am so thankful to those who generously gave their time to review a chapter: Savannah Campbell, Martha Kovack, Christina Winter, Amie Burkholder, Stephanie Stollar, Lindsay Kemeny, Nathaniel Swain, and Heather O'Donnell.

I owe special thanks to Stephanie Stollar, who has taught me so much through her Reading Science Academy, and who wrote the foreword for this book. She is always generous with her time and resources, and I continue to learn from her.

I couldn't have taken a year to write a book without the support of my incredible team, who in addition to their regular work painstakingly read and reviewed every chapter: Laura Cherney, Rachel Boerner, Heather Groth, René Parsons, and Regina Hendricks.

Thank you to the many others who shared opinions and suggestions, including Rachel Beiswanger, Kate Winn, Stephanie Darling, Jessica Farmer, Elise Lovejoy, Lexi O'Brien, Sara Marye, Sarah Paul, and Gin Quinn-Mooney.

Thank you also to Sam Ofman, Moses Ashirvad, Kezia Endsley, Christina Verigan, Sharmila Srinivasan, and the rest of the Wiley team for bringing this book to life.

Most of all, I thank my Savior, Jesus, who has blessed me beyond measure.

About the Author

Anna Geiger, M.Ed., is a former teacher with classroom experience from first through fifth grade. She currently serves educators through her website, The Measured Mom, where she has shared hands-on lessons, thoughtful articles, and printable resources since 2013.

Anna is Orton-Gillingham certified and has earned a Reading Science graduate certificate from Mount St. Joseph University. She hosts a weekly podcast called *Triple R Teaching*, provides thousands of resources to members of her membership site for PreK–3rd grade educators, and is a frequent presenter at virtual workshops, summits, and conferences.

Introduction

I began my teaching career in 1999, just a few years after Irene Fountas and Gay Su Pinnell published their first edition of *Guided Reading*. I read Lucy Calkins' *The Art of Teaching Reading* on a Florida beach, highlighting passages as I imagined how magical my classroom would be after spring break. Running records, miscue analysis, and other practical topics in my master's degree program only fueled my excitement.

I didn't use research articles to study the efficacy of a theory or method. Instead, I trusted my professors, my favorite authors, my experience, and my intuition.

I clung to the mantra that I knew my students best. I envisioned researchers as technicians in lab coats who hadn't spent a day in the classroom. How could their studies contradict what I knew to be true based on my own experience and others' anecdotal evidence?

Research professor Mark Seidenberg described my point of view perfectly: "The scientific perspective is seen as sterile and reductive, incapable of capturing the ineffable character of the learning moment or the chemistry of a successful classroom."[1]

When I first read the transcript of Emily Hanford's audio documentary "At a Loss for Words," I didn't take it seriously. In the documentary she criticized three-cueing, which was central to my beliefs about teaching reading. Surely a journalist couldn't know more than experienced teachers! As I reread the transcript, however, I began to question what I had believed for so long.

This led me on an unexpected journey of relearning what it means to teach reading well.

This is the book that I wish I'd had as a reading teacher! In its pages I explain why many of the balanced literacy practices I held dear do not align with research. I provide summaries in key areas of the science of reading and include practical routines, tips, and strategies to give you a clear path forward.

How This Book Is Organized

Chapter 1 provides an overview of the reading wars and a summary of how the brain learns to read. I share important theories that provide the background knowledge you'll need for the chapters that follow.

Chapter 2 explains why the knowledge of how students learn to read isn't enough to teach literacy. Teachers also need to understand how students *learn*—and how best to teach them. The importance of explicit instruction and frequent review are emphasized in this chapter and throughout the book.

Oral language is the foundation of literacy. Chapter 3 highlights the complexity of oral language and provides practical ways to make your classroom language-rich.

Chapter 4 explains how phonemic awareness develops and lists step-by-step routines for building phonemic awareness and the alphabetic principle.

Chapter 5 covers phonics. This is the longest chapter in the book—not because the science of reading is concerned only about phonics, but because we have a beautifully rich and complex language. You will learn guidelines for effective phonics instruction, get strategies for teaching high-frequency words, and find useful charts that you can reference whenever you need them.

Chapter 6 emphasizes the importance of automaticity in word reading and shares specific ways to build fluency at the letter, word, and text level.

Vocabulary is closely tied to comprehension, so I wrote Chapter 7 to help you decide which words to teach and to give you meaningful ways to make those words stick.

Chapter 8 demonstrates how to build comprehension at the sentence level, explains the importance of background knowledge, and shares research-based ways to teach reading comprehension strategies.

While this is not a book about writing, I included Chapter 9, which links reading and writing, because writing is such a powerful way to improve reading comprehension. You'll get tips for teaching handwriting, spelling, sentence writing, and paragraph writing—all with the ultimate goal of helping students use writing to better comprehend the text they read.

Chapter 10, on dyslexia, is an important one because children with dyslexia struggle to learn to read with balanced literacy methods. This chapter addresses dyslexia myths, shares common signs of dyslexia, and lists the steps you should take if you suspect this learning disability.

Finally, Chapter 11 describes an evidence-based framework for applying the science of reading. This system can help you deliver high-quality, research-based instruction to all students.

Each chapter includes a summary of the key points, links to learn more, and a QR code that will send you to free resources on my website that you can use immediately. Ready to reach all readers? Let's get started!

Note

1. Seidenberg, M. (2017). *Reading at the Speed of Sight,* Basic Books, 10.

CHAPTER 1

The Big Picture

Debates about how best to teach reading are nothing new. The reading wars, which are essentially a disagreement about the proper role of phonics in reading instruction, began almost two centuries ago (Figure 1.1).

The Whole Word Method

In the mid-1800s, education reformer Horace Mann argued against explicit instruction in letters and sounds. He described letters as "skeleton-shaped, bloodless, ghostly apparitions"[1] and advocated a whole word method instead. The **whole word method** taught children to read words as individual units based on shape.

This method gained traction, and major reading programs in the 1930s and 1940s adopted the look/say approach. *Dick and Jane*, a popular basal reading series of the time, repeated the most common high-frequency words in its stories.

Oh, Jane.
Look, Jane, look.
Look, look.
Oh, look.

Why Johnny Can't Read

Rudolf Flesch published his sensational book *Why Johnny Can't Read* in 1955. Flesch argued that phonics instruction is the most natural way to teach reading.[2] The book became a bestseller, and the reading wars intensified.

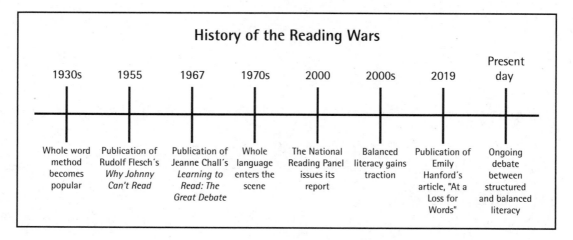

Figure 1.1   History of the reading wars.

Jeanne Chall's Research

In the 1960s, Jeanne Chall, a leading researcher from Harvard, analyzed research studies comparing different approaches to beginning reading. She studied widely used basal reading programs and observed how reading is taught in over 300 classrooms.

Her conclusion?

A focus on systematic, sequential phonics instruction is the best approach for teaching beginning readers. It produces better outcomes in word recognition in the early grades and even helps reading comprehension improve up to fourth grade.[3]

To those who described phonics instruction as lifeless and boring, Chall noted that students' engagement was independent of the program but rather depended on the atmosphere created by the classroom teacher.[4]

Whole Language

The first edition of Jeanne Chall's book, *Learning to Read: The Great Debate*, should have ended the reading wars. But they were just heating up.

In the 1970s, the **whole language** method entered the scene. Whole language proponents believe that learning to read is very much like learning to speak: it's natural. If we surround children with quality literature and environmental print, and we read aloud to them, they'll pick up reading without a lot of explicit instruction.

Ken Goodman, one of the founders of whole language, wrote: "Reading is a psycholinguistic guessing game. It involves an interaction between thought and language. Efficient reading does not result from precise perception and identification of all elements, but from skill in selecting the fewest, most productive cues necessary to produce guesses which are right the first time."[5]

The Report of the National Reading Panel

In 1997, The United States Congress convened the National Reading Panel (NRP) to determine what research had to say about reading. In 2000, the NRP concluded that five key factors are essential in learning to read: phonemic awareness, phonics, fluency, vocabulary, and comprehension.[6]

Balanced Literacy's Beginnings

Around the time that the NRP began its work, **balanced literacy** was born. Balanced literacy was an attempt to end the reading wars between the whole language and phonics camps by taking the best from each approach. It became immensely popular in the early 2000s.

Balanced literacy has no agreed-upon definition; the balanced literacy I describe is rooted in Ken Goodman's work. Teachers typically teach beginning readers using predictable leveled books, which contain many words with sound-spellings that students have not yet been taught. In order to identify these words, students must use MSV: cues from context or pictures (<u>m</u>eaning), cues from the structure of the sentence (<u>s</u>yntax), or cues from the letters on the page (<u>v</u>isual). This is known as **three-cueing.**

I was a balanced literacy teacher. I used running records to assess my students' reading levels and taught them to read using leveled books. I thought that children learn to read by reading, so my first graders spent most of the literacy block reading leveled books at their independent level.

I feared that too much phonics instruction would get in the way of comprehension and fluency, so I was careful not to overdo it. I taught phonics in fewer than 10 minutes a day during our word study lessons. If students were reading and encountered a word with a pattern we hadn't examined yet, I encouraged them to use the picture or context to "solve" the word.

Most of my students appeared to read their predictable books fluently, applying phonics with varying levels of success and moving through the guided reading levels.

When I had students who floundered, I increased their diet of leveled books and encouraged their parents to read more to them at home. I am sorry to say that I did not consider that something in my approach could have been wrong.

Emily Hanford's Reporting

In 2017, APM Reports released an audio documentary called "Hard to Read," with correspondent Emily Hanford, about why so many children with dyslexia have a hard time getting the help they need in school. The following year, Hanford reported that many educators either don't know what research reveals about how reading works or actively resist it.

It was Hanford's follow-up audio documentary "At a Loss for Words," published in 2019, that finally got my attention. A teacher commented on my website, asking what I thought about Hanford's reporting. When I read the transcript of the documentary, this paragraph jumped out at me:

> For decades, reading instruction in American schools has been rooted in a flawed theory about how reading works, a theory that was debunked decades ago by cognitive scientists, yet remains deeply embedded in teaching practices and curriculum materials. As a result, the strategies that struggling readers use to get by—memorizing words, using context to guess words, skipping words they don't know—are the strategies that many beginning readers are taught in school. This makes it harder for many kids to learn how to read, and children who don't get off to a good start in reading find it difficult to ever master the process.[7]

I was taken aback by Hanford's condemnation of three-cueing (not to mention completely insulted by her use of the word "guess"), but I was also relatively sure that a journalist could not know more about how reading works than an experienced teacher. I planned to write a post refuting "At a Loss for Words," point by point.

On each of my daily walks, I tried to formulate what was sure to be a convincing rebuttal. But I never got very far; as it turned out, I didn't know as much about how reading works as I thought I did.

I began looking into the research myself. It didn't take long to discover that Hanford was right.

THE MODERN READING WARS: BALANCED VERSUS STRUCTURED LITERACY

Hanford's continued reporting has inspired me and countless others to take a closer look at balanced literacy, which is still the most prominent method for teaching reading in kindergarten through second grade in the United States.[8]

The ultimate goal of balanced literacy is to teach children to love reading. The ultimate goal of structured literacy is to teach children how to read.

Most balanced literacy teachers teach phonics, but this instruction is often unsystematic and disconnected from the other reading and writing their students do. Balanced literacy is defined in terms of *activities that we do:* reading aloud, shared reading, guided reading, and independent reading.

Structured literacy is an umbrella term coined by the International Dyslexia Association. It refers to an approach that provides systematic, explicit instruction in the alphabetic code. Structured literacy is focused on the *elements that we teach*: phonology, sound-symbol relationships, syllables, syntax, semantics, and morphology.[9]

Perhaps the most striking difference is the emphasis of each approach. Balanced literacy focuses on meaning right from the start. The ultimate goal of balanced literacy is to teach children to love reading. Structured literacy's early emphasis is the code. While it would be wonderful if children learned to love reading, the ultimate goal of structured literacy is to teach children *how* to read.

It's not that no one learns to read with balanced literacy instruction; about 40 percent of children learn to read as long as they receive broad instruction. But for at least 50 percent of all students, explicit, code-based instruction is absolutely essential for learning to read, and a systematic approach is advantageous for *all* students.[10]

Scientifically-Based Research

The science of reading is not a philosophy. It is not a "phonics first and only" approach. Nor is it a program or curriculum.

DEFINING THE SCIENCE OF READING

The Reading League is an organization whose mission is to promote the use of evidence-aligned instruction. It defines the **science of reading** as:

> a vast, interdisciplinary body of scientifically-based research about reading and issues related to reading and writing. This research has been conducted over the last five decades across the world, and it is derived from thousands of studies conducted in multiple languages. The science of reading has culminated in a preponderance of evidence to inform how proficient reading and writing develop; why some have difficulty; and how we can most effectively assess and teach and, therefore, improve student outcomes through prevention of and intervention for reading difficulties.[11]

If you remember just one thing from that definition, let it be this: the science of reading is a body of research. A body of research is not a pendulum swing or a fad. It just is. Even if discussions of the science of reading disappear from social media, the research will remain.

A body of research is not a pendulum swing or a fad. It just is.

WHY MANY TEACHERS DON'T STUDY RESEARCH

As a teacher, I pored over professional books as often as I could. If someone had asked me if my teaching methods were based on research, I would have replied, "Oh yes! They're based on the writings of Fountas and Pinnell, Lucy Calkins, Regie Routman, and Sharon Taberski." These authors' books left me encouraged and inspired. I had no idea that much of what I read was based on a faulty theory of how reading works.

It didn't occur to me to track down a true research article; I hardly knew what one was. Besides, after a long day of teaching, I wouldn't have had the mental energy to decipher one. I would have agreed with the authors of *The Reading Glitch*: "The average scientific report is as digestible as a bowl of cold sauerkraut."[12]

If you feel the same way, take heart! I wrote this book to give you a clear understanding of the research and how to apply it.

RESEARCH-BASED VERSUS EVIDENCE-BASED

Research-based practices are teaching methods based on what we've learned from research. **Evidence-based practices** are based on the research as well, but these practices have also been proven to work in a controlled setting. Just because a teacher or author calls something research- or evidence-based, doesn't mean that it is. Ask for proof; ask for links to the scientifically-based research.

Once you get your hands on a full research article, you may not have the time, energy, or (let's be honest) interest in reading through dozens of pages. Do the following to get the gist of the article:

◆ Read the abstract and discussion/implications sections, which will give you a lot of valuable information.
◆ Look at the study participants. Find out what intervention they received. How was the intervention different from what the control group received?
◆ Finally, check what outcomes were measured. How were they measured? What was the effect size?

STATISTICAL SIGNIFICANCE AND EFFECT SIZE

Comprehending the jargon of a research study is difficult, but you're well on your way if you have a general understanding of two concepts: statistical significance and effect size.

If the results of a study are statistically significant, you can be confident that the results of the intervention aren't due to chance alone. **Statistical significance** is measured using p. The smaller the p value, the greater confidence you can have that the results weren't random.

Statistical significance doesn't mean much if the effect size is low. **Effect size** is a way of measuring the size of the difference between two groups: the students who received the intervention and the students who did not. An intervention could be many different things. It could be teaching a specific method for reading multisyllabic words or having students reread their decodable texts with a partner for 10 minutes a day. The effect size tells us whether the intervention actually made a difference in student learning.

For example, imagine that a researcher wants to find out whether explicit instruction in phonemic awareness improves reading outcomes. The researcher gives a pretest to two groups of similar students. One group receives the intervention (explicit phonemic awareness instruction) in addition to regular reading instruction. The control group only receives regular instruction. When the students are tested again six months later, the researcher finds an effect size of 0.5.

Cohen's *d* is one of the most common ways to measure effect size. Usually an effect size of below 0.2 does not have much practical significance. Values between 0.2 and 0.5 are considered to be small effects, values between 0.5 and 0.8 are considered to be medium effects, and values over 0.8 are considered large.[13] The higher the effect size, the greater the likelihood that the practice will accelerate student learning.

THE IMPORTANCE OF CONVERGING EVIDENCE

It's important to find *multiple* studies that point to a particular conclusion. This is called **converging evidence**, which is present when different and independent sources support a single conclusion.

Ideally, you will find a **meta-analysis**. A meta-analysis summarizes the results of multiple independent studies to yield an overall effect size. A high quality meta-analysis is arguably the best way to determine whether a teaching practice is effective.[14]

WHEN RESEARCH DOESN'T HAVE THE ANSWERS

As psychologist Steven Dykstra explains, some of our practices are based on bullseye science, which is as close to absolute truth as science gets. Bullseye science tells us that good readers are proficient at decoding. It tells us that phonemic awareness is important for success in reading. It tells us that teaching phonics is better than not teaching it. However, "You can't teach just in the bulls-eye. There isn't enough there to get the job done. You're going to have to make choices and decisions with the best evidence and reasoning available."[15]

Science hasn't answered all our questions. For example, we know phonics is important, but science doesn't give us a scope and sequence, a pacing guide, or the exact terminology to use.

Most of what teachers do in the classroom is an interpretation of the science. The teacher's job is to learn the science and make the best possible teaching decisions in light of it.

The Simple View of Reading

The Simple View of Reading (SVR) is a theoretical model that was developed by Gough and Tunmer in 1986 to simplify what is needed for a student to become a strong

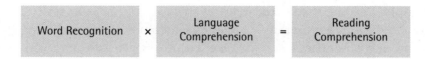

Figure 1.2   The Simple View of Reading (SVR).

reader. According to the SVR, word recognition times language comprehension equals reading comprehension (Figure 1.2).[16]

This simple theory has been supported by research many times in the decades since.[17] No one has been able to falsify it.[18]

The Simple View of Reading does not assert that the reading process is simple; it merely separates the complexity into two parts. I consider it a bird's-eye view of the skills reading requires. See Table 1.1.

The SVR shows that you don't have to choose between the phonics and meaning camps; students need proficiency in both word recognition *and* language comprehension to understand what they read.

The SVR also contradicts three-cueing. When I was a balanced literacy teacher, I assumed that having my students identify the words using context, pictures, or partial phonics was appropriate because they were still arriving at the words. In fact, however, they were not truly reading the words. A score of "0" for word recognition times "1" for language comprehension still equals "0." There was no reading comprehension because they were not actually reading.

Table 1.1   Examining the Simple View of Reading

Domain	Definition	Underlying Competencies
Word Recognition (Also called Decoding)	The ability to read isolated words quickly and accurately[19]	• Letter-sound knowledge • Phonemic awareness • Phonic decoding • Orthographic knowledge • Sight recognition
Language Comprehension (Also called Linguistic Comprehension or Listening Comprehension)	The ability to understand the oral language in a text if someone else reads it aloud[20]	• Background knowledge • Morphological awareness • Syntactic awareness • Vocabulary • Inference making • Perspective taking • Text structures • Comprehension monitoring

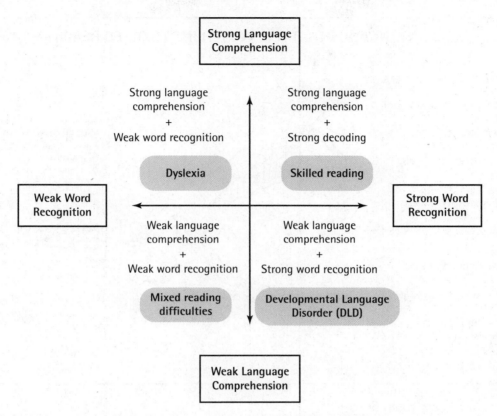

Strong Language Comprehension

Strong language comprehension + Weak word recognition

Strong language comprehension + Strong decoding

Dyslexia

Skilled reading

Weak Word Recognition

Strong Word Recognition

Weak language comprehension + Weak word recognition

Weak language comprehension + Strong word recognition

Mixed reading difficulties

Developmental Language Disorder (DLD)

Weak Language Comprehension

Figure 1.3   The Simple View of Reading is useful for defining different types of reading difficulties.

Finally, the SVR helps define different types of reading difficulties.[21] As you can see in Figure 1.3, just one quadrant (the top right) represents a skilled reader. The other three quadrants show the three types of reading difficulties.

Scarborough's Reading Rope

Developmental psychologist and researcher Hollis Scarborough created the rope (see Figure 1.4) in 1992 as a visual metaphor to help parents and teachers understand the complexities involved in learning to read. Scarborough's Reading Rope consists of two bundles, language comprehension and word recognition. The strands of each bundle are the subskills of the two domains.[22]

In Scarborough's view, the most important feature of the rope is its emphasis on the change over time in the nature of the relationships among the developing strands and bundles. If any strand gets frayed, it can hold back the development of other strands and weaken the entire rope.[23]

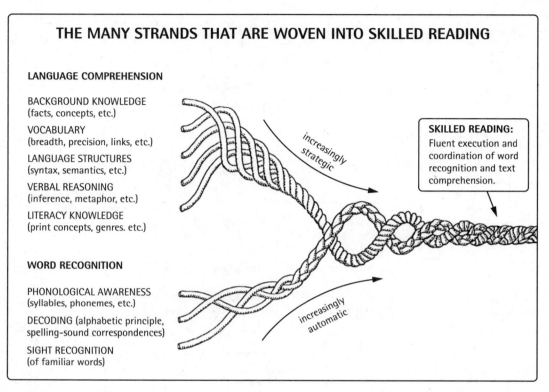

Figure 1.4   Scarborough's Reading Rope.

Image by Hollis Scarborough, published by Guilford Press

How the Brain Learns to Read

Stanislas Dehaene, a cognitive neuroscientist, has lamented that "it's a shame that teachers know more about the workings of their car than they know about the working of the brain of their children."[24] If you'd like all the particulars, check out Dehaene's book *Reading in the Brain*. I share only the most essential information here.

WHAT HAPPENS WHEN A PROFICIENT READER READS A WORD

Functional magnetic resonance imaging (fMRI) measures small changes in blood flow when different parts of the brain are activated. Through this technique, scientists have observed what happens when a person reads a word. There is not just one area of the brain that lights up when a person reads, because different parts of the brain must work together for reading to occur. Scientists have observed that when a person reads a word, activity unfolds from the back of the brain to the front, looping several times.

    1. Upon seeing the word, the visual information enters the brain via the occipital lobe at the back of the brain.

2. The information quickly moves into an area in the left hemisphere called the visual word form area. Dehaene calls it "the brain's letterbox." The brain's letterbox is where you store letters, letter combinations, and words you know by sight.
3. Finally, there's an explosion of activity into at least two networks in the left hemisphere. One network concerns meaning, and the other concerns pronunciation.[25]

The brain's letterbox is an area that exists before a person learns to read. Before reading, it reacts to faces and objects instead of words. When a person learns to read, however, faces and objects trigger brain activity in the other side of the brain. When people describe reading instruction as rewiring the brain, this is what they're talking about. Dehaene calls this "a sort of reorganization when children learn to read."[26] You could also say that the area used for picture recognition is hijacked and moved to another part of the brain so that the original area can be repurposed for recognizing words.

WHY YOU SHOULD NOT TEACH WORDS AS WHOLE UNITS

Because proficient readers recognize words in a tiny fraction of a second, it might seem like you read words as wholes. According to Dehaene, "It's just an illusion. The brain still processes every single letter and doesn't look at the whole shape. Whole word reading is a myth, basically."[27]

I used to advocate a "sight word first" method of teaching beginning readers. It felt easier to teach beginners to memorize a set of words instead of expecting them to "sound it out." I was right about one thing; this method does feel easier, at least at first. Unfortunately, students will hit a wall when their brain reaches its capacity for storing these images.

HOW TO REWIRE THE BRAIN

Unlike learning to speak, learning to read is not a natural process. Your students' brains must be trained to connect their visual system with their spoken language system. The important question is: How does this happen? In other words, how do you rewire the brain? According to Dehaene, learning letter-sound correspondences is the fastest way for students to learn to read words and comprehend what they read.[28]

Teaching students to memorize words or identify them without attending to each letter is a big mistake because it directs brain activity toward an inadequate circuit of the brain in the right hemisphere.[29]

Rewiring the brain happens quickly for some and slowly for others. However, all of your students' brains learn to read the same way. Dehaene states, "It is simply not true that there are hundreds of ways to learn to read. Every child is unique . . . but when it comes to reading, all have roughly the same brain that imposes the same constraints and the same learning sequence."[30]

How We Learn Words

As a literate adult, you recognize 30,000 to 70,000 words by sight.[31] How? People used to believe that readers used shapes of words or visual features of letters to store words in memory, but too many words have similar shapes to make this feasible. In addition, you instantly recognize the same word whether it's in uppercase, lowercase, or even mixed case.

Consider the word *bear*. The upper and lowercase letters are entirely different, but you recognize the word whether it's written as bear, BEAR, or BeAr. Whether the word is written in cursive, print, or a different font, you recognize it automatically.

Word learning is not a visual memory process. Instead, written words are stored in memory when **graphemes** (single letters or groups of letters that represent sounds) are connected to **phonemes** (the smallest units of speech in spoken words that can distinguish one word from another) along with meaning.

Imagine that you encounter an unfamiliar medical term, such as *sphenopalatine ganglioneuralgia* (the brain freeze you get after eating ice cream too quickly). The first time you see these words, you won't recognize them instantly. You'll need to slowly sound them out. You will probably need to do this multiple times. But after you've decoded the words enough times, you'll read them automatically. It's not because you've memorized how they look; it's because the spellings are bonded to their pronunciations in your memory.

ORTHOGRAPHIC MAPPING

This mental process is called **orthographic mapping**. According to David Kilpatrick, "orthographic mapping is the process readers use to store written words for immediate, effortless retrieval."[32] Put more simply? Orthographic mapping is the process readers use to remember words.

Each word has three forms: its sounds, spelling, and meaning. Through orthographic mapping, readers connect sounds and letters of words, along with meaning, as instantly recognizable words.[33]

Researchers call these instantly recognizable words "sight words." Unlike the common belief that sight words are words we must memorize because they are irregular, **sight words** are any words recognized automatically, without needing to sound out or guess.

HOW TO BECOME PROFICIENT AT ORTHOGRAPHIC MAPPING

Orthographic mapping takes time. If it was instant, you wouldn't see kindergartners sound out the same word after just reading it on the previous page. And you

Orthographic mapping is a mental process, not a skill we can teach or something we can include in our lesson plans. However, we can teach the skills that allow it to occur.

wouldn't need to sound out *sphenopalatine ganglioneuralgia* multiple times before recognizing the term instantly.

Orthographic mapping is a mental process, not a skill we can teach or something we can include in our lesson plans. However, we can teach the skills that allow orthographic mapping to occur. These are phonemic awareness, letter-sound correspondences, and phonic decoding. Once students become proficient at orthographic mapping (usually by third grade), they only need to read a word 1–4 times to recognize it instantly.[34]

WHY THIS MATTERS

All of this explains why early readers benefit from systematic phonics instruction that includes practice reading decodable texts (texts that primarily include the sound-spellings they've been taught). When students are taught to read using predictable leveled texts instead, they simply memorize the pattern and use picture cues. This type of "reading" bypasses orthographic mapping because students hardly need to look at the words.

THE FOUR-PART PROCESSING MODEL FOR WORD RECOGNITION

The four-part processing model explains how the brain reads and understands words. When looking at a word (see the bottom right of Figure 1.5), you first activate the orthographic processor (an area of the brain where you store images of letters and letter combinations) and the phonological processor (an area of the brain where you

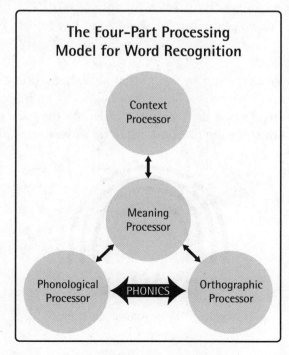

Figure 1.5 The four-part processing model for word recognition.

store speech sounds). In other words, you connect the sounds to the letters as you read the word in a fraction of a second. Once you've read the word, you activate the meaning processor to generate possible word meanings. Finally, you use the context processor to help you establish the meaning of the word in its particular context.[35]

While this model is a simplification of how reading works, it's a helpful reminder of the importance of phonics when teaching reading. Word identification comes before comprehension.

EHRI'S PHASES OF WORD LEARNING

No matter what grade you teach, you've surely seen a vast difference in students' literacy development. It's helpful to acquaint yourself with Linnea Ehri's phases of word learning so you can determine what your students need to learn next.

Based on her research, Ehri has described the course of learning to read and spell words as a series of four phases.[36]

The Pre-alphabetic Phase

In the pre-alphabetic phase (Figure 1.6), children have very little knowledge of letters and sounds. They may recognize their names or words in environmental print, but only by visual shape or context. If these children attempt to spell, they produce random strings of letters or letter-like forms.

Some kindergartners begin the year in this phase. To move children to the next phase, teachers should teach phonemic awareness along with letter names and sounds.

The Partial Alphabetic Phase

Many children begin kindergarten in the partial alphabetic phase (Figure 1.7), when they know the names and sounds of some letters and have limited phonemic awareness. They may begin to decode very simple words, but they are more likely to try to predict words using context or the first and last letter of words. Students may recognize

DTRMKL

Figure 1.6   The pre-alphabetic phase.

Image by Rocio Zapata

Figure 1.7 The partial alphabetic phase.
Image by Rocio Zapata

a few words by sight using the letter-sound correspondences they know. When spelling, they may spell words with just a few consonants (KR for CAR).

To help students progress to the next phase, teachers should teach their students to break words into their sounds and then spell those sounds. They should teach letter-sound correspondences and give students practice reading decodable books so they can apply this knowledge.

The Full Alphabetic Phase

Ideally, children will enter the full alphabetic phase (Figure 1.8) by late kindergarten or early first grade. During this phase, students know the sounds of all 26 letters and are learning other phonics knowledge as well. They begin to decode simple words by attending to every letter. Students in this phase learn to recognize words automatically after reading them several times. They spell words phonetically and start to remember correct spellings.

To move students along, teachers should continue to teach phoneme blending and segmenting. They should continue to teach spelling patterns as they move to more advanced phonics concepts.

Figure 1.8 The full alphabetic phase.
Image by Rocio Zapata

Figure 1.9   The consolidated alphabetic phase.
Image by Rocio Zapata

The Consolidated Alphabetic Phase

The goal is for children to enter the consolidated alphabetic phase (Figure 1.9) some time in second grade. In this phase, students know all or nearly all grapheme-phoneme correspondences. They have advanced phonemic awareness skills. When decoding, they use chunks rather than individual phonemes. Their sight vocabulary is increasing rapidly, and they are developing a proficient memory for correct spellings.

When teaching these students, teachers should help students focus on various chunks in words as they teach the reading of multisyllabic words.

 ## Key Things to Remember

- The science of reading is a body of research related to reading and writing.
- There is not enough research to prescribe or confirm everything teachers do in the classroom; the teacher's job is to learn the science and make the best possible teaching decisions in light of it.
- The SVR simplifies what is needed to become a strong reader.
- Scarborough's Reading Rope communicates the complexities involved in learning to read.
- The brain does not have just one area responsible for reading; rather, multiple parts of the brain work together. Explicit instruction in phonemic awareness and letter-sound correspondences rewires the brain for reading.
- Readers learn to read words automatically through a mental process called orthographic mapping. For orthographic mapping to occur, the reader must connect sounds to letters along with meaning. If you teach beginners to read by memorizing words or using three-cueing, you bypass orthographic mapping. This limits your students' ability to store words for future instant retrieval.
- Children need instruction in phonemic awareness and phonics to move through Linnea Ehri's phases of word learning.

Learn More

◆ Read *The Reading League's Defining Guide* e-book: www.thereadingleague.org/what-is-the-science-of-reading/defining-guide-ebook/

◆ Read *At a Loss for Words* by Emily Hanford. www.apmreports.org/episode/2019/08/22/whats-wrong-how-schools-teach-reading

◆ Listen to podcast episodes about the science of reading. For an index to episodes organized by topic, visit themeasuredmom.com/podcast-index.

Notes

1. Mann, H. (1842). *Common school journal for the year 1842,* Vol. IV, 27.
2. Flesch, R. (1955). *Why Johnny can't read*. Harper & Brothers.
3. Chall, J. (1967). *Learning to read: The great debate*. McGraw-Hill.
4. Ibid.
5. Goodman, K. S. (1967). Reading: A psycholinguistic guessing game. *Literacy Research and Instruction, 6*(4), 127.
6. National Reading Panel (U.S.) & National Institute of Child Health and Human Development (U.S.). (2000). *Report of the National Reading Panel: Teaching children to read: An evidence-based assessment of the scientific research literature on reading and its implications for reading instruction*. U.S. Dept. of Health and Human Services, Public Health Service, National Institutes of Health, National Institute of Child Health and Human Development.
7. Hanford, E. (2019). *At a loss for words*. APM Reports. https://www.apmreports.org/episode/2019/08/22/whats-wrong-how-schools-teach-reading.
8. Schwartz, S. (2019, December 3). The most popular reading programs aren't backed by science. *Education Week*. https://www.edweek.org/teaching-learning/the-most-popular-reading-programs-arent-backed-by-science/2019/12.
9. Cowen, C. D. (2016). What is structured literacy? International Dyslexia Association. https://dyslexiaida.org/what-is-structured-literacy/.
10. Young, N. (2023, August 3). The Ladder of Reading & Writing 2023 Update. Nancy Young. https://www.nancyyoung.ca/blog.
11. The Reading League. (2022). *Science of reading: Defining guide*. The Reading League.
12. Sherman, L., & Ramsey, B. (2006). *The reading glitch*. R & L Education, 133.

13. Wheldall, K., Wheldall, R. Buckingham, J. & Bell, N. (2023). In K. Wheldall, R. Wheldall, & J. Buckingham (Eds.), *Effective instruction in reading and spelling* (2–18). MRU Press.

14. Hansford, N. (2022). *The scientific principles of reading instruction.* Nathaniel Hansford.

15. Dykstra, S. (2021). *How science works: Teaching beyond the science we have without violating that science.* [Webinar]. Moving in the same direction: Partners in the science of reading. The Reading League. https://thereadingleague.uscreen.io/programs/conference2021session4.

16. Gough, P. B., & Tunmer, W. E. (1986). Decoding, reading, and reading disability. *Remedial and Special Education, 7*(1), 6–10.

17. Kilpatrick, D. A. (2020). The article that introduced the simple view of reading. *The Reading League Journal, 1*(2), 13–14.

18. Savage, R. (2020). A Simple View of Reading: A scientific framework for effective teaching. *The Reading League Journal, 1*(2), 41–45.

19. Moats, L., Kilpatrick, D., Blachman, B., et al. (2020). Frequently asked questions about the simple view of reading. *The Reading League Journal, 1*(2), 6–8.

20. Ibid.

21. Gough, P.B., & Tunmer, W.E. (1986).

22. Scarborough, H. S. (2001). Connecting early language and literacy to later reading (dis)abilities: Evidence, theory, and practice. In S. Neuman & D. Dickinson (Eds.), *Handbook for research in early literacy* (97–110). Guilford Press.

23. SoR-What I Should Have Learned in College. (2020, August 15). *Q & A with Hollis Scarborough.* [Video]. YouTube. https://www.youtube.com/watch?v=83tfzOFpBak&t=3223s.

24. WISE Channel. (2013, October 25). *How the brain learns to read – Prof. Stanislas Dehaene.* [Video]. YouTube. https://www.youtube.com/watch?v=25GI3-kiLdo&t=1s, 1:43.

25. Ibid.

26. Ibid, 10:19.

27. Ibid, 13:14.

28. BrainFacts.org. (2016, November 1). *The Brain Prize presents: Stanislas Dehaene.* [Video]. YouTube. https://www.youtube.com/watch?v=wlYZBi_07vk.

29. WISE Channel. (2013).

30. Dehaene, S. (2009). *Reading in the brain.* Penguin Books, 218.

31. Kilpatrick, D. A. (2015). *Essentials of assessing, preventing, and overcoming reading difficulties.* Wiley.

32. Ibid., 4.

33. Sedita, J. (2021, November 4). *The role of orthographic mapping in learning to read*. [Video]. Vimeo. https://vimeo.com/642494306.

34. Kilpatrick, D.A. (2015).

35. Adams, M. J. (1990). *Beginning to read*. The MIT Press.

36. Ehri, L. C. (2022). What teachers need to know and do to teach letter-sounds, phonemic awareness, word reading, and phonics. *The Reading Teacher*, *76*(1), 53–61.

CHAPTER 2

The Science of Learning

Anita Archer, an internationally recognized literacy leader, reminds us that the science of reading tells us *what* to teach. But the science of instruction is equally important in terms of *how* to teach.[1] The science of instruction—how we teach—is informed by the science of learning.

The **science of learning** is what we've learned from the field of cognitive psychology, usually defined as the study of the mind. When we put the science of learning into practice, our students learn more effectively and more efficiently.

> *The science of reading tells us **what** to teach. The science of instruction tells us **how** to teach.*

What's Memory Got to Do with It?

Long-term memory holds the information you've learned and stored semi-permanently. I find it fascinating that there are no known limits to long-term memory. Weirdly, I can still remember the color of socks I was wearing when, one day in sixth grade, a neighbor boy rang our doorbell and, horrifyingly, asked me out (yellow).

Unlike long-term memory, **working memory** is a temporary holding place. It's the small amount of information you can hold in your mind while working through a problem. Think of it as your workspace for thinking.

Figure 2.1   The average person can only hold about four pieces of information in working memory at one time.
Image by Rocio Zapata

The authors of *Uncommon Sense Teaching* compare working memory to an octopus juggling a set of balls (see Figure 2.1). The balls represent thoughts that bounce over and over again as long as you can keep them in your working memory. The average person can only hold four thoughts at once before the ideas begin to slip.[2]

Your students use working memory when they follow multi-step directions, remember the sounds in a word as they sound it out, or remember what they just read as they make sense of a paragraph. Students have different amounts of working memory. Some can hold just three items at once; others, six or more.[3]

Unfortunately, there's no evidence that you can increase students' working memory capacity, but there's good news. When students have more information in their *long-term* memory, they can use that information to help them process new information. The important question is this: How can you help students move information from their working memories into their long-term memories?

The answer begins with an understanding of cognitive load theory. **Cognitive load** refers to the amount of information working memory can hold at one time. John Sweller published his **cognitive load theory** (CLT) in 1988.[4] According to CLT, teachers must be aware of the limits of working memory. If they overwhelm their students' working memory, their teaching will be less effective.

There are two kinds of cognitive load. *Intrinsic* cognitive load refers to the difficulty of the task when compared to the background knowledge of the learner. For children who are first learning to read, sounding out D-O-G can be quite difficult. If a

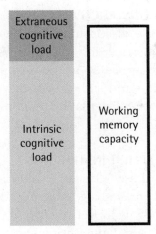

Figure 2.2   Cognitive load and working memory capacity.

child has orthographically mapped the word, however, this task requires no working memory at all.

Extraneous cognitive load is anything that makes it harder to learn. It's generated by the way you present the material and by what is happening in the learning environment. If you overcomplicate your lessons or allow too many distractions, you increase extraneous load. Your goal should be to decrease extraneous load as much as possible.[5]

Total cognitive load consists of both intrinsic and extraneous load. If the combination exceeds working memory capacity, learning will be compromised[6] (see Figure 2.2).

Explicit Instruction

Explicit instruction refers to both how lessons are designed and how teachers deliver those lessons. According to Archer and Hughes, "explicit instruction is systematic, direct, engaging, and success oriented."[7] The teacher explains concepts clearly, models the learning process, and guides students as they practice until mastery has been achieved.

You help your students move information from working memory to long-term memory when you provide explicit instruction.

When your lessons are clear and concise, you decrease extraneous load. You lessen the limits of working memory when you present new concepts in small chunks.[8] You help your students move information from working memory to long-term memory when you provide explicit instruction with practice and feedback.

EXPLICIT INSTRUCTION VERSUS CONSTRUCTIVISM

Explicit instruction is the opposite of constructivism, which is based on the belief that students learn best when they discover information for themselves.

As a teacher, constructivism appealed to me. I equated "explicit instruction" with "drill and kill." It sounded boring and stifling, which was exactly the opposite of the teacher I wanted to be. I failed to realize that many of my students required the explicit instruction that I wasn't giving.

WHAT RESEARCH SAYS ABOUT EXPLICIT INSTRUCTION

Project Follow Through remains the world's largest educational experiment.[9] Researchers conducted the billion-dollar study over nearly three decades, comparing 22 different models of instruction as they were used with over 200,000 students. After nine years, researchers found that the students who were taught using Direct Instruction—a teacher-directed model of explicit instruction designed by Seigfried "Zig" Engelmann—outperformed other students on tests of academic skills. It wasn't even close. Direct Instruction blew the other approaches out of the water. In addition, these children were better at problem-solving skills and had higher self-esteem and self-confidence—even when compared to students whose programs were designed for the express purpose of raising self-esteem!

Later studies showed that the students who were taught using Direct Instruction were more likely to finish high school and pursue further education.[10]

While it's important to distinguish between Engelmann's Direct Instruction program and direct instruction in general, Project Follow Through's results clearly support a direct, explicit approach to teaching.

THE FORMAT OF AN EXPLICIT LESSON

Rosenshine and Stevens summarized research-based principles of instruction in 1986. The following lesson framework incorporates these principles.[11]

The Structure of an Explicit Lesson

Introduction

    1. State the goal of the lesson.
    2. Review previous learning.

Lesson

    1. I DO: Present the new content/skills.
      • Present new materials in small steps.
      • Model procedures using clear language.
      • Ask a large number of questions and check for understanding.

2. WE DO: Provide guided practice with corrections and feedback.
   - Work through problems with the students.
   - Give students many opportunities to respond.
   - Provide timely feedback and corrections.
   - Have students continue practice, providing scaffolding if needed.
   - Reteach material when necessary.
3. YOU DO: Assign independent practice.
   - Monitor students' first practice attempts to be sure they understand.
   - Have students practice until the skills are automatic.

Closing
1. Review.
2. Assign independent work.

Sample Explicit Phonics Lesson: Spelling /ā/ with AI or AY

Introduction
1. Today you will learn two more ways to spell the long a sound.

basis	shake

2. You have already learned that you can spell /ā/ with an *a*, as in the word *basis*. You can also spell /ā/ with a-consonant-e, as in the word *shake*.
3. Today you will learn to spell /ā/ with the letters *ai* and *ay*.

Lesson

I DO:

1. We can spell /ā/ with *ai* at the beginning or in the middle of words. We can spell /ā/ with *ay* at the end of words.
2. (Hold up the *ai* card). When you see this card, say "A-I spells /ā/." Say it with me. "*A-I* spells /ā/." (Hold up the *ay* card). When you see this card, say "A-Y spells /ā/." Say it with me. "A-Y spells /ā/."

3. Watch me read each of these words. (Point to each grapheme as you say each sound and then blend the sounds together to read each word. Underline the *ai* or *ay* with your finger as you say its sound, to remind students that the two letters spell a single sound.)

main	play	chain	clay

WE DO:

1. Let's practice reading these words. Say the sound as I point to each spelling. Then say the whole word when I draw a line under the word with my hand.

plain	braid	day	play	stain

2. Let's read these blending lines together.

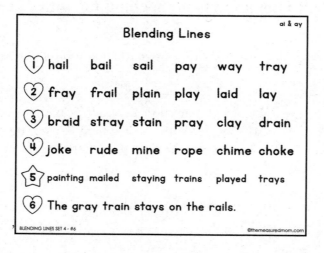

Blending Lines   ai & ay

① hail   bail   sail   pay   way   tray
② fray   frail   plain   play   laid   lay
③ braid   stray   stain   pray   clay   drain
④ joke   rude   mine   rope   chime   choke
⑤ painting   mailed   staying   trains   played   trays
⑥ The gray train stays on the rails.

BLENDING LINES SET 4 - #6   ©themeasuredmom.com

YOU DO:

1. I am giving each of you a copy of the blending lines to read chorally with your partner.

2. After you've read the lines together, take turns reading the lines. Ones should begin. (Circulate, offering support as needed.)

I DO:

1. Let's practice spelling words with *ai* and *ay*. Remember that *ai* goes at the beginning or in the middle of words, but *ay* goes at the end.

s n ai l

2. If I'm going to spell the word *snail*, I start by counting the sounds. /s/ /n/ /ā/ /l/. How many sounds? (Four) So how many blanks do I need? (Four) The first sound is /s/. What spelling? *(s)*. The second sound is /n/. What spelling? *(n)*. The third sound is /ā/. Is this sound in the middle or end of the word? (middle) So will we use *ai* or *ay*? (ai). The final sound is /l/. What spelling? *(l)*

WE DO:

1. Get out your dry-erase board. Let's spell together. The word is *sway*. The branches *sway* in the wind. Tap the sounds with me. /s/ /w/ /ā/. How many sounds? (three) Draw three lines on the board.

2. The first sound is? *(/s/)* What spelling? *(s)* The second sound is? *(/w/)* What spelling? *(w)* The final sound is? *(/ā/)* What spelling? *(ay)* Let's blend the sounds together to read the word. Ssswwwwaaaaay. *Sway.*

YOU DO:

1. Your turn! The word is *chain*. The lock had a *chain*. (Wait while students tap the sounds, draw the lines, spell the word, and read it.) Chain is spelled C-H-A-I-N. (Circulate and give feedback as needed. Repeat with *stain, faint, hay,* and *tray*).

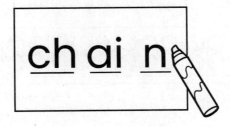

WE DO:

1. We're going to do a word chain. The first word to write on your board is *way*. I know the *way* to the park. Check your spelling: W-A-Y. Change one letter to make the word *say*. I *say* the answer. (Wait.) Check your spelling: S-A-Y. Add a letter to spell *stay*. I tell my dog to *stay*. (Wait.) Check your spelling: S-T-A-Y. Now you're going to change one vowel spelling and add a letter at the end. Ready? The word is *stain*. I have a *stain* on my shirt. (Wait.) Check your spelling: S-T-A-I-N.

Closing

1. Today you learned that *ai* and *ay* are two spellings for /ā/. *Ai* comes at the beginning or in the middle of words, and *ay* comes at the end. Let's review our flash cards. ("AI spells /ā/. AY spells /ā/.")
2. Tomorrow you'll read a book with these spellings.
3. Get a die out of your desk and play this Roll and Read game with your partner. (As students play, visit different pairs and support students as needed.)

Roll & Read

LONG A VOWEL TEAMS AI, AY

⚀	⚁	⚂	⚃	⚄	⚅
aid	pain	maid	way	bay	stay
tray	clay	day	bail	fray	gray
sail	pay	slay	hay	vain	mail
wait	waist	pray	faith	jay	lay
rail	braid	pail	yay	sway	train
way	nay	stray	stain	brain	play
claim	aim	laid	gray	may	paint
main	tail	say	plain	snail	ray

HOW TO OPTIMIZE INSTRUCTIONAL TIME

1. **Make sure your materials are well-organized and ready to go.** Being ill-prepared is asking for trouble. As Anita Archer says, "Avoid the void, for they will fill it!"[12]

   a. If you teach students in differentiated small groups, get a set of plastic drawers and put the materials for each group in a different drawer.

   b. If lessons will include letter tiles or other manipulatives, design a system that will have these supplies ready to go when the lesson begins.

   c. If students will be doing differentiated work at centers, store each group's materials in a different colored folder.

2. **Use instructional routines.** Routines reduce cognitive load for you and your students. They also keep you on track and reduce stress for everyone.

   a. Teach a blending routine. For example: Point to each grapheme of a word and prompt, "Sound." Students say the sound of each grapheme as they are prompted. Then point to the whole word and prompt, "Word?" As you underline the word with your finger, students read the word in unison. (See Figure 2.3)

Figure 2.3 Teaching a blending routine
Image by Rocio Zapata

   b. When doing a spelling activity such as *Say It Move It*, use a routine. For example: Say the word. Students repeat it. Next, students say each sound of the word as they move chips into boxes. Finally, students repeat each sound as they move its chip out of the way and write a grapheme in its place. Finally, they blend the sounds to read the word (See Figure 2.4.).

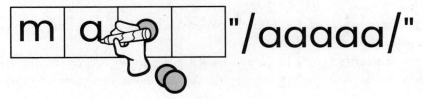

Figure 2.4 Say It Move It
Image by Rocio Zapata

HOW TO INCREASE OPPORTUNITIES FOR STUDENTS TO RESPOND

It's time to retire the age-old practice of asking a question and waiting to call on students who raise their hands. Anita Archer calls this "teaching the best and leaving the rest."[13] She encourages teachers to establish a no-hands raised environment. Students should only raise their hands if they have a public (and on topic!) question, or if the teacher says, "Raise your hand."

Asking a question and calling on hand-raisers is a very hard habit to break! But it's important to provide frequent opportunities for *everyone* to respond. When students respond more frequently, they are more attentive and on task. In addition, they are practicing the information and increasing the likelihood that they will remember it.[14]

1. **Have students respond in unison.** Research shows that asking for unison responses increases on-task behavior and academic learning.[15] Unison responses are appropriate when the answers are short and the same.

   a. **Teach a cue so that students know you're waiting for a choral answer**, such as, "Everyone?" Then provide a visual cue (such as holding out your hand) and have them say the response in unison. For example: "How do we spell the sound /ch/ after a long vowel or consonant? (pause) Everyone? (C-H) How do we spell the sound /ch/ after a short vowel? (pause) Everyone? (T-C-H)"

      Always be sure to give appropriate wait time before asking students to give the answer in unison.

   b. **Have each student write an answer on a dry erase board and hold it up at the same time.** You can make a homemade dry erase board by putting a piece of white cardstock inside a clear page protector. Kids can write with dry-erase markers and erase their writing using rags or old socks.

   c. **When the answer will be one of several options, have students write each potential answer on an index card and hold up the correct answer.** For example, if you are teaching students to differentiate between the short vowel sounds of *a* and *i*, have them hold up the appropriate letter card as they listen to consonant-vowel-consonant (CVC) words with *a* or *i*.

   d. **If doing a yes/no or true/false activity, have students respond with a hand signal.** If the answer is YES or TRUE, they should hold a thumbs up close to their chest. If NO or FALSE, they show a thumbs down. For example: "*I was absolutely furious when my parents got me a set of my favorite books for my birthday.* Did I use the word *furious* correctly? Put your thumb up or down."

2. **Have students work in pairs.** Structured partner responses are appropriate when answers are long or varied. When assigning partnerships, consider

privately listing your students in order from least to most proficient. Cut the list in half and line up the two halves. In a class of 24, students 1 and 13 would be partners, students 2 and 14, and so on.

a. **Give each partner a name such as "One" or "Two."** "Ones, tell the answer to your partner. Twos, be prepared to tell us what your partner shared."

b. **Teach effective listening strategies such as look, lean, and whisper.** "Look at your partner, lean toward your partner, and whisper the answer."

c. **Use the turn-and-talk procedure.** Ask a question, let students think for a moment, and prompt them to share with a partner. "Uh oh! Mrs. O'Grady has fallen into the magic pot! What do you think will happen next? Think about it for a bit." (Wait.) "Twos, tell your partner what you think will happen next."

d. **Give sentence starters to help partners get started.** "We've finished reading today's chapter in *Charlotte's Web*. Twos, lean to your partner and finish this sentence: 'Wilbur was brave when he . . .'"

e. **Always give a job to the listener as well.** "Ones, repeat your partner's answer."

3. **Occasionally call on individuals.** When a question can have multiple answers, or the answer depends on students' own experience, it's appropriate to call on individuals. But you can still hold everyone accountable by having students share their answer with a partner first. Then randomly call on a student to share their answer with the class.

HOW TO SCAFFOLD INSTRUCTION

Years ago, my family and I lived in Hong Kong for a semester. As I pushed our three small children around the city in their triple stroller, I marveled at the bamboo scaffolding used in construction. Apparently, bamboo is cheaper, faster to assemble, and stronger than steel. A lot of scaffolding is used at the start of construction; however, as the building comes together, scaffolding is gradually removed.

Similarly, teachers scaffold instruction so that students can do a task that they are not ready to do independently. Teachers provide high levels of initial guidance and support, gradually reducing support as students learn to perform the task on their own. I've added examples to several of Archer and Hughes' suggestions for **scaffolding** instruction.[16]

◆ **Break tasks down into smaller components.**

Example: When teaching kindergartners to spell CVC words, teach them to say the word, segment it into its sounds, and spell each sound. Eventually you can remove the scaffold of having children segment the word before spelling it.

- ◆ **Order skills so that they build on each other.**

    Example: When you teach phonics skills, begin with letter sounds and CVC words. Move on to more difficult skills such as consonant digraphs, CCVC and CVCC words, long vowels, r-controlled vowels, and diphthongs.

- ◆ **Gradually increase task difficulty.**

    Example: When teaching students to count phonemes in words, start with words that only have two phonemes. Gradually move on to words with three, four, and five phonemes.

- ◆ **Use visual aids to help students remember the steps of a process.**

    Example: After teaching students the 1-1-1 doubling rule, display a checklist.

    ☐ Does the word have one syllable?

    ☐ Does the word have one vowel?

    ☐ Does the word have one final consonant?

    Do you have three checkmarks? Double the final consonant before adding the ending!

HOW TO PROVIDE FEEDBACK

Feedback (any response to a student's performance or behavior) should be immediate whenever possible; the longer the delay, the less likely students will learn from it.

Archer and Hughes encourage teachers to vary feedback depending on the students' response.[17]

- ◆ **When students answer quickly**, affirm and move on. "Correct!" or "Great job!"

- ◆ **When students answer correctly but hesitantly**, affirm the answer and repeat the fact or review the concept.

    Example: If a student reads *rate* hesitantly, looking at you for confirmation, you could say, "Great job! That word is *rate*. The *a* spells /ā/ because of the silent e at the end of the word. (Display the word *rat*.) This word is *rat* because there's no *e* to change the vowel's sound. But when I add the *e* (display the word *rate*), the vowel's sound changes. Read the word again."

- ◆ **When students respond incorrectly because they don't understand**, utilize "I Do It, You Do It."

    Example: If students read the word *club* as *cub*, you could respond this way: "We need to say the sounds of every letter. Watch me say the sounds as I point to the letters. /k/ /l/ /ŭ/ /b/. Cllluuub. People with the same interests might join a *club*. Let's try another word. (Display the word *drag*). Your turn. Point to each spelling as you say the sounds. (/d/ /r/ /ă/ /g/.) Now read the word. If a bag is too heavy, you can *drag* it. (Repeat with other CCVC words as needed.)

- ◆ **When students respond incorrectly because they have forgotten a procedure or rule**, guide them as they apply it.

> *Example:* You spelled *tell* t-e-l. The FLOSS rule says that when a one-syllable word ends with /f/, /l/, /s/, or /z/ after a short vowel, we double the final consonant. Is *tell* a one-syllable word? Does it have a short vowel? Does it end with /f/, /l/, /s/ or /z/? Yes, it ends with /l/. So we spell *tell* t-e-l-l." (Practice with additional words such as *puff, chess,* and *fuzz.*)

♦ **When students read a word incorrectly**, point to the misread part of the word and guide students as they correct it.

> *Example:* If a student reads *bread* as *breed*, point to the letters *ea*. "What else can these letters represent? Try /ĕ/. What's the word?" If students cannot arrive at the correct answer, tell them the word. Have them repeat and reread the sentence. "The word is *bread*. What's the word? Now read the sentence again."

How to Ensure Your Students Remember What You Teach

To ensure that information stays in students' long-term memory, you must incorporate frequent review.

RETRIEVAL PRACTICE

Cognitive scientists often refer to the three stages of learning.[18]

1. Encoding (when we absorb the information)
2. Storage (where we hope we will remember it)
3. Retrieval (when we practice remembering it)

It feels like the most learning happens during the encoding stage—when you get the information into your students' heads. Indeed, that's where teachers typically spend the most time. But research says that you need to spend even more time getting the information *out* of your students' heads.[19] This is called **retrieval practice**.

Giving students many opportunities to retrieve information from their memories is the key to helping them master basic knowledge.

When you think about it, retrieval practice makes perfect sense. If you want to remember something, you should practice remembering it. The more you practice remembering something, the more firmly that information lodges in your long-term memory. Neural pathways get stronger when a memory is retrieved and students practice what they've learned.

Flash cards are the classic example of retrieval practice, but many teachers recoil at the thought of using

Giving students many opportunities to retrieve information from their memories is the key to helping them master basic knowledge.

them with their students. As a teacher, I thought that drilling basic facts was soul-killing and a hindrance to higher-level thinking. I didn't understand that students can't think critically without core knowledge. In their book, *Make It Stick,* Brown et al. write, "Pitting the learning of basic knowledge against the development of creative thinking is a false choice . . . Just as knowledge amounts to little without the exercise of ingenuity and imagination, creativity absent a sturdy foundation of knowledge builds a shaky house."[20]

When students practice basic skills to automaticity, they free up space in their working memories for critical thinking.

Examples of Retrieval Practice During Reading Instruction

- ◆ **Quiz your students on sound-spellings.** At least twice a week, use paper or digital flash cards to briefly quiz your students on the sound-spellings you've taught in your phonics lessons.
- ◆ **Quiz your students about nonfiction read-alouds on subsequent days.** The day after you read a book about plants to your kindergartners, ask questions. Remember not to call on volunteers; have your students whisper the answer to their partner. Then call on a random student.
  - • Which part of the plant makes food?
  - • What part of the plant takes in nutrients from the soil?
  - • Which part of the plant holds it up?

  Don't expect your students to be automatic in every retrieval practice. In fact, retrieval practice is most effective when students have to struggle to remember information but are still able to do so. Each time they practice retrieving the information, the more likely they are to remember it in the future.

- ◆ **Use the Two Things strategy.**[21] In the middle of a nonfiction read-aloud, pause and ask, "What are two things you've learned so far?" (Wait.) "Turn to your partner. Ones, tell your partner one thing you've learned. Twos, tell your partner a different thing that you've learned." At the end of a fiction read-aloud, ask, "What is one thing from this story that reminds you of your own life?" (Wait.) Twos, tell your partner one thing. After you're finished, Ones, tell your partner one thing."
- ◆ **Use random questions to review core knowledge daily.** After teaching information to your students through read-alouds or whole-group text reading, write a few questions about the text and put them in a basket. (Even better: Have your students dictate the questions!)

  Spend a few minutes each day pulling a few random questions from the basket. Make sure to give all students a chance to retrieve the information by having them think, pair, and share. Ask for a unison response or call on a random student.

- How is a fable different from a fairy tale?
- What is the name of our continent?
- What is one way a mammal is different from a bird?

Return the questions to the basket so students can practice retrieving the same information in the future!

Retrieval Practice: Teaching Tips

- **When doing retrieval practice, ask specific questions.** Instead of asking "What do you remember about frogs and toads?" ask questions like these: "What kind of animal are frogs and toads? Describe the frog's life cycle. What do frogs and toads eat?"
- **Give feedback during retrieval practice.** If you are doing a flash card drill to review sound-spellings and you notice that only a few students remember that *igh* spells /ī/, stop and review. "*Igh* spells /ī/. Look at these words. (Write *fight* and *high* on the board.) Let's read them together. (As you sound out the words together, underline the *igh* in each of them.) "Let's practice this card again. Listen first. *Igh* spells /ī/. Your turn."
- **Ask more than basic fact questions.** If you've taught your students the word *exhausted*, don't just ask for the definition. "Give an example of a situation where a mom might feel *exhausted*."
- **Remember that retrieval practice is about learning, not testing.** Flash card drills, the Two Things strategy, and other retrieval practice activities should not be graded.

SPACED PRACTICE

Retrieval practice is most effective when you've given your students time to forget the information. That's where spacing comes in. **Spacing** is engaging in retrieval practice multiple times, over time. For example, when you teach new vocabulary words, don't forget to review them weeks or even months later. Reconstructing learning from long-term memory will strengthen the mastery and memory of it.[22]

INTERLEAVING

Interleaving is when you layer the study of related topics, rather than engaging in massed repetition of a single topic. For example, when teaching beginning readers, don't spend too much time on a single short vowel. If students spend weeks reading short-*a* CVC words, they don't have to think very hard. Mix it up with another short vowel as soon as possible. Similarly, don't get stuck on a particular long vowel pattern for too long. As much as possible, have students play games that include mixed sets of vowel patterns.

Unfortunately, we don't know a lot about interleaving yet. We don't know exactly what type of material should be interleaved, nor do we know how similar the material should be.[23]

 ## Key Things to Remember

- The science of learning helps us understand how to teach.
- According to cognitive load theory, working memory can only hold about four items at a time. The goal is to decrease extraneous load so that information can move from working memory to long-term memory.
- Explicit instruction is a systematic, direct, and engaging way of teaching.
- To be more effective, teachers should optimize instructional time, increase opportunities for students to respond, provide frequent feedback, and scaffold instruction.
- You can increase the likelihood that your students will remember what you teach by using research-based practices such as retrieval practice, spaced practice, and interleaving.

Learn More

- Watch video clips of Dr. Anita Archer's masterful teaching in action: https://explicitinstruction.org/video-elementary/.

Notes

1. ReadWA. (2021, October 8). *The science of instruction: Bringing life to the science of reading with Anita Archer.* [Video]. YouTube. https://www.youtube.com/watch?v=dK04MEXDGVg.
2. Oakley, B., Rogowsky, B., & Sejnowski, T. (2021). *Uncommon sense teaching.* TarcherPerigee.
3. Cowan, N. (2010). The magical mystery four: How is working memory capacity limited, and why? *Current Directions in Psychological Science, 19*(1), 51–57.
4. Sweller, J. (1988). Cognitive load during problem solving: Effects on learning. *Cognitive Science, 12*(2), 257–285.
5. Sweller, J. (2010). Element interactivity and intrinsic, extraneous, and germane cognitive load. *Educational Psychology Review, 22,* 123–138.
6. Lovell, O. (2020). *Sweller's cognitive load theory in action.* John Catt Educational Ltd.

7. Archer, A., & Hughes, C. (n.d.) *Effective and efficient teaching*. Explicit Instruction https://explicitinstruction.org/.

8. Ashman, G. (2019). Explicit instruction. In Boxer, A., Ed. *The researchED guide to direct instruction* (pp. 29–35). John Catt Educational.

9. National Institute for Direct Instruction. (n.d.) *Project follow through*. National Institute for Direct Instruction. https://www.nifdi.org/what-is-di/project-follow-through.

10. Ibid.

11. Rosenshine, B., & Stevens, R. (1986). In Wittrock, M. C., & American Educational Research Association. (1986). *Handbook of research on teaching* (3rd edition, 376–391). Macmillan.

12. Archer, A. (2023, October 4). *Getting them all engaged – The power of active participation*. [Conference session] The 7th Annual Conference of the National Reading League, Syracuse, NY.

13. Ibid.

14. Archer, A., & Hughes, C. (2010). *Explicit instruction*. The Guilford Press.

15. Heward, W. L., Courson, F. H., & Narayan, J. S. (1989). Using choral responding to increase active student response. *Teaching Exceptional Children*, *21*(3), 72–75.

16. Archer, A., & Hughes, C. (2010).

17. Ibid.

18. The Derek Bot Center for Teaching and Learning. (n.d.) *How memory works*. Harvard University. https://bokcenter.harvard.edu/how-memory-works.

19. Roediger III, H. L., & Karpicke, J. D. (2006). The power of testing memory: Basic research and implications for educational practice. *Perspectives on Psychological Science*, *1*(3), 181–210.

20. Brown, P. C., Roediger III, H. L., & McDaniel, M. A. (2014). *Make it stick*. The Belknap Press, p. 30.

21. Agarwal, P. K., & Bain, P. M. (2019). *Powerful teaching*. Jossey-Bass.

22. Brown, et al. (2014).

23. Weinstein, Y., Sumeracki, M., & Caviglioli, O. (2019). *Understanding how we learn*. Routledge.

CHAPTER 3

Oral Language

Oral language development begins at birth, and children come to early childhood teachers with vastly different levels of oral language proficiency.[1] This gap is disheartening and may lead you to wonder if it's too late to improve oral language skills. It's not! Lyn Stone writes, "A child with lower oral language may make a teacher's job harder, but it also makes a teacher's job more important."[2]

Oral language is the complex system through which we use spoken words to communicate. Oral language influences reading through a variety of indirect pathways;[3] researcher Pamela Snow calls it "the central driver for reading acquisition."[4] To understand the complex system of oral language, it's helpful to identify its five key domains.[5] Each of these domains plays an important role in language development.

The Five Domains of Oral Language

◆ **Phonology** is the study of how we distinguish, order, and say sounds in words.
   Example: English syllables do not end with the /h/ sound.
◆ **Syntax** is the system of rules governing word order in phrases, clauses, and sentences.
   Example: In English, indefinite articles come before nouns, as in *the apple*.
◆ **Semantics** refers to the meaning of words and phrases.
   Example: *Crane* can refer to a bird, a type of machine, or the movement of one's neck to see something.

- **Morphology** is the study of morphemes, which are the smallest meaningful units of words (prefixes, suffixes, roots, and bases).

  Example: The word *preheat* contains the suffix *pre-* and the base word *heat*.

- **Pragmatics** is a system of rules and conventions for using language in social settings, going beyond literal meaning.

  Example: When someone politely asks, "How are you?" they usually don't want a detailed answer.

What the Research Says

Oral Language Skills and Reading Skills Are Related

- **Children's oral language skills are the foundation** for both word reading and language comprehension.[6]
- **Children with reading problems often have accompanying oral language deficits.**[7]

Early Oral Language Abilities Help Us Predict Later Skills

- In one study, **poor comprehenders in fifth grade had deficits in oral language throughout early childhood.**[8]
- **Kindergarten scores of oral language** (receptive vocabulary, narrative production, and emergent literacy) **are highly predictive of their scores on reading comprehension and vocabulary in fourth and seventh grades**.[9]
- **Composite measures of oral language** (including measures of vocabulary, syntax, and/or listening comprehension) **are the strongest predictors of word reading and language comprehension**, compared to studies that focus on a single predictor such as vocabulary or grammar.[10]

We Can Improve Oral Language Skills

- **A focus on a range of oral language skills in preschool leads to improvements in oral language** and spoken narrative skills.[11]
- **Explicitly teaching word meanings through interactive read-alouds may help narrow the vocabulary gap** among students.[12]

- ◆ A focus on **building vocabulary alone may not be sufficient for improving oral language** and reading outcomes.[13]
- ◆ **Dialogic reading**, in which the adult actively involves the child in discussions about the read-aloud, **powerfully affects language development**.[14]
- ◆ **Interventions that focus on a broad range of oral language skills** (including grammar, syntax, narrative skills, and inferring) **are most likely to help** children develop reading comprehension skills. [15]

Oral Language Routines

There is no quick fix for oral language difficulties, but your students' oral language skills will improve when you work on active listening, vocabulary, and oral narrative skills.[16] Consider implementing one or more of these routines into your school day.

MORNING MESSAGE

The Morning Message is a daily message that is written together as a shared writing experience. It generally communicates information about what will happen in the classroom later in the day or about a topic that students have been learning about.

The Morning Message is useful for teaching syntax and new vocabulary.

The Morning Message lets children see how speech is translated into print, draws attention to specific letter-sound relationships, and highlights concepts of print.[17] In addition, the Morning Message is useful for teaching syntax and new vocabulary. Very little research has been conducted on the Morning Message. However, this list of best practices is based on other early literacy research.[18]

Morning Message Best Practices

- ◆ Plan your Morning Message in advance. Then write the message in front of your students.
- ◆ As often as possible, use the Morning Message as an opportunity to build knowledge about key concepts in the larger curriculum. Make sure to include at least one key vocabulary word that the students are learning.
- ◆ As you write the message, draw attention to directionality, spacing, word-to-print matching, and other concepts of print.

- Whether or not you choose to have your students write part of the message (single letters or words), make sure that you model proper letter formation, spelling, sentence structure, and punctuation.
- As you write, draw attention to letter-sound correspondences that students are learning in their phonics lessons.

After the message has been written, use it as a springboard for discussion in which all students have opportunities to speak.

Sample Morning Message

1. Imagine that you've been teaching your first graders about the parts of a plant. You are growing bean seeds in a milk carton on the window sill, and they've begun to sprout. As you get ready for the school day, jot down what you will write in your morning message.

"Good morning, first graders! It's time for our morning message. I notice that our plants have begun to sprout! Today's message is going to be about what I see on the window sill."

---

2. Later, as you write the message on a large chart in front of your students (see Figure 3.1), talk aloud about your use of upper- and lowercase letters, spacing between words, and punctuation. If you have taught a particular high-frequency word or letter-sound relationship, invite students to help you with the spelling as you write. Call attention to new vocabulary words as well.

Figure 3.1 Sample Morning Message
Image by Rocio Zapata

"My first sentence will be: *Our bean seeds have germinated quickly.* Will my first letter be upper or lowercase? (Pause.) Everyone? Yes, an uppercase letter because it's the first word of the sentence. *Our . . . bean . . . seeds . . . have. . . germinated.* Say *germinated.* Say it again and clap the syllables. Ger-min-a-ted. Watch me spell all four parts. Ger. . . min. . . a. . . ted. *Germinated* means that a seed has begun to grow. What word means that a seed has begun to grow?

". . . *quickly!* I'm using an exclamation mark here because I'm so excited that the seeds have already sprouted!

"My second sentence will be: *I see little green plants in the milk cartons. I . . . see . . .* first graders, you know how to spell *see!* Let's tap the sounds. /s/ /ē/. How do we spell /s/? How do we spell /ē/ in this word? Read the word. *See.*

". . . *little . . . green . . . plants . . . in . . . the . . . milk . . . cartons.* I'm ending the second sentence with a period because it's a telling sentence."

3. After writing the message, read it aloud. Have your students read it with you. (Even if your students cannot read the words on their own yet, they need many opportunities to speak complete sentences and add new words to their oral language vocabulary.)

"Listen to me read today's message (point to each word as you read aloud.) *Our bean seeds have germinated quickly! I see little green plants in the milk cartons.* Now read it with me."

4. Ask questions about the message to promote conversation and oral language development.

"One of the words in today's message means that a seed has begun to grow. Find that word in the message. Now turn to your partner and whisper the word that means a seed has begun to grow. (Pause.) What's the word . . . everyone?

"What's your favorite vegetable? Turn and tell your partner. Start by saying, 'My favorite vegetable is . . .'

"_____, what is your partner's favorite vegetable?

"What is a vegetable that you *don't* like? Turn and tell your partner, 'I don't like . . .'

QUESTION OF THE DAY

Like Morning Message, Question of the Day can be part of your daily routine. Post a question, read it to your students, and guide them as they answer the question in a complete sentence. After you record your students' answers on a large chart, challenge them to extend their sentence using a conjunction such as *and, but, so,* or *because*.

Examples

If your question is, "What is your dream vacation?" have your students use this sentence framework: "My dream vacation is _____ *because* _____."

If your question is, "What desserts do you like?" have your students use the word *and* to answer the question. "I like to eat chocolate cake *and* brownies."

If your question is, "What is something you like to do at home?" have your students use the word *but* to extend the sentence. "I like to play outside, *but* I don't like to clean my room."

SHARED READING OF ENLARGED TEXT

As you're thinking about oral language routines, consider doing shared reading of an enlarged text several times a week.

Shared Reading's Unsavory Origins

Let's come right out and say it. Shared reading, in which the teacher and students read together from an enlarged text, originated with Don Holdaway, a fierce advocate of whole language.

Holdaway believed that shared reading of predictable text would lead children to easily recognize whole sentences and provide cues for reading individual words. He found shared reading preferable to word-by-word processing because it sounded like fluent language. He believed that the explicit teaching of phonics out of context served no useful purpose and that what he called the Shared Reading Experience was much more effective than direct instruction.[19]

Holdaway created this model to replicate the experience of enjoying a beloved book with a parent—an admirable goal. But the idea that shared reading will teach children to read without explicit instruction in phonemic awareness and phonics goes against everything you've read in Chapters 1 and 2.

A common caution among teachers who are moving from balanced to structured literacy is to not throw the baby out with the bathwater. In the case of shared reading, however, we need a fresh tub! Shared reading should not be used as a bridge between read-alouds and independent reading. It should not be used to teach children to lift words from the page.

Use Shared Reading to Teach Concepts of Print and Support Letter Learning

Shared reading can be used to teach concepts of print and support letter learning through **print referencing**. Print referencing is when an adult directs children's attention to features of written language. This strategy is most effective when the text includes print that is noticeable,[20] making shared reading with enlarged text ideal for teaching concepts of print.

The term **concepts of print** refers to an awareness of how print works; early knowledge of the following print concepts is predictive of future reading success.[21]

- Print holds meaning.
- A book has a front and back cover and must be held right side up.
- A book lists its title, author, and illustrator on the cover.
- A book's pages may be numbered.
- Pages are read from top to bottom and left to right.
- Print may be accompanied by illustrations or graphics.
- Words are made of letters, and sentences are made of words separated by spaces.
- Sentences begin with capital letters and end with punctuation.
- Print represents spoken language; each word we speak matches a word in print.

Concepts of print are easy to teach when you use an enlarged text. Simply point out the various features as you read a big book or display another text using a document camera. When you choose a text your students already know, such as a familiar song, poem, or predictable text, they will be able to follow along with you and observe that print represents spoken language.

Shared reading with enlarged text also makes it easy to draw attention to particular letters and sounds. In one study, preschoolers whose teachers did this kind of print referencing had significant gains in alphabet knowledge as compared to preschoolers experiencing typical reading sessions.[22]

Use Shared Reading to Build Vocabulary, Oral Language, and Knowledge

Shared reading is a way of giving your students access to beautiful vocabulary, advanced language structures, and—best of all—knowledge. Yes, you can do this with read-alouds in which students can't follow along, but shared reading lets your students see the words and join in the reading as they are able.

1. **Choose an engaging text that will challenge your students but is still within their reach.** Whenever possible, choose a poem or other text that addresses the concepts you're teaching in other subject areas. If I'm teaching a unit about ocean life to my first graders, we might read *The Narwhal's Predators and Prey* (Figure 3.2).

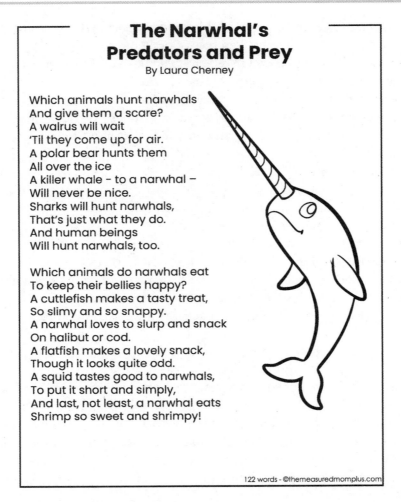

The Narwhal's Predators and Prey

By Laura Cherney

Which animals hunt narwhals
And give them a scare?
A walrus will wait
'Til they come up for air.
A polar bear hunts them
All over the ice
A killer whale - to a narwhal –
Will never be nice.
Sharks will hunt narwhals,
That's just what they do.
And human beings
Will hunt narwhals, too.

Which animals do narwhals eat
To keep their bellies happy?
A cuttlefish makes a tasty treat,
So slimy and so snappy.
A narwhal loves to slurp and snack
On halibut or cod.
A flatfish makes a lovely snack,
Though it looks quite odd.
A squid tastes good to narwhals,
To put it short and simply,
And last, not least, a narwhal eats
Shrimp so sweet and shrimpy!

122 words - ©themeasuredmomplus.com

Figure 3.2   Shared reading poem

2. **Introduce the text and read it aloud.** Remember to track the print so your students can follow along.

3. **Call attention to previously taught sound-spellings or high-frequency words.** This is not a substitute for explicit instruction, but it's a great opportunity to apply skills you've already taught. "You learned that -*y* at the end of words can spell the /ē/ sound. Let's find and read words with this spelling in the second stanza" *(happy, tasty, slimy, snappy, simply, shrimpy).*

4. **Draw attention to vocabulary.** "This poem has many different synonyms for *eat*. A *synonym* is a word that means the same thing as another word. Listen to me read the second stanza. Find a word that means *eat*" *(slurp, snack).*

5. **Build knowledge.** "In the first stanza, I read about five narwhal predators. Follow along as I reread stanza one. Then turn to your partner and see if the two of you can list all five."

6. **Read the text again, inviting students to join you as they're able.** Consider having them join in on words they can sound out, on rhyming words, or on particularly fun phrases ("shrimp so sweet and shrimpy!"). Make it very clear that if your students can't read some (or any) of the words yet, that's okay. "I haven't taught you all these spelling patterns yet. But we'll get there!"

7. **If your students are ready, provide copies of the text for them to read in pairs throughout the week.** Revisit the text on later days, spending fewer than 10 minutes each session. Consider performing the text for school staff or another class at the end of the week.

Make Your Classroom Language-Rich

If it feels like oral language development is one more thing you have to fit into your school day, I have good news! The following strategies only require simple tweaks to what you're already doing.

USE TURN AND TALK

As I shared in Chapter 2, it's time to abandon the age-old practice of asking a question and calling on volunteers. Instead, ask a question and give students a moment to think about their answer. Then have them respond to their partner. Finally, call on non-volunteers to share their answers with the class. This routine is called *turn-and-talk* or *think-pair-share*. Expect each exchange to take about three minutes.[23]

> *It's time to abandon the age-old practice of asking a question and calling on volunteers.*

Be sure to teach the turn-and-talk routine explicitly. Model and practice the following skills: taking turns, answering the question in one or two sentences, showing you are listening by making eye contact and nodding, speaking at an appropriate volume, and refraining from interrupting. Be ready to reteach these speaking and listening skills when your students need a reminder!

If you notice that some pairs have difficulty getting started, staying on topic, or having a meaningful conversation, seat them near you. Then, during turn-and-talk, give feedback and ask follow-up questions with a particular pair. Research shows that children's language benefits from multiple conversations with adults.[24]

USE ACADEMIC VOCABULARY

Academic vocabulary is the vocabulary of school. These words rarely appear in everyday conversation, but teachers and writers of school texts often assume that students know what they mean. We'll get into the specifics of how to teach vocabulary in a later chapter, but for now it's enough to know that you should be using these words often.[25] For the complete academic vocabulary list developed by Gardner and Davies, visit www.academicvocabulary.info.

Consider these examples of academic vocabulary:

◆ What is your **response** to the question?
◆ Please **explain** why you chose that answer.
◆ With your partner, **discuss** the **problem** and **solution** of *Stone Soup*.
◆ I'm going to **assess** your **understanding** with a few questions.
◆ The **objective** of today's lesson is to learn two new ways to spell the /ē/ sound.
◆ Check to make sure that your spelling is **accurate.**
◆ It is **essential** that every sentence begins with a capital letter.
◆ What is one reason that people still remember Johnny Appleseed? Give **evidence** from the passage to **support** your answer.
◆ Use the **context** to **determine** the meaning of the word *hasty*.

DO INTERACTIVE READ–ALOUDS

Make your read-alouds interactive by choosing several stopping points to ask both low- and high-level questions. Low-level questions have limited response options and typically require students to recall information; they're useful for testing knowledge. For example, "Are owls active during the day or at night?" High-level questions require critical thinking and more in-depth responses. For example, "Why did the character make that decision?"

Both types of questions are useful, but read-alouds are most effective when you focus less on low-level questions and more on questions that will encourage students to reflect on big ideas.

Low-level questions to ask during interactive read-alouds
◆ Who is the story mostly about?
◆ When and where does the story take place?
◆ What problem does _____ face?
◆ What happened after _____?
◆ What happened at the end of the story?

High-level questions to ask during interactive read-alouds

- What do you think the character was thinking when _____ ?
- How would you describe the main character?
- How is the setting important to this story?
- What do you think the character will do next, and why?
- What do the character's actions tell you about them?
- What clues did the author use to help you predict the ending?
- Was this story realistic? Why or why not?
- Did that feel like a satisfying ending? Why or why not?
- What lesson do you think the author wants you to learn after listening to this story?
- What do you already know about this topic?
- How does this connect to something you already knew?
- How are _____ and _____ different?
- Why do you think the author chose to _____?

SCAFFOLD ORAL LANGUAGE

It can be discouraging when open-ended questions fall flat, but don't despair! You can support your students in a variety of ways.

Use Sentence Starters

Sentence starters, also called sentence stems, are a type of oral language scaffold and are useful for all grade levels. After asking a question, instruct students to begin their answer with a particular sentence starter. This will help them frame their answer while giving them practice forming complete sentences. Here are a few:

- "I believe that . . ."
- "At the beginning of the story . . ."
- "One thing I learned today is . . ."
- "One surprising fact I learned is that . . ."

Help Students Elaborate on Their Responses

If your first question doesn't yield a meaningful response, Isabel Beck and Margaret McKeown encourage you not to simply ask more questions, but rather to follow up on your students' responses in productive ways. Doing this encourages children to elaborate their language and invites other children to connect to their ideas.[26]

Try these phrases to follow up on student responses:

- ◆ "I heard you say that . . ." or "So are you saying that . . ."
- ◆ "Tell me more about that."
- ◆ "What does that mean?"
- ◆ "How did you figure that out?"
- ◆ "Listen to me reread part of the text before I ask the question again."

Some children may not be ready to elaborate; they struggle to come up with any answer at all. One way to help these students is to offer choices. "Why did the wolf bang on the third pig's door? Was it because he wanted to make a friend, because he wanted to share dessert, or because he wanted to eat the pig?" Another way to scaffold is to turn an open-ended question into a yes or no question. "Is *smart* a good way to describe the third little pig?" You might give a phonological clue. "What was the second little pig's house made of? The answer begins with the /s/ sound."

Use Talk Moves

Researchers have analyzed productive classroom discussions and identified general talk moves that make discussions work. Talk moves are strategic moves by the teacher to open up the conversation and support student participation.[27]

Use the following talk moves to facilitate productive classroom discussions.

Say more	• "Can you say more about that?" • "Can you give an example?"
So, are you saying . . .?	• "Let me see if I understand. Are you saying that . . .?"
Who can rephrase or repeat?	• "Who can put what _____ said into their own words?"
Ask for evidence or reasoning	• "Is there anything in the text that made you think that?" • "Why do you think so?"
Agree/disagree and why	• "Do you agree with ____? Why or why not?" • "Are you saying the same thing as _____, or something different?"
Add on	• "Who can add on to _____'s idea?"
Explain what someone else means	• "Who can explain what _____ means when he says that?" • "Who can explain why they think _____ came up with that answer?"

Adapted from Michaels, S. & O'Connor, Cs. (2012). /https://inquiryproject.terc.edu/shared/pd/TalkScience_Primer.pdf/ last accessed on 16.02.2024

Give Clear Instructions

Some children in your classroom will need more repetitions, more opportunities for practice, and clearer instructions than their peers. Make the language of instruction accessible for everyone by using these techniques:

◆ When giving directions, make sure you are facing your students. If you have a particular student who struggles to follow directions, make eye contact and get down on their level.
◆ After you give directions to the whole class, repeat each step in short, simple sentences.
◆ If students struggle to follow multi-step directions, have them repeat the instructions in their own words.
◆ Use gestures, pictures, and demonstrations whenever possible.

 ## Key Things to Remember

◆ Oral language skills are the foundation for both word reading and language comprehension.
◆ Routines such as Morning Message and Question of the Day can improve oral language skills.
◆ Shared reading of enlarged text can be used to teach concepts of print, support letter learning, and build knowledge and oral language.
◆ Methods such as turn-and-talk give students more opportunities to build oral language skills.
◆ When planning interactive read-alouds, teachers should prepare a list of low- and high-level questions.
◆ You can scaffold oral language by using sentence starters, helping students elaborate on their responses, using talk moves, and giving clear instructions.

Free Resources

◆ List of questions for Question of the Day
◆ Poems for shared reading

www.themeasuredmom.com/bookresources/

Learn More

- Read *Strive-for-Five Conversations* by Tricia Zucker and Sonia Cabell.
- Get Davies' and Gardner's full academic vocabulary list by visiting this link: www.academicvocabulary.info.

Notes

1. Gilkerson, J., Richards, J. A., Warren, S. F., Montgomery, J. K., Greenwood, C. R., Kimbrough Oller, D., Hansen, J. H., & Paul, T.D. (2017). Mapping the early language environment using all-day recordings and automated analysis. *American Journal of Speech Language Pathology, 26*(2), 248–265.
2. Stone, L. (2019). *Reading for life*. Routledge, 9.
3. Dickinson, D. K., Golinkoff, R. M., & Hirsh-Pasek, K. (2010). Speaking out for language: Why language is central to reading development. *Educational Researcher, 39*(4), 305–310.
4. Snow, P. C. (2021). SOLAR: The science of language and reading. *Child Language Teaching and Therapy, 37*(3), 222.
5. Honig, A. S. (2007). Oral language development. *Early Child Development and Care, 177*(6–7), 581–613.
6. Shanahan, T., & Lonigan, C. (2012). The role of early oral language in literacy development. *Language Magazine, 12*(2), 24.
7. Catts, H. W., Fey, M. E., Zhang, X., & Tomblin, J. B. (2001). Estimating the risk of future reading difficulties in kindergarten children: A research-based model and its clinical implementation. *Language, Speech, and Hearing Services in Schools, 32*(1), 38–50.
8. Justice, L., Mashburn, A., & Petscher, Y. (2013). Very early language skills of fifth-grade poor comprehenders. *Journal of Research in Reading, 36*(2), 172–185.
9. Dickinson, D. K., & Tabors, P. O. (2002). Fostering language and literacy in classrooms and homes. (2002). *Young Children, 57*(2), 10–19.
10. National Early Literacy Panel (U.S.), & National Center for Family Literacy (U.S.). (2008). *Executive summary: Developing early literacy: Report of the National Early Literacy Panel*. National Institute for Literacy.

11. Fricke, S., Bowyer-Crane, C., Haley, A. J., Hulme, C., & Snowling, M. J. (2013). Efficacy of language intervention in the early years. *Journal of Child Psychology and Psychiatry, 54*(3), 280–290.

12. Coyne, M. D., Simmons, D. C., Kame'enui, E. J., & Stoolmiller, M. (2004). Teaching vocabulary during shared storybook readings: An examination of differential effects. *Exceptionality, 12*(3), 145–162.

13. National Early Literacy Panel (U.S.) & National Center for Family Literacy (U.S.). (2008).

14. Arnold, D. H., Lonigan, C. J., Whitehurst, G. J., & Epstein, J. N. (1994). Accelerating language development through picture book reading: Replication and extension to a videotape training format. *Journal of Educational Psychology, 86*(2), 235–243.

15. Ibid.

16. Snowling, M. (2019, November 12). *Oral language: The foundations of reading and reading intervention.* [Video]. YouTube. https://www.youtube.com/watch?v=U_pP4DbkrBk.

17. Wasik, B. A., & Hindman, A. H. (2011). The morning message in early childhood classrooms: Guidelines for best practices. *Early Childhood Education Journal, 39*, 183–189.

18. Ibid.

19. Park, B. (1982). The big book trend – a discussion with Don Holdaway. *Language Arts, 59*(8), 815–821.

20. Justice, L. M., Skibbe, L., Canning, A., & Lankford, C. (2005). Pre-schoolers, print, and storybooks: An observational study using eye movement analysis. *Journal of Research in Reading, 28*(3), 229–243.

21. Levy, B. A., Gong, Z., Hessels, S., Evans, M. A., & Jared, D. (2006). Understanding print: Early reading development and the contributions of home literacy experiences. *Journal of Experimental Child Psychology, 93*(1), 63–93.

22. Justice, L. M., Kaderavek, J. N., Fan, X., Sofka, A., & Hunt, A. (2009). Accelerating preschoolers' early literacy development through classroom-based teacher-child storybook reading and explicit print referencing. *Language, Speech, and Hearing Services in Schools, 40*(1), 67–85.

23. Hindman, A. H., Wasik, B. A., & Anderson, K. (2022). Using turn and talk to develop language: Observations in early classrooms. *The Reading Teacher, 76*(1), 6–13.

24. Ibid.

25. Nagy, W., & Townsend, D. (2012). Words as tools: Learning academic vocabulary as language acquisition. *Reading Research Quarterly, 47*(1), 91–108.

26. Beck, I. L., & McKeown, M. G. (2001). Text talk: Capturing the benefits of read-aloud experiences for young children. *The Reading Teacher, 55*(1), 10–20.

27. Michaels, S., & O'Connor, C. (2012). *Talk science primer.* TERC. https://inquiry project.terc.edu/shared/pd/TalkScience_Primer.pdf.

CHAPTER 4

Phonemic Awareness and the Alphabetic Principle

Phonemic awareness, the conscious awareness of individual speech sounds in spoken words, is essential for reading success. English has an alphabetic writing system, so children must be able to identify and manipulate sounds in words in order to match them to letters. Indeed, phonemic awareness may be the missing key for children who struggle with early reading skills.[1]

Phonological Awareness

Phonological awareness is the awareness of sound structures in spoken words. Phonological awareness skills include word awareness, an understanding of rhyme and alliteration, counting syllables, identifying onsets and rimes, *and* phonemic awareness.

Phonological and phonemic awareness are not equivalent. Phonemic awareness is a *component* of phonological awareness; it concerns the smallest units of sound within a spoken word that can distinguish one word from another.

The "Phon" Words

phonology: The study of the speech sounds of a language

phonological awareness: The awareness of sound structures in spoken language

phonemic awareness: The conscious awareness of individual units of sound in spoken words

phoneme: The smallest unit of sound within a spoken word that can distinguish one word from another

phonological sensitivity: Awareness of sounds larger than phonemes (words, syllables, rhymes, and onsets and rimes)

phonics: Reading instruction that teaches letters and the sounds they represent

PHONOLOGICAL SENSITIVITY SKILLS

Phonological sensitivity refers to an awareness of sounds larger than phonemes. Let's take a quick look at phonological sensitivity skills before diving into phonemic awareness.

Word Awareness

Word awareness is the ability to separate a spoken sentence into words. To teach word awareness, point to each word as you read aloud during shared reading activities. Draw students' attention to the spaces between words. You can also teach word awareness when writing the Morning Message. Say the sentence *before* you write it, counting the words with your fingers. Then say each word again as you write the sentence, thinking aloud as you leave spaces between words.

Sensitivity to Rhyme

When two words **rhyme**, the onsets are different, but the rimes sound the same. For example, the words *snail* and *tale* rhyme because their onsets, *sn* and *t*, are different, but their rimes (*ail* and *ale*) sound the same (see Figure 4.1).

Playing with rhyming words is fun and is best done when enjoying rhyming books, nursery rhymes, and rhyming poetry. As you read a rhyming book aloud, leave out the second word of a rhyming pair and let your students fill it in.

While some researchers argue that rhyming ability is important for reading and spelling,[2] many have concluded that rhyming is not necessary for learning to read. In 2002, Macmillan published a meta-analysis on rhyming and concluded that teaching

Figure 4.1 Rhyming words.

rhyming as part of a beginning reading program "is likely to have no effect whatsoever on children's reading ability. It may even hinder progress by necessitating a much slower pace of letter-sound instruction."[3]

The bottom line? Have fun with rhyming, but save your instruction and intervention time for phonemic awareness. Rhyming is not an essential pre-reading skill.

> *We need to let go of the idea that rhyming is an essential pre-reading skill.*

Alliteration

Alliteration is the repetition of the initial sound in two or more words, as in *busy bee*. Technically, alliteration is a beginning phonemic awareness skill because it requires attention to the initial phoneme(s) of words. An example of an alliteration task would be, "Which word has a different first sound: *chair, chess, cheese,* or *cot?*"

Syllables

A **syllable** is a spoken or written unit that has a vowel or vowel sound. The word *basket* has two syllables: bas | ket.

You can draw attention to syllables during shared reading and writing experiences. "Our seeds have begun to *germinate*. Listen to the parts of the word: ger-min-ate. Say the parts with me: ger | min | ate. Watch me spell each syllable."

Playing with syllables is fun, and awareness of syllables will be important when students are reading and spelling multisyllabic words. However, syllable awareness does not need to be mastered (or even taught) before phonemic awareness instruction.[4]

Onset-Rime

Onset-rime is the last of the phonological sensitivity skills. Onsets and rimes are smaller units of sound within a syllable. The **onset** is the part of a syllable before the vowel. The **rime** is the string of letters that begins with the vowel. Not every word or syllable has an onset. *In*, *am*, and *off*, for example, do not have onsets; however, every syllable has a rime (see Figure 4.2).

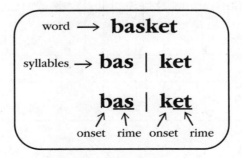

Figure 4.2   Onset and rime.

As with other phonological sensitivity skills, an understanding of onsets and rimes is a poor predictor of reading performance when compared to phonemic awareness.

A FINAL WORD ABOUT PHONOLOGICAL SENSITIVITY SKILLS

Figure 4.3 is useful for showing the complexity of phonological awareness skills. However, children do not always develop these skills from left to right.[5]

Unfortunately, this continuum (often pictured as a staircase) has led to a decades-long misunderstanding that children learn these skills in order, and that they cannot reach a later skill without mastering those earlier in the sequence.

Students do not need to master phonological sensitivity skills before phonemic awareness instruction.

We now know that phonemic awareness is most important for learning to read and that students do not need to master phonological sensitivity skills before phonemic awareness instruction.

Phonemic Awareness: An Overview

Phonemic awareness is the conscious awareness of individual units of sound in spoken words (phonemes). Research clearly shows that early phonemic awareness is a strong predictor of later reading success.[6] Why might this be?

To understand the alphabetic principle, our learners must first become aware of individual phonemes in spoken words.

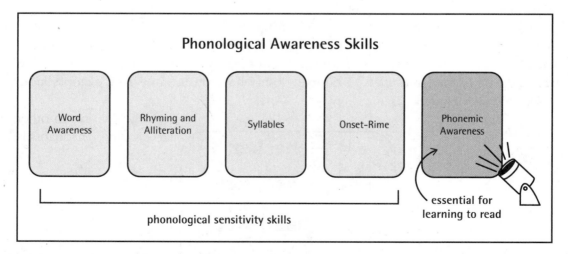

Figure 4.3   Phonological awareness skills.

To understand our alphabetic writing system, we need to recognize that symbols represent units of sound. This understanding is called the **alphabetic principle**. To understand the alphabetic principle, our learners must *first* become aware of individual phonemes in spoken words. In other words, they must have phonemic awareness.[7] Not only does phonemic awareness have a causal relationship with reading achievement, it also has a reciprocal relationship. This means that you can and *should* teach phonemic awareness alongside early decoding instruction.[8]

ALL ABOUT PHONEMES

Even linguists do not agree on the number of phonemes in English, with the total count ranging from 40 to 52.[9] This variance is due to the inexactness of phonemes and differences in dialect.

Consonant Phonemes

A **phoneme** is the smallest unit of sound that can distinguish one spoken word from another. For example, the words *slap* and *snap* differ only by their second phoneme. A **grapheme** is a letter or letters that represent(s) a phoneme. For example, the grapheme *ph* represents the phoneme /f/.

A **consonant phoneme** is a closed speech sound in which the breath is at least partly obstructed by the lips, teeth, and/or tongue. It is very important to pronounce consonant phonemes correctly, without adding a schwa or /ŭ/ sound. For example, teach your students to say /p/, not /puh/.

Consonants may be voiced or unvoiced. **Voiced** consonants are made with engaged vocal cords; **unvoiced** consonants do not engage the vocal cords. When saying a consonant phoneme, put your hand on your throat. If you can feel a little vibration, the consonant is voiced. If not, the consonant is unvoiced. The phoneme /b/ is voiced. The phoneme /p/ is unvoiced. See Figure 4.4.

Consonant phonemes may be **stops** or **continuants**. Unlike stop sounds, you can sustain continuant sounds until you run out of breath. The sound /t/ is a stop sound. The sound /s/ is a continuant sound.

One way to classify consonant phonemes is by the place of articulation—in other words, where the sound is formed in the mouth. Another way to classify consonants is by the manner of articulation—how the sound is made. Figure 4.4 shows this information organized in a single graphic.

Vowel Phonemes

If someone asked you to list the English vowels, what would you say? Many of us would respond, "a, e, i, o, u, and sometimes y." But vowel *phonemes* are different from vowel *graphemes*. Actually, English has up to 19 vowel phonemes.

Consonant Phonemes

🔊 = denotes a voiced phoneme

Place of articulation: WHERE the sound is made

Manner of articulation: HOW the sound is made

		Lips together — BILABIAL	Teeth on lip — LABIODENTAL	Tongue between teeth — INTERDENTAL	Front of mouth — ALVEOLAR	Roof of mouth — PALATAL	Back of mouth — VELAR	In the throat — GLOTTAL
Flow of air is stopped, followed by a puff of air	**STOP**	/p/ /b/			/t/ 🔊/d/		/k/ 🔊/g/	
Air is forced through the nose when the mouth is closed	**NASAL**	🔊/m/			🔊/n/		🔊/ng/	
A hiss or friction through a narrow air channel	**FRICATIVE**		/f/ 🔊/v/	/th/ 🔊/th/	/s/ 🔊/z/		/sh/ 🔊/zh/	/h/
Stop + fricative	**AFFRICATE**					/ch/ 🔊/j/		
Formed in a way similar to vowels	**GLIDE**	🔊/w/					🔊/y/	
Formed by slightly interrupting airflow without causing friction	**LIQUID**				🔊/l/	🔊/r/		

Figure 4.4　Consonant phoneme chart.

Adapted from Moats, L. C. (2020); Blevins, W. (2023).

Vowel phonemes are open speech sounds that are not consonants. A vowel phoneme is included in every spoken syllable. Vowel phonemes may be stressed or unstressed, tense (long) or lax (short). We distinguish vowels from each other based on the place of articulation.

A macron is used to represent long vowel sounds, as in /ā/, /ē/, /ī/, /ō/, and /ū/. A breve is used to represent short vowel sounds, as in /ă/, /ĕ/, /ĭ/, /ŏ/, and /ŭ/.

A **diphthong** is formed by the combination of two vowel sounds; it feels like one vowel sound is gliding into another. The words *boy* and *voice* include the diphthong /oi/. The words *cow* and *house* include the diphthong /ou/. Some programs also classify the /aw/ sound as a diphthong, as in *saw* and *pause*.

The **schwa** is the most common vowel sound in English. It occurs in unstressed syllables and sounds like a lazy /ŭ/ or /ĭ/. In the word *banana*, the first and final vowel sounds are the schwa.

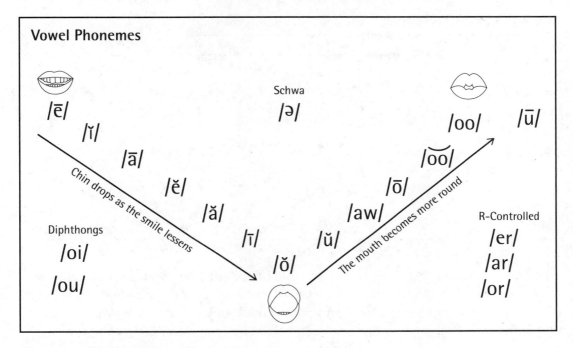

Figure 4.5   Vowel phoneme chart.
Adapted from Moats, L. C. (2020); Blevins, W. (2023).

When a vowel comes before *r*, its sound changes. You can hear **r-controlled vow-els** in *car* - /ar/, *form* - /or/, and *purse* - /er/. Figure 4.5 presents the vowel phonemes according to place of articulation.

WHAT'S THE POINT?

There's no need to memorize the phoneme charts, and you certainly don't need to teach the terminology to your students. But having this information at your fingertips may give you insights into students' difficulties with reading and spelling. For example, if a student mixes up *b* and *p* when spelling, you can see from the consonant phoneme chart that this isn't a surprising mistake. The letters' sounds are formed in the same part of the mouth; they only differ in that /b/ is voiced and /p/ is not. If a student mixes up short a and short e when reading, that's not a surprise either. Notice how close these sounds are on the vowel phoneme chart.

COUNTING PHONEMES

As you can see in Table 4.1, the number of letters in a word does not necessarily match the number of phonemes. This is because a single letter can represent two phonemes (as with the letter *x*), and multiple letters can represent a single phoneme (*igh* spells /ī/).

Table 4.1   Counting phonemes in words.

Word	# of Phonemes	Phonemes
sun	3	/s/ /ŭ/ /n/
land	4	/l/ /ă/ /n/ /d/
twitch	4	/t/ /w/ /ĭ/ /ch/
store	3	/s/ /t/ /or/
charm	3	/ch/ /ar/ /m/
quiz	4	/k/ /w/ /ĭ/ /z/
joy	2	/j/ /oi/
fox	4	/f/ /ŏ/ /k/ /s/
light	3	/l/ /ī/ /t/

While counting phonemes is pretty straightforward once you get the hang of it, there are different opinions when it comes to the /or/ and /ar/ sounds. Because the *r* influences the vowel sound, most programs count an r-controlled vowel as a single phoneme.

PHONEMIC AWARENESS TASKS

A set of tasks can be used to test students' phonemic awareness skills (see Table 4.2). The simplest task is **phoneme isolation**, which involves having students identify individual (such as initial, medial, or final) phonemes in words. **Phoneme blending** is when students combine phonemes to make a word. This skill is essential for decoding words. **Phoneme segmentation** is breaking a word apart into its phonemes; children need this skill when they begin to spell. Finally, **phoneme manipulation** involves adding, deleting, or substituting phonemes.

Table 4.2   Phonemic Awareness Tasks

Phoneme isolation	• Say *chat*. What sound did you say at the beginning of *chat*? • Say *sheep*. What sound did you say in the middle of *sheep*? • Which word has the same first sound as dog? Fish, cat, duck, or goat? • Which word does not belong? Mouse, mushroom, map, or book?
Phoneme blending	• Blend these sounds together to make a word: /s/ /ŭ/ /n/
Phoneme segmentation	• Say the sounds in the word "flip."
Phoneme manipulation	• Add /t/ to the end of "well." What's the new word? • What is "slap" without the /l/? • The word is "west." Change the /s/ to /n/. What's the word?

SEQUENCE OF PHONEMIC AWARENESS DEVELOPMENT

The location of a phoneme in a word influences how easy it is for students to be aware of it. For example, students are aware of initial phonemes (such as /d/ in *dinosaur*) before they demonstrate an awareness of final phonemes (such as /ch/ in *beach*).

Figure 4.6 shows the sequence of phonemic awareness development.[10] Knowing this sequence helps you plan instruction. In addition, understanding this sequence is useful when analyzing students' spelling errors, which can alert you to errors in phonemic awareness development. For example, if a child spells *bt* for *bat*, they may not yet be aware of medial phonemes in spoken words. If a child spells *jump* as *jup*, they may not be aware of internal consonants in final blends.

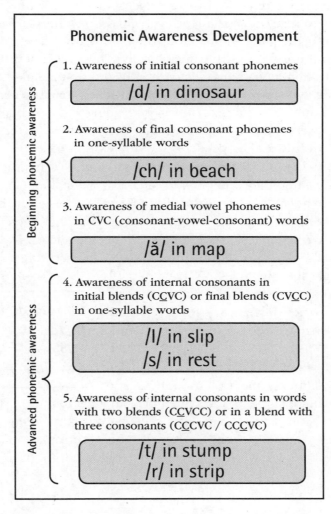

Figure 4.6 Sequence of phonemic awareness development.

What the Research Says

Here's a quick refresher on effect sizes. An effect size measures whether the instruction made a difference on student learning. An effect size lower than 0.2 doesn't have much practical significance, which basically means that we can't be sure that the instruction made any difference. A value between 0.2 and 0.5 is small, a value between 0.5 and 0.8 is medium, and an effect size greater than 0.8 is considered large.

- **Phonemic awareness training helps students acquire phonemic awareness.** Children will acquire *some* phonemic awareness naturally as they learn to read and spell. However, children with explicit instruction in blending, segmenting, and manipulating phonemes achieve a much higher level than those who learn it incidentally. The NRP found that phonemic awareness training had an effect size of 0.86 on phonemic awareness.[11]

- **Phonemic awareness training helps children learn to read and spell.** The NRP found an effect size of 0.53 on reading and 0.59 on spelling.[12]

- **Phonemic awareness training has the greatest effect size when taught to children in preschool.** Start early! The NRP found a larger effect size when phonemic awareness was taught to children in preschool and kindergarten than when it was taught to older students.[13]

- **Phonemic awareness training is most effective when it focuses on just 1-2 tasks at a time.** The National Reading Panel found an effect size of 0.71 when a single skill was taught per session and 0.79 when two skills were taught. The effect size dropped to 0.27 when three or more skills were taught in a single lesson.[14]

- **Phonemic awareness instruction is most effective when letters are incorporated.** For years we've been told that phonemic awareness instruction should not include letters, and that if we add letters we've switched to phonics. But phonemic awareness and

> *Phonemic awareness instruction is most effective when letters are incorporated.*

phonics can be taught at the same time. Students *must* be using phonemic awareness alongside their phonics skills because they blend and segment phonemes when they read and spell. The NRP found an effect size of 0.61 when letters were manipulated, compared to 0.34 when letters were not.[15]

- **Less is more.** According to the NRP, the ideal amount of total phonemic awareness instruction is 5–9.3 hours, yielding an effect size of 1.37, or 10–18 hours, with an effect size of 1.14. You might think that more is better, but when the children received instruction for longer time periods, the effect size was 0.65.[16] If you spread 10–18 hours over a typical school year, that's just 3–6 minutes a day.
- **Students learn phonemic awareness best when they are taught in small groups**. The NRP found an effect size of 1.38 when phonemic awareness was taught in small groups, compared to 0.67 when it was taught to the whole class.[17]
- **Phonemic awareness is a means rather than an end.** Phonemic awareness is not meaningful in and of itself; it only matters in the context of reading instruction.[18] That's why it's so important to incorporate letters in phonemic awareness instruction whenever possible.

Teaching Phonemic Awareness

Phonemic awareness is best learned by pronouncing spoken words and segmenting them in order to spell them.[19] This is good news! You don't need a separate, oral-only phonemic awareness program that takes 10–15 minutes per day. Instead, integrate your phonemic awareness instruction into your phonics lessons.

While it's true that you'll want to integrate letters as soon as possible, it's helpful to establish phonemic awareness as a listening activity first. Think of it as warming up the ears for what students will work on in print.

TEACH STRETCHED SEGMENTING

In her book, *Teaching Word Recognition,* Rollanda O'Connor recommends the following oral procedure.[20]

Teacher	My word is *fish*. Fish swim in the ocean. Listen to me say *fish* really slowly. *Fffffiiiiisssshhh*. Say it with me.
Students & Teacher	*Fffffiiiiisssshhh. (The teacher signals when to move to the next phoneme by moving their hand away from their body with each new phoneme.)*
Teacher	Your turn.
Students	*Fffffiiiiisssshhh (Again, the teacher uses hand motions to help children know when to move into each phoneme.)*

WORDS TO USE FOR STRETCHED SEGMENTING

Use words with continuous phonemes for this activity. Start with the bold words, since they begin *and* end with continuous phonemes.

fan	led	meet	**nose**	rug	shed
feed	lid	**mom**	not	**run**	**shin**
feet	**loaf**	**moon**	note	sack	ship
fin	mad	mop	nut	sad	shop
fog	make	mope	rag	sag	sit
lake	**man**	mud	rake	**Sam**	soak
lane	made	mug	**ram**	same	soap
late	**mane**	**name**	read	sat	sub
leaf	**mash**	neat	red	**seal**	**sun**
lean	**math**	neck	rich	seed	**van**
leap	**meal**	need	rip	**seem**	**vase**
leash	**mean**	**noon**	robe	shape	**zoo**

TEACH STRETCHED BLENDING

The following procedure is also based on one shared by O'Connor in *Teaching Word Recognition.*[21]

Teacher	We have a set of four pictures. After I name each picture, repeat it. Van.
Students	Van.
Teacher	Fish.
Students	Fish. (etc.)

Teacher	I'm going to stretch out one of these words. The word is ssssoooaaaap. Say it with me.
Students & Teacher	Ssssoooaaaap.
Teacher	Which of these words was that?
Students	Soap.

Continue with the rest of the words on the card. When students are ready, do the activity without pictures. Simply stretch one word at a time, and have students say the word.

TEACH STUDENTS HOW TO ISOLATE THE INITIAL, FINAL, OR MEDIAL SOUND IN WORDS

Start with words whose first sound can be sustained, as in *mmmmmmoon*. When using words whose first sound cannot be stretched, emphasize the first sound in a staccato fashion, as in *p-p-pot*.

Teacher	My word is *moon*. What's the word?
Students	Moon.
Teacher	Listen to me stretch the word into its sounds. /mmmooonnn/. Your turn.
Students	/mmmmooooonnnnn/.
Teacher	Say it again, but this time I'll stop you on the first sound.
Students	/mmmm-/
Teacher	Stop. What sound did you say?
Students	/m/
Teacher	/m/ is the first sound in *moon*.

TEACH STUDENTS TO PLAY SIMPLE PHONEME ISOLATION GAMES

When students understand how to identify initial, final, or medial phonemes, teach them to play simple games with a partner.

Tic-tac-toe

To place a piece, students should say the picture's name and then isolate its initial, final, or medial sound.

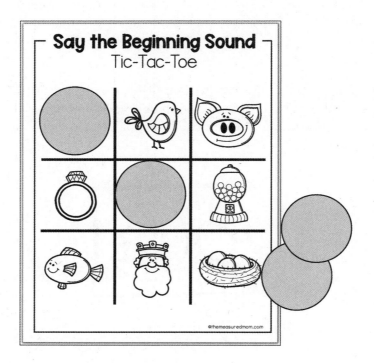

Say the Sound

When they roll the die and land on a space, students should say the picture's name and its initial, final, or medial sound.

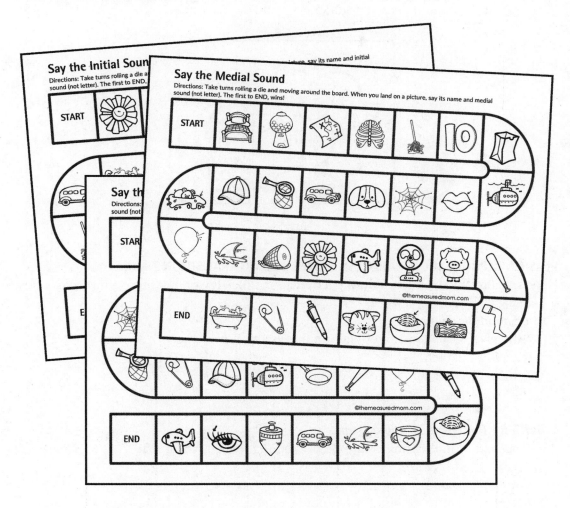

Where Is the Sound?

The teacher should ask students to listen for a particular phoneme. Is it at the beginning, middle, or end of the word? (The sound is /m/. My word is *man*. Say the word. Where is the /m/ sound in *man*?) Students should put their chip in the appropriate space.

PLAY ORAL PHONEMIC AWARENESS GAMES DURING TRANSITION TIMES

Need to calm students down during a transition time? Try one of these simple activities.

Turtle Sound Blending

Teacher	My sounds are lllllluuuuunnnnnch. What's the word?
Students	Lunch.
Teacher	My sounds are boooooot. What's the word?
Students	Boot.

What Am I Thinking? Blending Game

Teacher	I'm thinking of a type of clothing. Its sounds are /h/ /ă/ /t/. What's the word?
Students	Hat.
Teacher	I'm thinking of a type of sea animal. Its sounds are /k/ /r/ /ă/ /b/. What's the word?
Students	Crab.

Blending Detectives

Teacher	I've got a mystery food. Its sounds are /b/ /ē/ /n/ /z/. What's the mystery food?
Students	Beans.

Teacher	The sounds are /ch/ /ē/ /z/. What's the mystery food?
Students	Cheese.
Teacher	The sounds are /g/ /r/ /ā/ /p/. What's the mystery food?
Students	Grape.

Clap, Tap, or Stomp Phonemes

Teacher	Our first word is *shirt*. What's the word?
Students	Shirt.
Teacher	Say and clap the sounds with me.
All	*/sh/ /er/ /t/*
Teacher	Our next word is *belt*. What's the word?
Students	Belt.
Teacher	Say and clap the sounds with me.
All	*/b/ /ĕ/ /l/ /t/*

BEGIN PHONICS LESSONS WITH A PHONEMIC AWARENESS WARMUP

Before teaching a new sound-spelling, introduce the phoneme with a phonemic aware-ness warm-up featuring that sound. The following script could be used when teaching that *sh* spells /sh/.

Teacher	Listen to my silly sentence. *Shelly shared shampoo with a shark.* Say it with me.
Students & Teacher	Shelly shared shampoo with a shark.
Teacher	What sound did you say at the beginning of most of those words?
Students	/sh/
Teacher	What is your mouth doing when you say the sound /sh/?
Students	(Answers will vary.)
Teacher	Let's practice blending with the /sh/ sound. My sounds are /sh/ /ĭ/ /p/. What's the word?
Students	Ship. (Repeat with *mash, shut,* and *dish.*)
Teacher	Now we're going to break words into their sounds. Tap and say the sounds of *mush*.
Students	/m/ /ŭ/ /sh/ (Repeat with *cash, shed,* and *shell*)
Teacher	We spell the /sh/ sound with the letters *sh*.

Alliterative Sentences for Phonemic Awareness Warmups

- **A**nnie Astronaut asked for apples.
- **A**my's ape ate acorns.
- **B**ernie baked a batch of brownies.
- **C**ooper cut cooked carrots.
- **D**an danced the disco with his daughter.
- **E**dgar the Emperor emptied the envelope.
- **E**ve eats an eel.
- **F**ive feathers fell fast.
- **G**us gave gum as a gift.
- **H**ungry hippos have hamburgers.
- **I**sabel Insect itched and itched.
- **I**ris eyed ice cream.
- **J**ohnny Jaguar did a jumping jack.
- **K**im kept her kite in the kitchen.
- **L**ittle Lisa licked a lollipop.
- **M**any mice make music.
- **N**ora naps at noon.
- **O**llie operates on the octopus.
- **O**pal owns an overcoat.
- **P**ercy packed purple pants.
- **Qu**een Quinn quit quarreling.
- **R**andy raced Ralph to the red rug.
- **S**ally sat on the sofa and sewed.
- **T**wo tall turkeys told tales.
- **U**ncle's umbrella is ugly.
- **U**tticus used utensils.
- **V**ictor the vulture visited the village.
- **W**anda wore a white wig.
- Ma**x** put the toy T-Rex in a box.
- **Y**oung yaks yawn.
- **Z**elda zipped zero zippers.
- **Sh**elly shared shampoo with a shark.
- **Ch**ip chewed the charred chocolate.
- **Th**in Thelma thought.

ADD LETTERS TO PHONEMIC AWARENESS INSTRUCTION

As soon as you start teaching letter-sound correspondences, you can combine phonemic awareness and phonics instruction (yes, even in preschool!). As students break words into speech sounds and represent those sounds with letters, they learn the alphabetic principle.[22]

Use Sound Boxes

Sound boxes are an excellent tool for building phonemic awareness.

1. Give each student a strip of up to four boxes and a set of manipulatives.
2. Name a word with 2–4 phonemes.
3. Have students segment the word into its phonemes, pushing counters into boxes to represent the phonemes (see Figure 4.7).
4. Guide your students as they move each counter and write the letter that spells its sound (see Figure 4.8).

Figure 4.7   Sound boxes without letters.
Image by Rocio Zapata

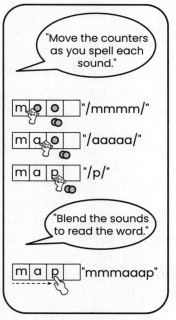

Figure 4.8   Adding letters to sound boxes.
Image by Rocio Zapata

Sound Box Tips

◆ Follow the sequence of development as noted in Figure 4.6. Start with three-phoneme words. Then move on to words with initial or final blends.
◆ Always remember that students should spell a *single phoneme* in each box, even if that phoneme's spelling includes more than one letter, as in *ch, sh, th,* or *ck*.

Use Letter Tiles

1. Give your students letter tiles featuring the graphemes you've taught so far.
2. Name a word. Count its phonemes as you segment the word into phonemes. Spell each phoneme using the letter tiles (see Figure 4.9).
3. As they move the letter tiles, encourage your students to say the letter's sound rather than its name.
4. Eventually have students change their word into a new word by switching a single grapheme.

Teacher	Point to each tile and say the letter's sound.
Students	/m/, /t/, /s/, /ă/.
Teacher	The first word you're going to spell is the word *sat*. Say *sat*.
Students	*Sat.*
Teacher	Let's stretch the word together.
Students	/sssssssaaaaaat/.
Teacher	What's the first sound in *sat?*
Students	/ssss/.
Teacher	Move the letter that spells /s/. (Students move the letter *s*.) What's the next sound in *sat?*
Students	/ă/.
Teacher	Add the letter that spells /ă/. (Students move the letter *a*.)
Teacher	What's the final sound in *sat?*
Students	/t/.
Teacher	Add the letter that spells /t/. (Students move the letter *t*.)
Teacher	Move your finger under the word and blend the sounds to read the word.
Students	Ssssaaat.
Teacher	Let's change the word *sat* to *mat*. Which spelling will you need to change? (Students point to the letter *s*.)
Teacher	Move out the /s/ and add the /m/. Then move your finger under the letters to read the word.

Figure 4.9 Using letter tiles.

Image by Rocio Zapata

Use Dry-Erase Boards

As your students become more proficient, switch to dry erase boards and markers. The following activity builds advanced phonemic awareness skills, since students will be working with internal consonants in blends (see Figure 4.10).

Teacher	The first word you're going to spell is *flip*. Say the word.
Students	*Flip*.
Teacher	Let's stretch the word together.
Students	/ffffflllllliiiip/.
Teacher	Let's tap the sounds.
Students	/f/ /l/ /ĭ/ /p/.
Teacher	Write the letters that spell the sounds. (Students write *flip*.)
Teacher	Your new word is *slip*. Say the word.
Students	Slip.
Teacher	How will you change *ffffflip* to *sssslip?* Point to the spelling you will change. (Students point to the letter *f*.)
Teacher	What spells /s/? Erase *f* and write the new letter. (Students change *f* to *s*.) Run your finger under the word as you read it.
Students	Slip.
Teacher	Your new word is *slap*. Which letter will you change? Point to it. (Students point to *i*.) Erase the *i* and write the new letter. (Students change *i* to *a*). Continue with this chain: *snap, snack*, and *smack*.

Figure 4.10 Using dry-erase boards.

Image by Rocio Zapata

Key Things to Remember

- Rhyming and syllable counting do not need to be taught before phonemic awareness instruction.
- Phonemic awareness is a predictor of reading success, but it also continues to develop as children learn to read and spell.
- Phonemic awareness instruction is most effective when letters are incorporated. This does not turn the activity into phonics; it merely adds phonics.
- The most powerful way to teach the alphabetic principle is to show children how to divide words into sounds, spell each sound, and read back the word they've spelled.
- Incorporate phonemic awareness into your phonics lessons.

Free Resources

- Pictures for stretched blending
- Printable games: Tic-tac-toe, "Say the Sound," "Where Is the Sound?"
- Word lists for phonemic awareness activities

www.themeasuredmom.com/bookresources

Learn More

- Read *Teaching Word Recognition,* by Rollanda E. O'Connor.
- Read the IDA fact sheet about building phonemic awareness: https://dyslexiaida .org/new-fact-sheet-building-phoneme-awareness/.
- Listen to this interview with Dr. Susan Brady: www.themeasuredmom.com/ phoneme-awareness-susan-brady/.

Notes

1. Stanovich, K. E. (2009). Matthew effects in reading: Some consequences of individual differences in the acquisition of literacy. *Journal of Education, 189*(1–2), 23–55.

2. Bryant, P. E., Bradley, L., Maclean, M., & Crossland, J. (1989). Nursery rhymes, phonological skills, and reading. *Journal of Child Language, 16*(2), 407–428.
Goswami, U. (1990). A special link between rhyming skill and the use of orthographic analogies by beginning readers. *Journal of Child Psychology and Psychiatry, 31*(2), 301–311.

3. Macmillan, B. M. (2002). Rhyme and reading: A critical review of the research methodology. *Journal of Research in Reading, 25*(1), 32.

4. Geiger, A. (Host). (2023, April 3). What we know about phoneme awareness with Dr. Susan Brady (No. 118) [Audio podcast episode]. In *Triple R Teaching*. Anna Geiger. https://www.themeasuredmom.com/phoneme-awareness-susan-brady/.

5. Seidenberg, M. [Reading Meetings]. (2021, September 12). *Phonemes, speech, and reading*. [Video]. YouTube. https://www.youtube.com/watch?v=bq_xA3NfO54.

6. Ball, E. W., & Blachman, B. A. (1991). Does phoneme awareness training in kindergarten make a difference in early word recognition and developmental spelling? *Reading Research Quarterly, 26*(1), 49–66.

7. Brady, S. (2020). A 2020 perspective on research findings on alphabetics (phoneme awareness and phonics): Implications for instruction. *The Reading League Journal, 1*(3), 20–28.

8. Perfetti, C. A., Beck, I., Bell, L. C., & Hughes, C. (1987). Phonemic knowledge and learning to read are reciprocal: A longitudinal study of first grade children. *Merrill-Palmer Quarterly, 33*(3), 283–319.

9. Moats, L. C. (2020). *Speech to print*. Paul H. Brookes Publishing Co.

10. Brady, S. (2020).

11. National Reading Panel (U.S.) & National Institute of Child Health and Human Development (U.S.). (2000). *Report of the National Reading Panel: Teaching children to read: An evidence-based assessment of the scientific research literature on reading and its implications for reading instruction.* U.S. Dept. of Health and Human Services, Public Health Service, National Institutes of Health, National Institute of Child Health and Human Development.

12. Ibid.

13. Ibid.

14. Ibid.

15. Ibid.

16. Ibid.

17. Ibid.

18. Yopp, H. K., & Yopp, R. H. (2000). Supporting phonemic awareness development in the classroom. *The Reading Teacher, 54*(2), 130–143.

19. Herron, J. (2022). Personal communication (Spell Talk listserv).

20. O'Connor, R. E. (2014).

21. Ibid.

22. O'Connor, R. E., & Jenkins, J. R. (1995). Improving the generalization of sound/syllable knowledge: Teaching spelling to kindergarten children with disabilities. *The Journal of Special Education, 29*(3), 255–275.

CHAPTER 5

Phonics

Phonics is a method of instruction that teaches students the relationships between letters and sounds and how to use those relationships to read and spell words.

Code Emphasis Versus Meaning Emphasis

As a balanced literacy teacher, I knew phonics was important. But I feared that a strong initial emphasis on phonics (the code) would detract from meaning and lead to a class of "word callers," children who could read words but couldn't make sense of what they read.

Even though I never considered myself a whole language teacher, I had bought into its alluring lie: that meaning should be emphasized from the start, because children did not need to learn the "basics" first. I believed that if I surrounded my students with quality literature, read to them often, and gave them real books to read, reading would develop naturally. Researcher Jeanne Chall wrote that whole language "is a romantic view of learning. It is imbued with love and hope. But, sadly, research has shown it to be less effective than a developmental view, and least effective for those who tend to be at risk for learning to read."[1]

THE RELATIONSHIP BETWEEN PHONICS AND COMPREHENSION

Structured literacy advocates do not deny the importance of comprehension. However, they understand that reading comprehension is not a major goal *right from the start*. Rather, reading comprehension is an *outcome*.

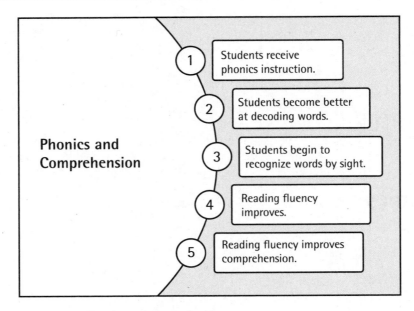

Figure 5.1 Phonics and comprehension.

As phonics expert Wiley Blevins points out, students first receive phonics instruction and begin to understand how to use letters to represent words. The more phonics instruction they receive, the better they become at decoding words. With more practice at decoding, students begin to recognize words by sight because they've orthographically mapped them. The more words students recognize by sight, the more their reading fluency improves. The more fluent readers are, the less mental energy they need for identifying words, thus freeing the brain to focus on comprehension (see Figure 5.1).[2]

WHY NOT THREE-CUEING?

As a balanced literacy teacher, it did not trouble me that my students could not yet decode many of the words in their leveled books. Because the books were predictable and had strong picture support, my students could usually land on the correct words using pictures and context, syntax, and the limited phonics knowledge they did have. Even though they couldn't read the words in isolation, they *did* understand the stories. And wasn't that the most important thing? (Spoiler alert: At this stage, it was not.)

My students quickly picked up on the patterns and "read" many of these books fluently. This masked their lack of decoding skills. I didn't realize that I was teaching them to *behave* like skilled readers without teaching them the skills to *become* skilled readers.

As described in Chapter 1, three-cueing is a model of reading based on the theory that skilled readers use meaning, syntax, and visual (phonics) cues to read (see Figure 5.2).

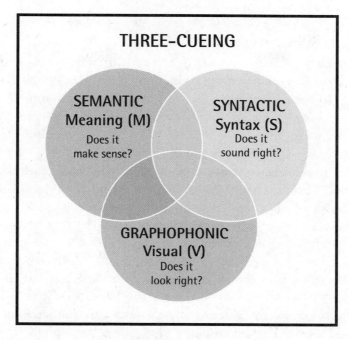

Figure 5.2 The three-cueing model.

Teachers who believe in three-cueing use prompts such as, "What would make sense?" "Use the picture to help you." "Did that sound right?" While three-cueing is presented as a Venn diagram giving each "cue" equal space, in practice the visual (phonics) cue is used as a last resort.[3]

I accepted three-cueing without reservation. Little did I know that this popular theory has no research support. Stanovich and West discovered this for themselves in 1989. While they initially believed that their research would substantiate three-cueing, it actually revealed that *poorer* readers, not the more skilled ones, rely more on context. "We *did* start with a theoretical bias, one consistent with the top down view. But in real science, one is eventually influenced by evidence, regardless of one's initial bias."[4]

As a balanced literacy teacher, I refused to believe that I was teaching students to guess at words. But guessing is a hallmark of three-cueing because, without the phonics knowledge to decode a word, students can't be sure of its identity. When I acknowledged that three-cueing encourages guessing, I began to understand that the system falls apart when students begin to read texts with complex vocabulary and fewer pictures. Three-cueing teaches students to rely on that which is unreliable, while the goal of phonics instruction is to ensure that students can read each and every word automatically.[5]

Three-cueing teaches students to rely on that which is unreliable.

What the Research Says

- **Students are more successful at reading when beginning reading instruction has a code emphasis.** Chall found that an initial code emphasis leads to better reading achievement by the beginning of fourth grade than a meaning emphasis. In other words, when teachers prioritize phonics *at the beginning*, students will be better at both identifying words and understanding what they read later on.[6]

- **Phonics instruction should be systematic and explicit.**[7] Systematic instruction includes routines in which sound-spelling relationships are taught in a logical order, from simple to more complex. Review is built in. When phonics instruction is explicit, teachers directly teach sound-spelling relationships. First, they model the new skill. Then they help students apply it. Finally, they release students to apply the skill independently.

- **Students need phonemic awareness to make sense of phonics.**[8] Phonemic awareness provides the foundation for decoding. When teachers combine phonemic awareness and phonics through spelling and reading exercises, they help their students understand the alphabetic principle.

- **Good phonics instruction leads to less reliance on decoding.** The more practice students have at sounding out words, the sooner they will orthographically map words and recognize them by sight.[9]

- **When struggling readers have phonics weaknesses, they should receive intense intervention.** Remediation in the early grades has been shown to have lasting results.[10]

- **Phonics is not a full reading program.**[11] Ehri writes, "The goal of making every child a reader is not easy. There is no magic pill to make it happen. Systematic phonics instruction by itself does not help students acquire all the processes they need to become successful readers."[12]

Types of Phonics Instruction

There are four main types of phonics instruction: synthetic, analytic, embedded, and analogy (see Figure 5.3).

- **Synthetic phonics** is direct and explicit. Students learn sound-spelling relationships and blend the sounds together from left to right. They practice reading words using short decodable books or passages.

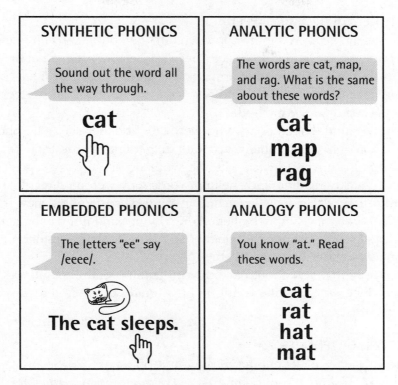

Figure 5.3   Four types of phonics instruction.

◆ With **analytic phonics**, students examine a set of words and try to find what sound they have in common. They are then taught to make a generalization about what spelling represents the sound.

◆ **Embedded phonics** is when the teacher teaches phonics on an "as needed" basis. During an individual reading conference, a teacher might notice that a student is stuck on the word *sleeps*. The teacher uses this opportunity to teach the student that *ee* is pronounced /ē/.

◆ **Analogy phonics** is also known as the word family approach. Students look for chunks in a word to help them read it. For example, if a child can read *at*, they can also read *cat, rat, hat,* and *mat*.

So, which type of phonics instruction is best? Most systematic, explicit phonics programs use the synthetic approach. The biggest benefit to this approach is that as soon as students know a handful of letter-sound relationships, they can start sounding out simple words like *mat*.

WHAT ABOUT THE WORD FAMILY APPROACH?

I used to favor using the word family approach (analogy phonics) with beginning readers because it felt easier. However, easier doesn't necessarily mean better.

A 2004 study found that kindergartners who were taught synthetic phonics had significantly better reading, spelling, and phonemic awareness than students who were taught using the word family method.[13]

A 2005 study found that students who were taught either synthetic phonics or the word family approach were equally accurate at reading words their programs had taught. However, those who learned with the synthetic phonics approach were significantly better at quickly reading and spelling words they weren't directly taught.[14]

The bottom line is that teaching reading using word families may seem like it's working, but children may simply be generating rhymes and not paying attention to all the letters in each word. Despite the tougher start, emphasizing attention to all letters, left to right, may be more beneficial in the long run.

This isn't to say that you should avoid word families entirely. But you might want to wait to introduce word families until mid-first grade or later as a way to reinforce spelling patterns.[15]

TYPES OF ENGLISH GRAPHEMES

A **grapheme** is a letter or letters that represent a phoneme. For example, the grapheme *sh* usually represents the phoneme /sh/. There are many names for letter-sound relationships like this one: sound-spellings, sound-spelling relationships, sound-spelling correspondences, sound-symbol relationships, letter-sound associations, letter-sound correspondences, and grapheme-phoneme correspondences (GPCs). Table 5.1 shows a list of English graphemes organized by type.

Table 5.1   Types of English Graphemes

Grapheme	Examples	Notes
A **single consonant letter** represents a phoneme that is formed by obstructing the flow of air with the teeth, lips, or tongue.	bus, cat, den, fig, get, ham, jug, kick, let, man, net, pig, rid, sun, tap, vet, wig, yes, zip	
Odd letter x is the only letter that represents two phonemes, /k/ and /s/.	fox	
Combination qu is unique because q is always followed by u in English words. Combination qu represents the sounds /k/ and /w/.	quiz	

Grapheme	Examples	Notes
A **single vowel letter** represents a phoneme that is produced with no obstruction of the vocal tract.	c<u>a</u>t, m<u>e</u>t, t<u>i</u>n, h<u>o</u>t, b<u>u</u>g	Words with the consonant-short vowel-consonant pattern are known as CVC words.
A **doublet** is a double consonant that represents a single phoneme.	pu<u>ff</u>, wi<u>ll</u>, hi<u>ss</u>, fu<u>zz</u>	Words with double ff, ll, ss, or zz after a short vowel are said to follow the FLOSS rule.
A **consonant digraph** is a combination of two consonant letters that represent a single speech sound different from each letter's individual sound.	<u>ch</u>op, <u>ph</u>ase, <u>sh</u>ip, <u>th</u>in, <u>th</u>en, <u>wh</u>en, du<u>ck,</u> cou<u>gh</u>	I include *ck* in this category even though both letters can represent the /k/ sound.
Initial consonant blends are two or three consonant letters at the beginning of a word whose sounds seem to blend together when spoken; however, each keeps its individual sound.	l-blends: <u>bl</u>og, <u>cl</u>ip, <u>fl</u>ag, <u>gl</u>ad, <u>pl</u>ug, <u>sl</u>ed r-blends: <u>br</u>ing, <u>cr</u>ib, <u>dr</u>ess, <u>gr</u>ill, <u>fr</u>og, <u>pr</u>ess, <u>tr</u>ip s-blends: <u>sc</u>at, <u>sk</u>ip, <u>sm</u>oke, <u>sn</u>ip, <u>sp</u>in, <u>st</u>ill, <u>sw</u>im, <u>sl</u>ap Others: <u>dw</u>ell, <u>tw</u>in 3-letter blends: <u>scr</u>atch, <u>str</u>ing, <u>spr</u>ung, <u>spl</u>at	Some experts prefer to use the word *blend* only as a verb. They often refer to consonant blends as *consonant clusters*. Teach children to read CCVC, CVCC, CCVCC, and CCCVC words, but don't teach each blend individually as a unit. I don't recommend putting blends on flash cards.
Final consonant blends are blends that appear at the end of a word or syllable.	pa<u>ct</u>, le<u>ft</u>, we<u>ld</u>, she<u>lf</u>, bu<u>lk</u>, be<u>lt</u>, ra<u>mp</u>, sa<u>nd</u>, a<u>nt</u>, a<u>sk</u>, cla<u>sp</u>, fi<u>st</u>, pu<u>lp</u>, we<u>pt</u>, te<u>xt</u>	
An **initial consonant digraph blend** is a three-letter blend at the beginning of a word that consists of a digraph and a consonant.	<u>shr</u>ink, <u>squ</u>int, <u>thr</u>ill, <u>sch</u>ool, <u>sph</u>ere, <u>chr</u>ome, <u>phr</u>ase, <u>thw</u>ack	*Squ-* is not technically a consonant digraph blend.
A **final consonant digraph blend** is a three-letter blend at the end of a word that consists of a consonant and a digraph.	wi<u>dth</u>, fi<u>fth</u>, fi<u>lch</u>, hea<u>lth</u>, lym<u>ph</u>, wre<u>nch</u>, te<u>nth</u>, war<u>mth</u>	Final consonant digraph blends can also include four letters, as in twe<u>lfth</u> and stre<u>ngth</u>.
Consonant trigraphs are three letters that represent a single sound	fe<u>tch</u>, bu<u>dge</u>	
The letters ng & nk may be referred to as **glued** or **welded sounds**, because it's difficult to hear the individual sound of each letter when combined with the vowel that precedes it. Many programs teach them as chunks.	thi<u>nk</u>, ba<u>nk</u>, bo<u>nk</u>, ju<u>nk</u>, ri<u>ng</u>, lo<u>ng</u>, sa<u>ng</u>, flu<u>ng</u>	Technically, *ng* is a consonant digraph and *nk* is a consonant blend.

(continued)

Table 5.1   (continued)

Grapheme	Examples	Notes
Vowel–consonant–e is a common spelling pattern for long vowel sounds. Words with this pattern may be called CVCE words, magic e words, or silent e words.	st<u>a</u>k<u>e</u>, h<u>e</u>r<u>e</u>, d<u>i</u>m<u>e</u>, l<u>o</u>n<u>e</u>, m<u>u</u>t<u>e</u>	Very few one-syllable words use the vowel-consonant-e pattern to spell long e (eve, here, theme, scene, Pete).
R-controlled vowel is the name given to a vowel-r combination. The r changes the sound of the vowel. These are also called bossy r or r-influenced vowels.	f<u>ar</u>m, c<u>or</u>n, h<u>er</u>, st<u>ir</u>, p<u>ur</u>se	Some programs give special attention to long vowels followed by r: ch<u>air</u>, h<u>ear</u>, st<u>are</u>, and so on.
Vowel teams are two, three, or four letters that represent a single vowel sound.	Long a: r<u>ai</u>n, p<u>ay</u>, st<u>ea</u>k, w<u>eigh</u>, v<u>ei</u>n, th<u>ey</u> Long e: sw<u>ee</u>t, h<u>ea</u>t, k<u>ey</u>, w<u>ei</u>rd, fi<u>e</u>ld, happ<u>y</u> Long i: p<u>ie</u>, th<u>igh</u>, fl<u>y</u> Long o: s<u>oa</u>p, t<u>oe</u>, sn<u>ow</u> Long u: st<u>ew</u>, gl<u>ue</u>, n<u>eu</u>tral, j<u>ui</u>ce, z<u>oo</u>m	The single letter y (as in happ<u>y</u> or fl<u>y</u>) is obviously not a team, but it fits well here. Some people call *oo* a variant vowel. Long oo appears in z<u>oo</u>m. Short oo appears in b<u>oo</u>k.
A **diphthong** is a vowel sound that glides in the middle; the mouth shifts during the production of the single vowel phoneme.	t<u>oy</u> / v<u>oi</u>ce; c<u>ou</u>ch / h<u>ow</u>l, s<u>au</u>ce / l<u>aw</u>	Some programs do not call au/aw spellings diphthongs; they may be called variant or complex vowels.
A **silent letter combination** is one in which only one consonant's sound is heard.	de<u>b</u>t, <u>g</u>nat, <u>k</u>nit, lam<u>b</u>, <u>p</u>sychiatrist, <u>rh</u>ombus, <u>w</u>rist	Some silent letter combinations are frequently called consonant digraphs (kn, wr).

Guidelines for Effective Phonics Instruction

Research does not tell us what order to teach sound-spellings. The following guidelines are useful when choosing your scope and sequence.

EFFECTIVE PHONICS INSTRUCTION FOLLOWS A SOLID SCOPE AND SEQUENCE
Teach a combination of consonants and short vowels at the very beginning so that students can read words as soon as possible. When choosing those first consonants, make sure that several are continuous consonants (such as *f, m, n, l, r,* and *s*), because their sounds are easier to blend.[16]

Teach skills in an order from simple to more complex.

A Possible Phonics Scope and Sequence

1. Consonants and short vowels
2. Consonant digraphs
3. Words that include initial and final consonant blends
4. CVCE words
5. Long vowel teams
6. R-controlled vowels
7. Diphthongs and variant vowels
8. Words with the consonant-le ending
9. Words with silent letters
10. Words with prefixes and suffixes

Separate concepts that are easily confused. For example, when teaching the alphabet, don't teach the letters *b* and *d* back-to-back because children often confuse these letters. It's also wise to separate similar short vowels like short *e* and short *i*.[17]

Teach the most common sound-spellings first. English has about 250 ways to spell approximately 44 phonemes. There isn't time (nor is it necessary) to explicitly teach each one. The chart in Table 5.2 displays the spellings for 44 phonemes, based on a 1966 study summarized by Edward Fry in 2004.[18] It can help you decide where to focus your instruction.

Table 5.2   English Grapheme Chart

Common Spelling		Less Common Spelling				Rare Spelling		
Phoneme	Graphemes							
/ă/	a cat							
/ā/	a basic	a–e ate	ai rain	ay play	eigh weigh	ea break	ei veil	ey they
/ar/	ar arm	ear heart						
/aw/	a all	au auto	o off	aw paw	a water	ough bought	augh caught	
/b/	b bat							
/ch/	ch chip	t picture	tch stitch					

(continued)

Table 5.2 (continued)

Common Spelling		Less Common Spelling			Rare Spelling		
/d/	**d** dog						
/ĕ/	**e** wet	**ea** head					
/ē/	**e** me	**-y** happy	**ee*** sweet	**ea*** team	**e-e** here	**ie** field	**ey** key	**ei** weird
	*We might teach ee and ea before teaching the -y spelling because they occur in single syllable words.						
/er/	**er** term	**or** doctor	**ur** purse	**ar** dollar	**ir** shirt	**ear** earth	**our** journey
/f/	**f** fox	**ph** phone	**ff** fluff	**gh** laugh			
/g/	**g** girl	**gh** ghost					
/h/	**h** hat	**wh** who					
/ĭ/	**i** win	**y** gym	**ui** build	**ai** captain			
/ī/	**i-e** nice	**i** pilot	**-y** my	**igh** fight	**ie** tie	**y-e** type	
/j/	**g** gem	**j** jug	**dge** bridge	**d** educate			
/k/	**c** cat	**k** king	**ck** duck	**ch** choir			
/l/	**l** lip	**ll** will					
/m/	**m** mat	**mb** lamb					
/n/	**n** net	**kn** knot	**gn** gnat				
/ng/	**ng** sing	**n** sink					
/ŏ/	**o** hot	**a** wand					
/ō/	**o** open	**o-e** home	**oa** soap	**ow** own	**ou** mould	**oe** toe	
/oi/	**oi** toil	**oy** boy					
Short oo	**u** put	**oo** look	**o** woman				

Common Spelling			Less Common Spelling			Rare Spelling		
/or/	**or** form	**ore** core	**our** pour	**ar** warm				
/ou/	**ou** couch	**ow** down						
/p/	**p** pig							
/r/	**r** red	**wr** write	**rh** rhombus					
/s/	**s** sun	**c** city	**ss** dress	**ps** psychic	**sc** science	**ts** tsunami		
/sh/	**t** action	**sh*** ship	**c** special	**ss** mission	**s** tension	**ch** chef		
	*Even though *t* is the more common spelling, we would teach *sh* first because it is found in single syllable words.							
/t/	**t** ten							
/th/	**th** think							
/th/	<u>**th**</u> they							
/ŭ/	**u** bug	**ou** touch	**o** son	**oo** flood				
Long /oo/	**u** student	**u-e** tune	**oo** soon	**ew** stew	**ou** you	**eu** neutral	**ue** glue	**o** move
/v/	**v** vet	**f** of						
/w/	**w** win	**wh** when	**u** suite					
/y/	**i** onion	**y*** yes	*Even though the *i* spelling is more common, we would prioritize the *y* spelling because it appears in single syllable words.					
/z/	**s** his	**z** zip	**zz** fuzz					
/zh/	**s** erosion	**g** genre	**z** seizure					
Schwa	**o** other	**a** away	**i** animal	**e** effect	**y** oxygen	**ie** patient	**eo** pigeon	

EFFECTIVE PHONICS INSTRUCTION DIRECTLY TEACHES ALPHABET RECOGNITION

Alphabet recognition involves learning the names, shapes, and sounds of the letters of the alphabet. Should you start with letter names or letter sounds? What order should you teach the alphabet? Should your instruction be multisensory? Let's examine what the research says and doesn't say.

Letter name knowledge is a strong predictor of reading achievement. In 1967, Bond and Dykstra found that the ability to recognize letters of the alphabet prior to beginning reading instruction was the best predictor of first grade reading achievement.[19]

Children who can recognize letters quickly will have an easier time learning letter sounds and word spellings.[20] It's also true that many letter names contain the speech sound they represent (m - /m/, f - /f/, etc.), making it easier to learn letter sounds once students know letter names.[21]

Letter name knowledge is not an end in itself. According to Allen and Neuhaus, "Fast and accurate letter reading is not the end goal; rather, it is the stepping-off point to automatic word reading that frees cognitive attention to focus on higher level skills, fluency, and reading comprehension."[22]

It may be best to teach letter names and sounds at the same time. You might be asking yourself, "Aren't the *sounds* the most important?" After all, we don't need to know letter names to decode words; we need their sounds. Why don't we start with sounds and leave letter names out of it? Wouldn't that reduce cognitive load and make learning easier?

In 2010, Piasta et al. found that students who learned letter names and sounds together had better sound knowledge than those who were initially taught just the letter sounds.[23] If you're concerned that teaching both at the same time will overwhelm students, research suggests that children will learn what they are taught (whether that's letter sounds, names, or both at the same time).[24] While there is no consensus yet, there is strong evidence that we should teach both letter names and sounds at the same time.[25]

Regardless of where you stand on this issue, learning a letter's name is useful for at least one reason: a letter's name is its only stable property. A letter's appearance changes depending on whether it's upper- or lowercase, print or cursive. A letter's sound may vary depending on its position in a word. But its name never changes. A letter's name is the anchor to which children can attach other information.

Teaching letter names and sounds out of context is effective. While students can gain alphabet knowledge through shared reading and print referencing,[26] we needn't fear teaching alphabet knowledge apart from text. A 2020 study compared children who learned letters and sounds in context (within their names, familiar words, and storybooks) with children who were directly taught letter names and sounds in isolation. Both groups learned letter names equally well, but the group who learned letters and sounds in isolation were more successful at learning letter sounds.[27] If this approach sounds like it will stifle motivation, guess what? The students who learned letters in isolation actually showed higher engagement!

Research isn't clear about whether we should teach upper- or lowercase letters first. It's possible that children learn lowercase letters more easily when they know their uppercase counterparts; the natural conclusion would be that we should teach uppercase first or both together. But this has not been tested.[28]

Research does not tell us the best possible order for teaching letters.[29] My opinion is that the order you teach the letters should depend on your purpose. If you are teaching preschool and a major goal is that students learn to write the letters, I would group the letters according to how they are formed. Start with straight letters, move on to letters with curves, and conclude with letters that include slants. This is a possible order for teaching the alphabet with this purpose in mind:

Lowercase: t, l, i, j, u, r, n, m, h, b, p, o, c, d, a, g, q, s, f, e, z, v, w, k, y, x

Uppercase: T, L, I, F, H, E, J, D, P, B, O, C, G, U, S, R, Q, A, M, N, Z, V, W, K, Y, X

If you are teaching kindergarten, you will want to order the letters in a way that allows students to read words as soon as possible, including as many continuous sounds as possible at the beginning of the sequence.

When designing my series of original decodable books, I included a few continuous sounds at the beginning. However, I also considered which letters would allow my students to read short a CVC words in the very simple books they would be reading. I also separated easily confused consonants (b/d) and vowels (a/e).

My order for teaching letter names and sounds in kindergarten is as follows: s, j, a, t, p, m, d, c, h, r, n, i, b, f, g, k, o, e, l, v, w, u, x, y, qu, z.

The traditional letter-of-the-week approach is not ideal. The pace is far too slow for kindergartners, who should begin to learn blending as soon as possible. A 2012 study found that kindergartners who were taught one letter per day, followed by periods of review, made better progress than students taught one letter each week.[30] A 2021 study found that kindergartners and first graders did better when 2–4 letters or digraphs were taught per week as compared to 1–3.[31] A 2020 study also showed an association between learning letters at a faster pace and stronger letter-sound knowledge.[32]

Choose keywords that do the best possible job of highlighting the letter's sound. You'll be teaching CVC words first, so it makes sense to choose keywords that highlight the vowels' short sounds. According to literacy expert Louisa Moats, keywords should be as undistorted as possible. In addition, keywords for consonants should not begin with consonant blends, as this can lead to confusion.[33] See Table 5.3.

Table 5.3   Possible Keywords for Teaching Letters and Sounds

Letter	Good Keywords	Keywords to Avoid
a	apple	ant, ambulance (nasalized) acorn (does not begin with a's short sound)
b	bat, book, ball	block (begins with a consonant blend)
d	dinosaur, duck, donut	drum (begins with a consonant blend)
e	edge, Ed, echo	elephant (easily confused with the letter name l) egg (may sound like it begins with long a)
f	fish	flower (begins with a consonant blend)
g	goat, gorilla	grape (begins with a consonant blend)
h	hat, house	
i	itch	insect (nasalized) ice cream (long i sound)
j	jump, jellyfish	
k	kite, kick	
l	lamp, ladder	
m	mountain, mouse, moon	
n	nose, nest, noodles	
o	octopus, ostrich	orange, owl, oval (do not begin with o's short sound)
p	penguin, pig	plum (begins with a consonant blend)
q	quilt, queen	
r	rat, rabbit	
s	sun, sock	snake (begins with a consonant blend)
t	tiger, turtle	train (begins with a consonant blend)
u	up	umbrella (nasalized) unicorn (does not begin with u's short sound)
v	vase, violin, volcano	
w	worm, web	
x	fox, box	xylophone (does not include the normal sound of x) X-ray (easily confused with the short e sound)
y	yawn, yo-yo	
z	zip	

Research is unclear about the benefits of multisensory methods when learn-ing the alphabet. Many teachers believe that adding gross motor movements and tactile experiences improves letter learning. However, the evidence is quite limited. We can agree that multisensory methods often increase engagement, and we can speak to our own experiences, but we can't claim that research backs us up—at least not yet.[34]

We don't yet have convergence of evidence that teaching articulatory aware-ness helps children differentiate and remember sounds. Increasing awareness of how sounds are formed in the mouth—by drawing attention to mouth position, air-flow, and whether the sound is voiced or unvoiced—may help children learning letters and sounds.[35] However, a 2019 study did not find an advantage to drawing attention to mouth position and movement.[36] My personal opinion is that it makes sense to briefly draw attention to mouth position, but we need more research.

Embedded mnemonics are an effective strategy for teaching letter sounds. When a letter shape is incorporated into a familiar object that begins with the letter's sound, students may do better at letter-sound learning. This is not the same as putting a picture *next* to a letter. A *d* that is shaped like a dinosaur (see Figure 5.4) is more effective than a card with a dinosaur next to the *d*.[37]

EFFECTIVE PHONICS INSTRUCTION DIRECTLY TEACHES SOUND–SYMBOL RELATIONSHIPS

Children benefit from explicit instruction in letters and sounds. In other words, you should directly tell your students the names of the letters and what sounds they repre-sent. A 2019 study found support for **paired-associate learning**, in which children are taught the printed letter while saying its name and sound.[38]

Routines lighten cognitive load when your students know what to expect, freeing their brains to focus on what's most important: the new concept. Here's one to try.

Figure 5.4 Embedded mnemonics

A Routine for Introducing New Sound–Symbol Relationships

1. Phonemic awareness warm-up
- Repeat each word after me. *Caaaat. Haaad. Maaap. Saaaack.*
- What sound did you say in the middle of each word?
- Now we're going to blend some sounds. Watch me first. The sounds are /mmmm/ /aaaaa /t/. The word is mat. Your turn! The sounds are /ssss/ /aaaa/ /d/. What's the word? (Repeat with *fan* and *lap*.)

2. Introduce the new symbol on a card and draw attention to the articulatory features of the phoneme.
- This is the letter *a*. *A* spells the vowel sound /ă/.
- When I say the /ă/ sound, I open my mouth like this. Say /ă/.
- When I say /ă/ I can feel that this is a noisy sound. Put your hand on your throat while you say /ă/.

3. Have students practice identifying the grapheme and its sound.
- When you see this card, say "*a* spells /ă/." Say it with me.
- I'm going to add this card to our review deck.

4. Have students practice writing the grapheme.
- When you make a lowercase *a*, begin in the middle. Curve around, up, and down. Let's practice finger-writing the letter in the sky and on our desks.
- Now let's write the letter on a dry-erase board (or with a pencil on handwriting paper). Each time you write the letter, say /ă/.

5. Add a grapheme card to your sound wall.
- Here is our /ă/ sound card. The key word is *apple*. Say *aaaapple*.
- Let's add our word card. We spell /ă/ with the letter *a*. Caaaat.

EFFECTIVE PHONICS INSTRUCTION MAY INCLUDE THE USE OF SOUND WALLS

As of this writing, no published studies have examined the effectiveness of using a sound wall in early reading instruction. However, many teachers find sound walls to be a useful tool for connecting speech to print.

A **sound wall** is a visual reference to help students when they are reading and spelling. Unlike a word wall, where words are displayed by their beginning letter, many sound walls display the 44 speech sounds by manner and/or place of articulation in the mouth. Sound walls often include mouth articulation pictures to represent what the mouth does when producing each phoneme. An anchor picture helps students remember what sound is represented. Sound walls also include a list of graphemes under each phoneme or a list of key words with the grapheme underlined (see Figures 5.5 and 5.6).

Incorporate your sound wall into your phonics lessons. For example, "Today you learned that two spellings for /ā/ are *ai* and *ay*. Our new key words are *rain* and *pay*. I'll put them under /ā/ on our sound wall." Teach your students to use the sound wall as a reference when reading and spelling.

Sound walls can indeed be a useful tool, but it's important to acknowledge that they are a popular trend without much research support. I question the value of long, detailed discussions about how a certain sound is formed in the mouth, and students shouldn't be expected to associate terms like *stop, fricative,* and *affricate* with particular phonemes. If you choose to incorporate a sound wall, use it in a way that makes sense to you and your students; don't get bogged down by the details.

EFFECTIVE PHONICS INSTRUCTION TEACHES STUDENTS HOW TO BLEND

As soon as your students have mastered four to six letter-sound correspondences that can be combined to form words, you can begin to teach blending. **Blending** is the stringing of letter sounds together to decode a word.

While most teachers understand that phonics is important, many do not teach a blending routine. Simply telling students to "sound it out" isn't teaching them *how*.[39] Blending must be modeled and practiced often.

It's tempting to teach words as wholes because it's faster than blending in the short-term; it even works for many children—at least at first. One study of struggling readers found that students who were taught to memorize the words and students who were taught blending did equally well on the immediate posttest. A week later, however, students in the blending group did better at remembering the words they were taught and were much better at applying the strategy to unfamiliar words.[40]

Tips for Teaching Blending

- **Start with letters with continuous sounds** (/f/, /l/, /m/, /n/, /r/, /s/, /v/, /z/) because it's easier to model how to move from one sound to the next.[41]
- **Start with successive blending. Successive blending** (also called **cumulative** or **continuous blending**) is when students start by blending the first two sounds together; then they say the third sound and add it to the first two blended sounds. They continue in this manner until all the sounds are blended. Successive blending reduces cognitive load because students don't have to hold all the sounds in their head at once. See Figure 5.7.

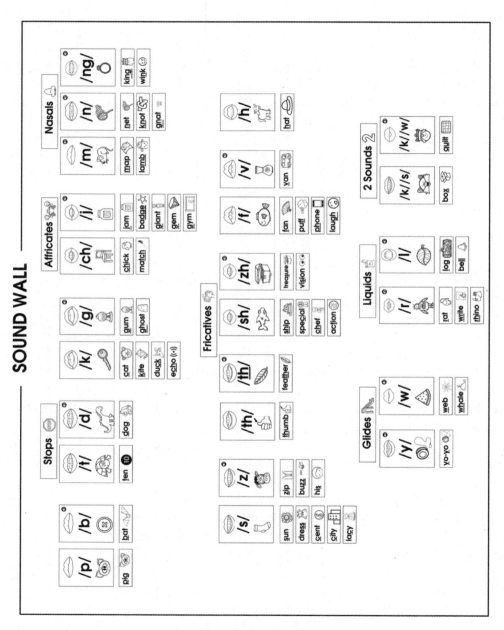

Figure 5.5 A sound wall for consonant phonemes.

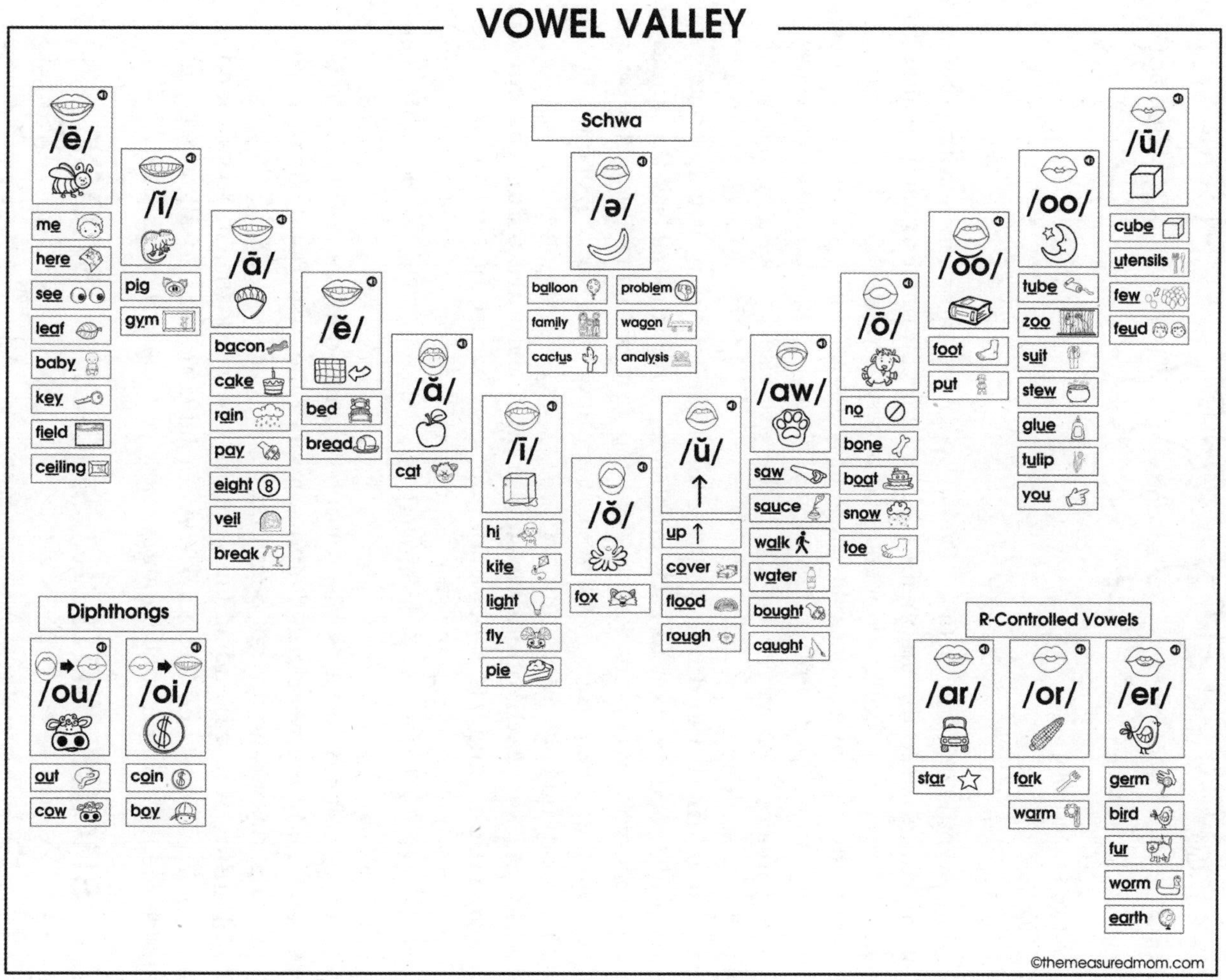

VOWEL VALLEY

Schwa

/ə/ — balloon, problem, family, wagon, cactus, analysis

/ē/ — me, here, see, leaf, baby, key, field, ceiling

/ĭ/ — pig, gym

/ā/ — bacon, cake, rain, pay, eight (8), veil, break

/ĕ/ — bed, bread

/ă/ — cat

/ī/ — hi, kite, light, fly, pie

/ŏ/ — fox

/ŭ/ — up, cover, flood, rough

/aw/ — saw, sauce, walk, water, bought, caught

/ō/ — no, bone, boat, snow, toe

/ŏŏ/ — foot, put

/oo/ — tube, zoo, suit, stew, glue, tulip, you

/ū/ — cube, utensils, few, feud

R-Controlled Vowels

/er/ — germ, bird, fur, worm, earth

/or/ — fork, warm

/ar/ — star

Diphthongs

/oi/ — coin, boy

/ou/ — out, cow

©themeasuredmom.com

Figure 5.6 A vowel valley for vowel phonemes.

101

Figure 5.7   Successive blending.

Image by Rocio Zapata

Start by modeling the activity. Begin by saying the sounds with your students as you point to the graphemes. Make sure you point to each spelling for at least a second. Allowing adequate time is very important.

Gradually release responsibility to your students. First omit the verbal cues, using only your finger to prompt students. Finally, have students do successive blending independently. Always finish the exercise by defining the word or using it in a sentence.

- ◆ **Move on to final blending.** By the end of kindergarten, if not sooner, you should only need to point to each grapheme. Have students say the sound of each grapheme as you point. Pause while you wait for them to blend the sounds together in their head. Then move your finger under the whole word as students read the word quickly. See Figure 5.8.

- ◆ **As students say each phoneme, make sure they are using the correct pronunciation.** Students should not add a schwa to the end of phonemes. Teach your students to clip the stop sounds and sustain the continuous sounds. The sound of the letter *b* is pronounced /b/, not "buh." The sound of the letter *l* is /llll/, not "luh."

  Another common issue is mispronouncing the sound of *r*. The sound is not /er/. Start to say the word *rabbit* and stop after the first sound: /rrrr/. If you're doing it right, your mouth will be round.

- ◆ **Use blending lines.** Blending lines are lines of words that students sound out using their phonics knowledge. They're a fantastic way to allow students to practice the new sound-spelling and review previously learned skills.

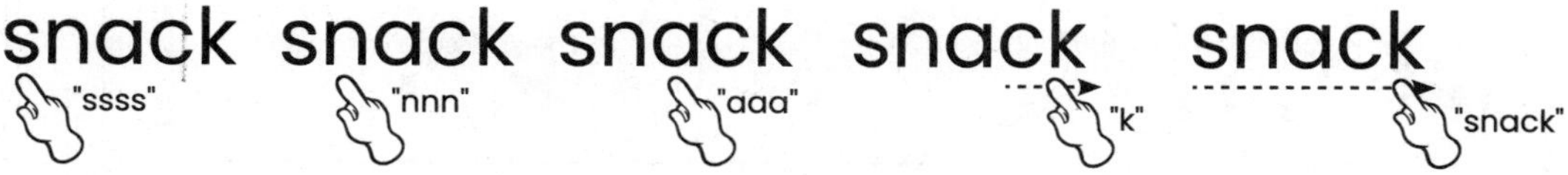

snack "ssss"   **snack** "nnn"   **snack** "aaa"   **snack** "k"   **snack** "snack"

Figure 5.8   Final blending.

Image by Rocio Zapata

When designing blending lines, start with **minimal pairs** (when words differ by a single phoneme). Each line should get more and more difficult. Later lines should include review words and challenge words. The final line or two should include a sentence featuring the new sound-spelling.

Wiley Blevins offers blending line tips in his book *A Fresh Look at Phonics*.

♦ Model only one or two words so that students do the bulk of the decoding work.
♦ The first time through the blending lines, have students read the words chorally.
♦ After this choral reading, point to words in random order and call on individual students to read them.
♦ Use the blending lines on multiple days; after the first day, blending lines can be used as a warm-up.
♦ Make copies of the blending lines for students to practice on their own and at home.[42]

The set of blending lines in Figure 5.9 could be used after teaching short i. In the first line, the words differ only by their initial letter. Lines 2–3 gradually get more difficult. Line 4 consists of review words. Line 5 is a set of challenge words. Line 6 is a sentence featuring the short *i* sound-spelling.

♦ **Help your students move beyond sound-by-sound decoding.** Saying each sound before blending is a necessary first step, but you don't want your students to get stuck there. If you have students who are solid on letters and sounds but still read words one sound at a time, these steps may help.[43]

Blending Lines					
1 dip	hip	lip	rip	sip	tip
2 pin	pit	pig	sit	nip	six
3 zip	him	did	lip	kid	fix
4 bag	nap	pat	rag	pan	hat
5 zips	kids	pigs	bins	rips	hits
6 The pig can dig.					

Figure 5.9 Blending lines.

- Have them whisper when sounding out the word.
- Have them sound out the word silently with their lips moving.
- Have them nod as they say each sound in their head, then say the word aloud.
- Have them only move their eyes as they sound out the word in their head.

EFFECTIVE PHONICS INSTRUCTION INCLUDES WORD BUILDING

Word building is a powerful way to support phonemic awareness, decoding, and word recognition because it draws students' attention to phonemes and spelling patterns.

With **word building**, students are given a set of grapheme tiles and asked to build particular words using the sound-spellings you've already taught them. The list of words that students build is often called a **word chain** or **word ladder**. A CVC word chain might look like this: cat, cot, pot, pit, sit. A 2003 study engaged struggling readers in 20 word-building sessions. They made greater progress on decoding, comprehension, and phonological awareness than the control group.[44]

If the idea of distributing and collecting hundreds of letter tiles each day makes you feel a little sick, here's a tip: print grapheme tiles on white cardstock. Then stick the page onto a large sheet of adhesive magnetic paper. Cut apart the tiles, and put them on a magnetic baking sheet for each student (don't give students all the grapheme tiles at once; distribute the new tiles as you teach the graphemes). Students can build their words at the bottom of the tray, returning each tile to its place when they switch out a grapheme (see Figure 5.10). At the end of each day's word-building activity, stack the trays—you're ready for next time!

Make sure you have your word chain ready before beginning a word-building activity. Use the link at the end of this chapter to get free word-chaining lists.

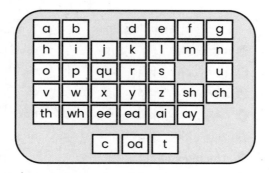

Figure 5.10   Magnetic grapheme tiles on a metal tray.

Sample word chaining: sample lesson

Teacher	Your word is *goat.* A goat is a small farm animal with horns. Say *goat.*
Students	Goat.
Teacher	Tap the sounds of *goat.*
Students	/g/ /ō/ /t/.
Teacher	Use your tiles to spell the word. (Move around the room, supporting students as needed.) Say the sounds and blend the word.
Students	/g/ /ō/ /t/. Goat.
Teacher	Change one letter to spell the word *coat.* (Move around the room, supporting students as needed.) Say the sounds and blend the word.
Students	/k/ /ō/ /t/. Coat.

EFFECTIVE PHONICS INSTRUCTION ADDRESSES HIGH-FREQUENCY WORDS

High-frequency words are words that are used most often in the English language. The goal is to help your students turn high-frequency words into **sight words**, words they recognize instantly without needing to sound out or guess.

Dolch published his list of 220 words in 1936. A few decades later, Fry compiled his list of 1000 words; of these, teachers typically focus on the first 100. Unfortunately, both Dolch and Fry were fans of the look-say method; they advocated teaching the words on their lists as whole units to be memorized.[45] Now that we understand how the brain learns to read, we can reject this notion.

It makes more sense to teach regularly spelled high-frequency words alongside their corresponding phonics pattern. If you're teaching CVC words, teach your students to decode *can, him, red,* and *big.* If you're teaching CVCE words, teach *make, like,* and *use.* No rote memorization necessary!

How to Introduce Irregular High-Frequency Words

But what about irregular high-frequency words? Words like *come, to,* and *could?* Readers store irregular words the same way they store regular words: by orthographically mapping them. You can facilitate orthographic mapping by using the sound mapping technique shared in Chapter 4.

Here's a routine for introducing irregular high-frequency words. Repeat the routine on subsequent days for any word that students struggle with.

1. Say the word.
2. Have students repeat the word.

3. Use the word in a sentence.
4. Ask students to tap the sounds in the word.
5. Spell each sound together, drawing attention to irregular parts of the word.
6. If desired, have students mark the irregular part of the word by highlighting it or marking it in some way (many teachers use a heart).
7. Have students read the word again.
8. Have students write the word apart from the sound boxes, saying each sound as they spell it.
9. Provide many opportunities for reading and spelling the word.

Teaching An Irregular High-Frequency Word: Sample Lesson

Teacher	Today you're going to read and spell the word *some*. Say the word.	
Students	Some.	
Teacher	I would like *some* carrots. Let's tap the sounds of the word *some*.	
Students	/s/ /ŭ/ /m/.	
Teacher	Watch me spell the word in my sound boxes. Do the same in your sound boxes. The first sound is /s/. We're going to use the letter *s* to spell /s/. The next sound is /ŭ/. What letter would you expect to see?	
Students	U.	
Teacher	It would seem like that, wouldn't it? But this word uses the letter *o* to spell /ŭ/. The final sound in *some* is /m/. How should we spell /m/?	
Students	M.	
Teacher	Correct. We've spelled all the sounds: /s/ /ŭ/ /m/. But there's one more surprising letter in the word *some*. It has a sneaky silent e, which I'm going to squeeze next to the *m*. I'm going to mark these tricky parts with a heart; these are the parts I need to memorize. Read the word *some*.	
Students	Some.	
Teacher	Now write the word. Say each sound as you spell it.	
Students	/s/ /ŭ/ /m/.	
Teacher	Turn to your partner, and use the word *some* in a sentence. Start by saying, I wish I had *some* . . .	

Sound boxes:

s		

s	o	

s	o	m

s	o	me

s	o	♡ me ♡

Ways to Practice Irregular High–Frequency Words

After you've explicitly taught high-frequency words with attention to their phonemes and graphemes, students will need opportunities to read and spell the words. Use the Cover, Copy, Compare technique, as shown in Figure 5.11. This procedure has been proven to be effective in helping students remember spellings.[46]

Stephanie Stollar shares this procedure for Cover, Copy, Compare in her Reading Science Academy.[47]

1. Prepare a list of up to 10 high-frequency words for spelling practice. Write them in the left column of a worksheet.
2. Students should read the first word, fold the page backward on the line to *cover* it, and *copy it from memory* in the first space. They should then open the page back up and *compare* their spelling to the model.
3. If correct, students should move on to the next word. If incorrect, students should cross out the incorrect spelling and try again, this time writing the word in the third column.
4. The teacher should track students' progress by noting when a student has written a word correctly on three consecutive days.

Cover, Copy, Compare

Word	Response #1	Response #2
1. would	~~wolud~~	would
2. put	put	
3. have	have	
4. should	should	
5. does	~~dose~~	does
6. could	could	
7. are	are	
8. said	~~seid~~	said
9. they	they	
10. very	~~vary~~	very

Figure 5.11 Cover, Copy, Compare technique.

See Figure 5.12 for a list of decodable high-frequency words organized by phonics pattern and Figure 5.13 for a list of irregular high-frequency words.

O'Connor shares Beat the Clock in her book, *Teaching Word Recognition*.[48] This review game can be played in pairs. Students will each need a stack of high-frequency word cards that they need to practice. See Figure 5.14.

Student 1 reads the words in his stack while the other player uses a countdown timer. How many words did Student 1 read in 1 or 2 minutes? The words that were read correctly are counted, and the number is recorded. Student 1 will try to beat this time the next time they play the game. Beat the Clock can also be a spelling game. Student 1 copies words from his stack of cards as quickly as possible. Student 2 checks to see how many words were correctly copied in 2–3 minutes. Over time, students will need fewer peeks at the words as they spell them.

DECODABLE HIGH FREQUENCY WORDS

VC and CVC*						DIGRAPHS		BLENDS		-NG, -NK
*Teach students early on that s can represent /z/. Students can also easily learn that a double consonant represents the single consonant's sound.						much then		and its		drink
						pick this		ask jump		long
am	can	has	is	ran	ten	shall when		best just		sing
an	cut	him	it	red	up	such which		black must		thank
as	did	his	let	run	us	that wish		bring stop		thing
at	get	hot	not	sit	well	them with		fast went		think
big	got	if	off	six	will			help		
but	had	in	on	tell	yes					

IND, OLD, OST			OPEN SYLLABLES		CVCE		LONG VOWEL TEAMS		
While you could call these words irregular, these patterns are common enough that we can teach them as patterns.			Teach students that when a syllable ends with a single vowel, the vowel spells its long sound.				clean	green	light
					ate	ride	each	keep	right
			a	me	came	take	eat	see	
find	cold	most	be	my	five	these	please	sleep	grow
kind	hold		by	no	gave	those	read	three	know
	old		fly	she	here	use			own
			go	so	like	while	may	soon	show
			he	try	made	white	play	too	
			I	we	make	write	say		good
								blue	look
							new		

R-CONTROLLED		DIPHTHONGS*		CONSONANT-LE	MULTI-SYLLABLE			
far	hurt	brown	found	little	about	away	going	seven
first	more*	down	house		after	before	myself	under
for	or	how	our		along	better	never	upon
girl	start	now	out		always	every	open	yellow
her			round		around	funny	over	
		draw*						
		saw*	boy					
*You might choose to include "more" with the CVCE words.		*"Aw" is not always classified as a diphthong.						

Figure 5.12   Decodable high-frequency words.

IRREGULAR HIGH FREQUENCY WORDS

END WITH V + E	O-E SPELLS /Ŭ/	-O SPELLS /OO/	AL SPELLS /AW/
give have live	come done some	to do Into today	all call fall small walk

OUL SPELLS /OO/	A SPELLS /Ŏ/ AFTER W	U SPELLS /OO/	RHYMING IRREGULAR PAIRS	
could should would	want wash	full pull put	any many	there where

IRREGULAR HIGH FREQUENCY WORDS THAT DO NOT FIT INTO SPELLING PATTERNS							
again animal are because been both buy	carry does don't eight four friend from	goes great laugh move of once one	only other people pretty said school sure	the their they through together two very	warm was were what who why work	you your	

Figure 5.13   Irregular high-frequency words.

Figure 5.14   Beat the Clock.

Image by Rocio Zapata

Try the Star Words activity, shared by Foorman, et al.[49] Have each student begin with a set of three to five high-frequency words on a metal ring. Throughout the week, each student should read their set of words to the teacher, an aide, or another adult. Each time a word is read correctly, the adult draws a star on its card. When a word receives three stars, more words can be added to the ring. See Figure 5.15.

Editable practice games are another fun and effective way to practice high frequency words. Simply type in the words your students need to practice, and have them play a simple memory or bingo game.

Figure 5.15   Star Words.
Image by Rocio Zapata

Is It Ever Okay to Have Students Memorize High-Frequency Words?
When students are beginning to decode words and know just a small number of letter-sound correspondences, it's actually effective to teach them to memorize a small number of functional words to get them on the path to reading.[50] For example, if students have only been taught the sounds of *s, a, t, p,* and *n*, it's still okay to teach them to recognize the word *the* so they can read connected text.

Linda Farrell and Michael Hunter, the founders of Readsters, recommend teaching the following words to students who are still learning letter-sound correspondences: *the, a, I, to, and, was, for, you, is,* and *of.*[51]

Other Tips for Teaching Irregular High-Frequency Words
Teach irregular high-frequency words in families (see Figure 5.13). *To* and *do* should be taught together. *Could, would,* and *should* are another family. *There* and *where* go together, as do *any* and *many*. Separate words that are easily confused, like *were* and *where*.

Teach high-frequency words before students encounter them in the decodable books they're reading. If they will be reading a phonetically regular word such as *like*, but have not been taught the corresponding phonics pattern, the word is temporarily irregular. Teach it as you'd teach other irregular high frequency words.

Incorporate review often; do not assume that a word a student read correctly a month ago is still remembered.

EFFECTIVE PHONICS INSTRUCTION INCLUDES PRACTICE WITH DECODABLE TEXTS
Decodable text can be sentences, a passage, or a book in which a majority of the words can be sounded out based on the sound-spellings the reader has been taught. It is also called phonetically controlled text or accountable text.

A text is decodable from the point of view of the reader. For you and me, almost every text we encounter is decodable. For a child who is just learning to read, a decodable text will contain mostly CVC words.

Why Use Decodable Text?

Decodable texts are important because they allow students to apply their phonics knowledge through decoding words from left to right, with attention to every letter.[52] The more times students decode a word, the closer they get to recognizing it instantly as a sight word.

Jocelyn Seamer writes:

> We can't just throw children in the deep end with books containing the whole alphabetic code and think that they'll 'pick it up.' We need to carefully scaffold experiences through decodable texts to allow children to experience success at each phase of the reading acquisition process. This approach, working from simple to complex, prevents cognitive overload and ensures that children's attention remains focused on the internal structure of the word rather than trying to remember words based on global shapes . . . it also focuses students on blending all through the word instead of using other 'cues' to lift words from the page.[53]

Leveled versus Decodable Books

As a balanced literacy teacher, I avoided decodable books. I felt they were stilted, confusing, and just plain boring. How could decodable books help my students learn to love reading? I taught phonics, but my students had few opportunities to apply what they'd learned because they read leveled books. In fact, I leveled my entire classroom library using the Fountas and Pinnell Text Level Gradient, also known as the guided reading levels.

Leveled books are typically ranked from A-Z. Levels do not take phonics patterns into account. Instead, books are leveled based on print features, text structure, content, sentence complexity, word count, word frequency, and other factors.[54] The early levels include predictable books with strong picture support. The words may be long or complex, but students can "read" them if they understand the pattern and use the pictures. See Figure 5.16.

Figure 5.16 Early leveled books are predictable with strong picture support.

Later levels have more lines of print and less picture support. The idea is that students will start to apply phonics knowledge as they are taught it, relying less on context and pictures. Unfortunately, it doesn't always work this way.

The type of texts we use affects students' learning. Blevins writes, "We can teach an award-winning phonics lesson, but if we follow that up (day after day, week after week) with texts to apply the phonics skills containing few decodable words, our efforts might be in vain."[55] In their 1985 study, Juel and Roper-Schneider concluded that "emphasis on a phonics method seems to make little sense if children are given initial texts to read where the words do not follow regular letter-sound correspondence generalizations."[56]

When I began to understand the science of reading, I wanted to hold on to my early leveled books. Couldn't beginning readers read both? A light bulb finally went off when I realized that the early leveled books are written *precisely to give students practice with three-cueing*. They *must* use context and pictures to "read" the words because they don't yet have the skills to read them any other way!

It's not easy for a kindergarten or first grade teacher to make the switch from leveled to decodable books. Suddenly students have to slow down and decode every word. Frankly, it's a bit painful to listen to. But hang in there—it's worth it! Dr. John Shefelbine explained that "the kindest thing you can do for beginning and struggling readers is to give them the time and encouragement they need to grunt and groan their way through sounding out words. You're rewiring their brains and it's hard work."[57]

> *Early leveled books are written precisely to give students practice with three-cueing.*

What the Research Says

- ◆ In 1985, Juel and Roper-Schneider conducted a study with first graders. After receiving identical phonics instruction, one group read from a basal with more decodable text; the other read from a basal with a focus on high-frequency words. Students reading the more decodable text were more likely to sound out words when reading.[58]
- ◆ A 2004 study found that average readers were more successful at reading decodable texts than text that was less decodable. The students with weaker reading abilities did not do as well with decodable text. This may be because they were not necessarily matched with books that featured phonics patterns they'd already been taught.[59]

- A 2004 study assigned at-risk first graders to tutoring in either highly decodable or less decodable texts; both groups received instruction in the same phonics program. The control group did not receive tutoring. Interestingly, both tutored groups showed improvement in their reading, but the decodability of the text did not seem to make a difference.[60] While some use this study to question the benefits of decodable texts,[61] Blevins counters that the decodable texts in this study were weak and stilted.[62]

- A 2005 study gave phonics instruction to two groups of first graders. One group was given highly decodable text to read after instruction; the other was given less decodable text. The students who read highly decodable texts applied their letter-sound knowledge to a greater extent than the control group. They were also more accurate in their reading.[63]

- Also in 2005, Blevins conducted a study in which one group of first graders used decodable text for practice; the other group read patterned and predictable text. The students who read decodable text achieved higher scores on a word identification test, a phonemic awareness assessment, and a decoding assessment. They were also less likely to report a dislike of reading.[64]

- In their 2007 study, Hiebert and Fisher evaluated how well first graders read texts that were mostly decodable or texts that included words with sound-spellings that had not yet been taught. Students read with greater speed, accuracy, and comprehension when reading the mostly decodable texts.[65]

- Cheatham and Allor synthesized the existing research on decodability in 2012. They found that students who are first learning to read do better at reading books that are more decodable than books that are less decodable. Cheatham and Allor also noted that we do not yet know the ideal level of decodability, and proposed that early reading text should address multiple criteria, not just decodability.[66]

What Makes a Good Decodable Book?

Good decodable books should sound the way we talk. "Ned did jump" is not the way we speak. I would much rather see a book introduce the -*ed* inflectional ending a little early, as in "Ned jumped," than inadvertently teach students that books sound funny.

Good decodable books should include a large percentage of words that are decodable based on sound-spellings that have been previously taught. Research does not give us an ideal percentage, but I do not aim for 100 percent decodability. This would prevent the inclusion of irregular high-frequency words, which help the text sound natural.

Good decodable books should be interesting and engaging. As an author of decodable books, I know how hard it is to tell a good story with a limited number of letters.

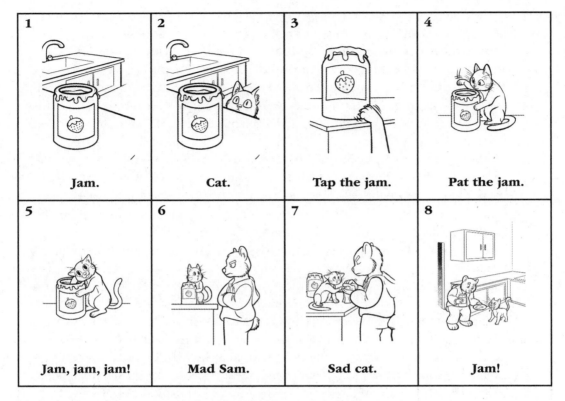

Figure 5.17   *The Cat* by Anna Geiger. Illustrated by Rocio Zapata.

That's where pictures come into play; when pictures support the story without teaching students to rely on them, they are invaluable. When I wrote the decodable text featured in Figure 5.17, I included just one high-frequency word (the) and eight letters: *s, j, a, t, p, m, d,* and *c.* The pictures helped me tell an interesting story.

If a decodable book claims it tells a story, the story should make sense. If asked, students should be able to retell the story. I have read decodable books that were so random I couldn't think of a single question to ask my students. The story in Figure 5.17, though simple, has a problem and solution. The teacher could ask the following questions to check student understanding:

- ◆ What is sitting on the kitchen counter?
- ◆ What do you think the cat is thinking on page 2?
- ◆ Describe how the cat is feeling on page 5. Why is the cat so happy?
- ◆ Why is Sam mad at the cat?
- ◆ How does the story have a happy ending?
- ◆ What do you think the cat should do the next time it sees a treat on the counter?

But Won't Decodable Books Kill a Love of Reading?

As a balanced literacy teacher, my biggest hang-up about decodable books was my fear that they would turn students off to reading. I failed to understand that decodable books give students success. Louisa Moats writes, "Adult distaste for decodable books fails to respect the child's need to exercise a skill: Children want to be self-reliant readers and are delighted when they can apply what they know."[67]

A Decodable Text Routine

After you introduce a new sound-spelling, guide your students in blending practice, word building, and spelling practice. If necessary, teach any new high-frequency words. Then introduce the new decodable text, whether that's a set of sentences, a passage, or a book.

Guide your students as they read the title and examine the cover illustration or picture. What do they think the story will be about? Consider teaching a new vocabulary word that's related to the story. For the story in Figure 5.17, I might teach the word *curious.* "In this book, the cat is *curious.* When you are curious, you want to learn about something. What do you think the cat will be curious about?"

For the first read, have your students read the book aloud, alone or with a partner. If a student misreads a word, point to the misread word and have them read it again. If needed, point to the missed or misread sound-spelling. After the child reads the word correctly (with your help if needed), they should reread the sentence.

Ask questions about the text. Next, have children orally retell the story to a partner. Depending on their level, they can finish a sentence about the story, write their own sentence, or write a retelling or story extension.

Give your students many opportunities to reread the text. I recommend giving each child a gallon-sized plastic bag and having them slip the new text into the bag. They can use their bag of texts for partner reading and rereading during other times of the day.

Decodable Books Should Not Be Used Indefinitely

The big reason to move your students beyond highly decodable text is that too much of it can lead to a misunderstanding about how English orthography (our spelling system) works. They need to learn that straight decoding will not always lead to the correct word. For example, if a student encounters the word *mother,* they might read it as moe-thur or mŏth-ur, both of which could be phonetically correct. But the student should recognize that this is not a real word and adjust the pronunciation to come up with the correct word: mother. This mispronunciation correction is called **set for variability.**[68]

Another thing to keep in mind is that there simply isn't enough time to teach all 250+ sound-spellings. According to David Share's self-teaching hypothesis, students with sufficient decoding skills can figure out the rest of the code over time as they attempt to read more difficult words (words that they won't find in highly decodable text).[69]

Finally, nondecodable text also gives students practice with statistical learning. As they read authentic text, they will notice that some sound-spellings appear more frequently. This will help them apply phonics patterns appropriately.

When to Move Students out of Decodable Books
Research doesn't say when students should move out of decodable text when practicing their reading; experts have various opinions.

- Researcher Heidi Mesmer has written that the appropriate transition is after 2–3 months of reading instruction, when students can easily blend CVC words.[70]
- Linda Farrell, founding partner of Readsters, says that typically developing readers are ready for nondecodable text when they can read single-syllable words with short vowels, digraphs and blends, and two syllable words with schwa, r-controlled vowels, and silent e at a rate of at least 35 words per minute.[71]
- Educational trainer Jocelyn Seamer believes that students should first learn the 75 core graphemes and be able to read about 70–90 words per minute.[72]

Decodable books are like training wheels; we remove them when they are no longer necessary. While I think that decodable text always belongs in a phonics lesson to reinforce the new sound-spelling, I think we should encourage students to practice their reading in authentic text when two things are true. First, their word identification strategy should always begin with putting their eyes on the word—not the picture or their teacher. Second, they know basic phonics skills (CVC words, CCVC and CVCC words, digraphs, CVCE words, some vowel teams, and r-controlled vowels) and can also read simple two-syllable words.

Decodable books are like training wheels; we remove them when they are no longer necessary.

If you question whether a student is ready to move beyond decodable text, have them read a simple book like *Henry and Mudge, Frog and Toad*, or *Fly Guy*. If the student can read one of these books independently, they are likely ready for less decodable text. For many students, this will be sometime between the middle and end of the first grade year.

Regardless of where they are in their reading journey, don't let decodable text be the only text your students experience. Build oral language and vocabulary through shared reading and read-alouds, and encourage your students to enjoy any book of their choice during free time.

EFFECTIVE PHONICS INSTRUCTION INCLUDES THE TEACHING OF PREFIXES AND SUFFIXES

A **prefix** is a word part that is attached to the beginning of a base word or root; a **suffix** comes at the end.

Prefixes usually alter the meaning of the root word. For example, the prefix *-un* means *not* or *opposite*.

There are two kinds of suffixes. **Inflectional suffixes** do not change a word's part of speech when they are added. These suffixes are mostly changes to words using *-s*, *-ed*, or *-ing*. The pronunciation of these endings varies. In the word *cats*, the *-s* ending is pronounced /s/. In the word *hugs*, the -s ending is pronounced /z/. The -ed ending can be pronounced in three ways: /ĭd/, /t/, or /d/. It's not necessary to teach rules for these pronunciations; rather, students should be taught the possibilities and be given opportunities to practice reading words with inflectional endings.[73]

A **derivational suffix** changes the meaning of a word and may also change its part of speech. The suffix *-ful* changes *beauty* to *beautiful*, turning a noun into an adjective.

Use the lists in Table 5.4 to help you decide which prefixes and suffixes to teach. Keep in mind that the first four rows of prefixes in the chart account for 58 percent of all words with prefixes. The first three rows of suffixes account for 65 percent of all words with suffixes.[74]

Table 5.4　Most Common Prefixes and Suffixes

Prefix	Meaning	Examples	Suffix	Meaning	Examples
un–	not, opposite of	untidy	–s, –es	more than one	bugs foxes
re–	again	repaint	–ed	past-tense verb	jumped
in–, im–, il–, ir–	not	inactive immature illogical irregular	–ing	present participle verb	reading
dis–	not, opposite of	disagree	–ly	characteristic of	sadly
en–, em–	cause to	entangle empower	–er, –or	one who	waiter actor
non–	not	nonfiction	–ion	act, process	attention imagination tension

(continued)

Table 5.4   (continued)

Prefix	Meaning	Examples	Suffix	Meaning	Examples
in–	in or into	infield	–able, –ible	can be done	comfortable
over–	too much	overdo	–al, –ial	having characteristics of	personal
mis–	wrongly	misspell	–y	characterized by	gloomy
sub–	under	submarine	–ness	state of	happiness
pre–	before	precook	–ity, –ty	state of	clarity
inter–	between	intersection	–ment	action or process	enjoyment
fore–	before, in front	foreground	–ic	having characteristics of	heroic
de–	opposite of	deactivate	–ous, –eous, –ious	possessing the qualities of	courageous
trans–	across	transport	–en	made of	wooden
super–	above	supernatural	–er	comparative	stronger
semi–	half	semicircle	–ive, –ative, –itive	adjective form of a noun	attentive
anti–	against	antiwar	–ful	full of	wonderful
mid–	middle	midway	–less	without	merciless
under–	under, too little	underground	–est	superlative	biggest
ex–	out, out of	exterior	–ance, –ence	state of	importance

Teaching a New Prefix or Suffix: Sample Lesson

Teacher   Today's new prefix is *R-E*. We read it as /rē/. What's the prefix?

Students   *R-E.*

Teacher   How do we read it?

Students   /rē/.

Teacher   Will we find a prefix at the beginning or end of a word?

Students   The beginning.

Teacher   Correct! The prefix *R-E* means *again* or *back*. (Write *reread* so students can see it.)

The word *reread* means "to read again." (Display the word *return*.) The word *return* means "to turn back." Can you think of another word that begins with the prefix *R-E?* Think for a moment and say the word to your partner. (Pause.) _____, tell us a word that begins with the prefix R-E.

Student   Redo (retie, reprint, redraw, etc.).

Teacher	Excellent! What does *redo* mean?
Students	To do something again.
Teacher	I have a list of words with the prefix *R-E*. I'm going to circle the prefix in each word. Read the word in your head. At my signal, read the word with me. (Follow this procedure with each word.)

redo
repaint
redraw
recall
rebuild
repay
refill
reboot
recharge
reheat

Now let's read the whole list.

I'm going to choose one word and use it in a sentence. My word is *reheat*. I will *reheat* my supper in the microwave. Choose a word from this list and take a minute to think of a sentence using that word. Then tell it to your partner.

EFFECTIVE PHONICS INSTRUCTION TEACHES STUDENTS TO READ MULTISYLLABIC WORDS

Many phonics curricula wait too long to introduce multisyllabic words.[75] This is unfortunate, because students need to be able to read multisyllabic words to be successful with authentic text.

If students reach third grade unable to read multisyllabic words, their comprehension will suffer. Anita Archer says that "no comprehension strategies are powerful enough to compensate for not being able to read the words within the text."[76]

According to Beck and Beck,[77] our students need three skills for reading longer words:

1. *Analysis:* Where to divide the word into syllables
2. *Pronunciation*: How to say the parts
3. *Synthesis*: How to combine the syllables into a word

Many children do not have these skills and simply guess when they encounter longer words. Thankfully, research has shown that when poor readers receive focused, spaced instruction on reading multisyllabic words, their decoding improves.[78]

Everyone can agree that students need strategies for reading multisyllabic words, but there are different opinions as to what those strategies might be.

Teaching Syllable Types

A syllable may form a whole word or part of a word. Many programs teach students to identify and read six different syllable types because knowing a syllable's type gives a clue as to how to pronounce its vowel.

The Six Syllable Types

- **Closed syllables** end in a single vowel and consonant. The vowel is typically short.

    nap | kin

- **Open syllables** end in a vowel. The vowel sound is typically long.

    <u>ro</u> | bot

- **Magic e** (silent e, or vowel-silent e) **syllables** include a vowel-consonant-e pattern; the vowel typically represents its long sound.

    com | <u>plete</u>

- **Vowel team syllables** include a vowel team or diphthong.

    ex | plain

- **R-controlled syllables** include a vowel followed by an r. The r affects the sound of the vowel.

    far | mer

- **Consonant-le syllables** include a consonant plus the letters *le*.

    ket | <u>tle</u>

I find that it makes the most sense to teach multisyllabic words after students have learned to read a particular syllable type. For example, after teaching closed syllables in CVC words, students can also learn to read closed syllables within compound words: bedbug, bobcat, catnip, and pigpen. When students have learned to read single-syllable CVCE words, they can also learn to read longer words: bathrobe, bedtime, costume, cupcake, and escape.

One way to practice reading different syllable types is to play Find the Match. Break two-syllable words apart and have students combine them to form words (see Figure 5.18). Forming and pronouncing nonsense words is a fun part of the process.

If you don't want to teach syllable types, consider teaching at least closed and open syllables, since these make up almost 75 percent of English syllables. You don't even

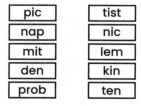

Figure 5.18   Closed-syllable activity: Find the Match.

have to call them closed and open. Closed syllables could be called "short vowel syllables" and open syllables could be called "long vowel syllables."

Teaching Syllable-Division Strategies

Some programs teach a rather complicated method of dividing words into syllables and identifying each syllable type. They teach students the four main syllable division patterns one at a time:

1. **VC|CV**: When a word has the vowel-consonant-consonant-vowel pattern, we divide between the consonants, as in nap|kin or rab|bit.
2. **V|CV**: When a word has the vowel-consonant-vowel pattern, we often divide after the first vowel. The vowel will usually spell its long sound, as in ro|bot or pi|lot.
3. **VC|V**: If dividing according to the V|CV pattern did not yield a word, try dividing after the consonant. Because the first syllable will now be closed, the vowel will typically spell its short sound, as in rob|in or clos|et.
4. **V|V**: When a word has two adjacent vowels that are not a vowel team, we divide between the vowels and pronounce the word, as in li|on or flu|id.

Applying these division strategies can be quite the process. While I question the time that it takes to teach and practice this process, many successful programs include it.

Sample Syllable-Division Exercise Using Syllable-Division Principles and Syllable Types

Teacher	Let's divide this word into syllables. Put a V under the first two vowels. Draw a bridge between the vowels. Look up. What do you see?
Students	Two consonants.
Teacher	Label them with C's. What pattern do you see?
Students	VC|CV.
Teacher	Correct. Divide the word. What type of syllable is the first?
Students	Closed.
Teacher	How do you know?
Students	It ends with a single vowel and a consonant.

compete
V   V

compete
V C C V

compete
V C C V

Teacher	Correct. Label it closed. What sound will the vowel make?	Cl
Students	Its short sound.	cŏmpete
Teacher	Correct. Code it. What about the second syllable?	V C C V
Students	Magic e.	
Teacher	How do you know?	Cl ME
Students	It has the vowel-consonant-e pattern.	cŏmpēte
Teacher	Correct! Label this syllable. What sound will the vowel make?	V C C V
Students	Its long sound.	
Teacher	Correct! Code it. Now read each syllable and put them together to read the word.	
Students	Cŏm. Pete. Com-pete.	
Teacher	Adjust the vowel sound of the first syllable. Try the schwa sound.	
Students	Cŭm. Pete. Compete!	

Should You Teach Syllable Types and Syllable-Division Strategies?

Many phonics programs, particularly those based on the Orton-Gillingham method, include extensive practice with syllable types and syllable division.

Kearns published a 2020 study to determine whether the syllable-division patterns work consistently. He found that two-syllable words with the VC|CV pattern, in which we'd expect the first vowel to be short, followed this pattern 78.8 percent of the time. In words that are more than two syllables, the first vowel in a VC|CV pattern had the short sound in only 62.5 percent of cases overall. The V|CV pattern is trickier. Here we'd expect the first vowel to be long because it's in an open syllable. Only 47.3 percent of cases showed this to be true. For words with more than two syllables, the percentage dropped to 32.7 percent.[79]

In the discussion of his findings, Kearns points out that dividing words into syllables according to syllable-division patterns is an effortful process that requires a great deal of cognitive load. If the patterns are so inconsistent, are syllable-division patterns worth teaching? It's hard to say.

My personal opinion is that syllable types are useful to know, but syllable-division patterns are questionable. A reasonable concern is that practicing an elaborate syllable-division strategy takes a great deal of time—time

A reasonable concern is that practicing an elaborate syllable division-strategy takes a great deal of time—time that is probably better spent reading connected text.

that is probably better spent reading connected text. And yet, could spending time in syllable-division help students internalize the patterns, though inconsistent, and therefore help them read longer words with greater accuracy and fluency? Kearns' study did not address this question.

Let's look at other methods for teaching students to read multisyllabic words.

ESHALOV

"Every syllable has at least one vowel," called ESHALOV, is a strategy that requires students to follow six steps.[80]

1. Underline all the vowels in a long word.
2. Join any vowel teams into one vowel sound.
3. Identify known parts of the word.
4. Count the number of word parts that you'd expect based on the number of vowels.
5. Break the word into syllables.
6. Try to pronounce the word. Flex it to make a real word.

Let's try out ESHALOV with the word *unavoidable*.

1. Students would first underline all the vowels.
2. Students would combine the *o* and *i* with a single line because these vowels go together.
3. Students could box the *un-* if they know this prefix and *-able* if they know this suffix.
4. It looks like the word has five syllables because we've underlined five vowels.

5. Students could then attempt to read the word . . . un-ay-void-a-ble. They could flex the sound of the first *a* to get to the word *unavoidable*, one they have in their oral language vocabulary.

BEST

With the BEST strategy,[81] students follow four steps.

1. **B**reak off the parts you know.
2. **E**xamine the base word and underline the vowels.
3. **S**ay each part.
4. **T**ry the whole word.

Let's try out BEST using the word *unsuccessful.*

1. Students could first break off the prefix *un-* and the suffix *-ful.*
2. Students could look at the base word, *success,* and make a guess about how to divide it.   **unsuccessful**
3. Students could then say each part of the word . . . un-suc-cess-ful.   **un|success|ful**
4. They could put the parts together and end with the word **un|suc|cess|ful**
   unsuccessful.

Other Tips for Teaching Students to Read Multisyllabic Words

- A helpful scaffold could be to present multisyllabic words already separated into syllables. Have students practice reading the parts and putting the syllables together to form real words. Eventually you can have them divide the words themselves.
- Teach the following simple syllable-division guidelines[82] as they come up during multisyllabic word reading practice.
  - When a word includes two adjacent consonants, divide between the consonants, as in nap|kin and rab|bit.
  - Do not separate letters in a consonant digraph or blend, in an r-controlled vowel, or in a vowel team.
  - Inflectional endings such as -ing, -er, -es, -ed, and -est can form separate syllables.
  - At the end of a word, when a consonant comes before -le, the consonant belongs with the -le, as in stum-ble or rat-tle.
  - Single vowels can stand for a single syllable, as in pres-i-dent.
- Students need to have longer words in their oral vocabulary if we expect them to be able to flex the vowels to make a real word. This is why it can be useful to preteach multisyllabic words before the reading of complex text.

Example: A sentence in the day's text may be, "The discovery of gold led many people to travel west." A second grade teacher knows that some children will have trouble with the word *discovery.* They post the word with a loop under each chunk. They then prompt students to read each part and then put the parts together to read the word. Research has shown this strategy to be effective in improving word recognition skills.[83]

discovery

Practice, Practice, Practice! When you choose one of these strategies and teach it to your students, they'll know they have a plan of attack when they encounter difficult multisyllabic words. Consider spending 10–15 minutes a day on a strategy for at least four weeks so students can internalize it.[84]

EFFECTIVE PHONICS INSTRUCTION INCLUDES SPELLING INSTRUCTION

Traditional spelling instruction involves giving children a list of words on Monday. Teachers expect their students to memorize the spellings of each word during the week and take a final test on Friday. Sometimes the words are related only in concept; they may not have similar spelling patterns.

The Problem with Traditional Spelling Instruction

Traditional spelling instruction emphasizes visual memory. Children are expected to memorize a string of letters or the shape of a word. They practice the words using flashcards or by writing the words multiple times. But good spellers do not necessarily have a strong *visual* memory. They have a strong *orthographic* memory. **Orthographic memory** has to do with knowing how sounds are represented in language.[85]

Teach Decoding and Spelling Together

Rather than teach spelling at a separate time of day, it makes sense to teach spelling and phonics together at least through first grade.[86] When you are teaching your students to read CVCE words, you should also be teaching them how to *spell* CVCE words.

Spelling instruction is worth your time! It improves reading proficiency because it reinforces sound and letter patterns.[87] Spelling instruction also helps with pronunciation and meanings.[88]

Spelling Dictation

Think of dictation as guided spelling practice, not assessment. You should include spelling dictation with every new sound-spelling that you teach with the goal of doing dictation at least twice a week.[89] It should begin as soon as students are reading CVC words, preferably at the beginning of kindergarten.

Dictation Procedure

1. Prepare a list of 5–7 words and 1–2 sentences that feature the new sound-spelling. Make sure at least 1–2 words include review patterns.
2. Provide a white board or worksheet for students to record their work. White boards are more fun and less time-consuming, but a prepared worksheet allows you to have a record of student work and encourages proper handwriting. You might want to switch between the two, depending on time constraints. A good practice might be to use a white board every third or fourth session.
3. If you are preparing a worksheet in advance, I recommend drawing a line for each phoneme so students can write a single grapheme on each line (see Figure 5.19).

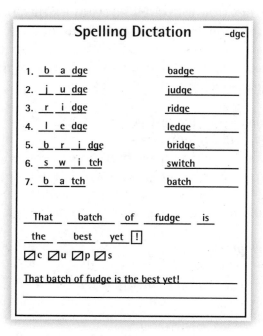

Figure 5.19 Spelling dictation.

4. After you dictate each word, have students repeat it. They should then say and tap the sounds in the word. As they spell each sound, walk around the room and give support as needed.

5. Write the correct spelling so everyone can see it. Have students check their work and correct their spelling if needed. Finally, they should rewrite the word correctly on a single line next to their original spelling (no lines or boxes this time).

6. Start small with sentence dictation. It's exhausting for young writers. Increase the length of the sentences as students are ready.

7. If your students are doing dictation on a worksheet, prepare a set of lines for each sentence (one line per word). After you dictate the sentence, have students repeat it as they point to one line for each word. They may need your help to repeat it again.

8. After students write a sentence, have them check it using CUPS:
    a. **C**apitalization: Does the sentence start with a capital letter? For older students: Are proper nouns capitalized?

b. **U**nderstanding: Does the sentence make sense? Have them read it aloud to make sure they didn't miss any words.

c. **P**unctuation: Does the sentence end with the proper mark? For older students: Are other punctuation marks used appropriately?

d. **S**pelling: Are all the words spelled correctly?

9. After checking their work with CUPS, have students rewrite the sentence.

10. To conclude the activity, have students read aloud their word list and sentences.

Sound Mapping

If you choose to give a weekly spelling list, sound mapping is an excellent way to introduce and practice the words. When introducing each new spelling word, have students "map" it using a phoneme-mapping grid. Sound mapping was inspired by phoneme-grapheme mapping, a process created by Kathryn Grace and shared in her book, *Phonics and Spelling Through Phoneme-Grapheme Mapping.*[90]

Here is the sound-mapping procedure:

1. Say the word. Have students repeat it.
2. Have students break the word apart into its sounds, tapping once for each sound.
3. Students should spell a single sound in each box.

Students should check their spelling against your example and fix any mistakes.

Note that each sound gets a single box, even if it takes more than one letter to spell a particular phoneme (see Figure 5.20). The letters of a consonant blend should each get their own box, while the letters of a consonant digraph or vowel team should share a box. The letter x should overlap two boxes, because it represents two sounds, /k/ and /s/. I like to squeeze the silent e next to the consonant that it follows.

EFFECTIVE PHONICS INSTRUCTION INCORPORATES REVIEW

Systematic phonics instruction includes frequent review. According to Blevins, new sound-spellings should be intentionally reviewed for the next four to six weeks.[91] Consider these ways to incorporate review into your phonics lessons:

♦ Do a **visual drill** two to three times a week using a grapheme deck. Students say the sound(s) of each grapheme as the teacher shows a paper or digital flash card. For example, if the card shows *igh*, students say the long *i* sound.

m	a	t							
t	e	x	t						
s	t	i	ck						
d	r	e	ss						
ch	i	l	d						
b	r	i	ng						
d	r	i	n	k					
sh	a	de							
b	a	tch							
s	l	u	dge						
s	p	ee	ch						
p	r	ay							
f	ir	s	t						
n	ur	se							
b	o	tt	le						
q	u	e	s	t					

Figure 5.20 Sound Mapping.

- Two-three times a week, do a **spelling drill** as students write the graphemes for a particular phoneme in a sand tray or on a dry-erase board. The teacher dictates a sound, such as /k/. Students repeat the sound and write the spellings they've learned as they speak them. For example, after the teacher dictates /k/, students might write c, k, and ck. While writing, they would say, "C spells /k/. K spells /k/. C-K spells /k/."
- **Blending lines** should include review patterns.
- **Sound mapping** should include previously learned sound-spellings.
- **Dictation** should include previously learned sound-spellings.
- Students should have many opportunities to **reread decodable passages and books**.

EFFECTIVE PHONICS INSTRUCTION FOLLOWS A PREDICTABLE LESSON FORMAT

While research has little to say on an exact lesson sequence, I recommend the following, with the understanding that this lesson may take two days to complete.

- Start with a review (this may include a visual and/or spelling drill).
- Do a phonemic awareness warm-up featuring the new sound.

- ◆ Explicitly teach the new grapheme(s). Include blending practice.
- ◆ Continue with sound-mapping and word building.
- ◆ If needed, teach your students one or more high-frequency words.
- ◆ Do spelling dictation.
- ◆ Conclude with the reading of decodable text.

Sample Phonics Lesson for the OA and OW Spellings

Introduction (30 s)	"Today you're going to learn two spellings for the long o sound."
Review (4 m)	Say the sound of each grapheme as I show the flash card.

Get out your dry erase board and marker for our spelling drill. The first sound is /s/. Repeat. (Students repeat the sound and write the spellings they've learned for /s/. Continue with other sounds you've taught.)

Phonemic awareness warm-up (2 m)	Repeat each word after me. Show. Toe. Throw. Snow. Joe. What sound did you say at the end of each word?
	I'm going to give you sounds to blend together. After I say the sounds, blend them together and say the word. /k/ /r/ /ō/. (Students: "Crow." Continue with other words: *cone, smoke, flow, coat.*)
	Today's sound is /ō/. What is your mouth doing when you say the /ō/ sound?
New sound–spelling (5 m)	We have two new ways to spell long o. O-A is one way to spell /ō/. O-W is another way to spell /ō/. When you see the OA card, say /ō/. When you see the OW card, say /ō/. Let's practice.
	(If you have a sound wall, post these spellings on the wall under the /ō/ phoneme.)
	Let's blend these /ō/ words that are listed on the board. (Guide students as they read *coat, goat, loaf, coach, toast, boat, cloak, blow, crow, grow, know, show, shown,* and *growth.*)
	As you look at these words, where do you see the OA spelling? Where do you usually see the OW spelling?

Now let's practice our spelling drill for /ō/ You know
four ways to spell /ō/ now – o, o-consonant-e,
oa, and ow.
The sound is /ō/. Repeat. (Students repeat the sound
and write the four spellings on their boards.)

Let's practice reading our
new blending lines with
OA and OW.
(If time allows, have students
read the blending lines in
pairs after you've read
them as a class.)

Blending Lines

oa & ow

①	snow	blow	blow	throw	coach	poach
②	moan	slow	foam	row	know	flown
③	goat	low	shown	blow	groan	coast
④	twine	close	brake	shade	globe	flute
⑤	roaming	towing	soaked	blowing	foams	coached
⑥	Sloan rowed his boat by the coast.					

©themeasuredmom.com

Word chaining (5 m)

Let's build words with the /ō/ sound. These words will
include some of the ways you've learned to spell /ō/:
o, o-consonant-e, OA, and OW. If the word you spell
doesn't look right, try again.
coat – goat – go – grow – grown – groan

Dictation (8-10 m)

Here's your dictation page. Repeat
each word after me, say its
sounds, and spell it.
boat, show, grow, goat, soap, cone,
rope
The goats roam near the big
oak tree.

Spelling Dictation
oa

Teacher: Say each word. Have students repeat the word, say each sound as they tap it, and then spell each
sound on a line. Finally, students should write the whole word on the long line.

1. _____   _____

2. _____   _____

3. _____   _____

4. _____   _____

5. _____   _____

6. _____   _____

7. _____   _____

Teacher: Dictate each sentence. Students should repeat the sentence, repeat it again as they tap on a line for
each word, and write the sentence. They should check it using CUPS and recopy the entire sentence.

_____ _____ _____ _____

_____ _____ _____ [ ]

[ ] C [ ] U [ ] P [ ] S

_____

C= Begins with a capital letter
U= Understanding (when read aloud, does it make sense?)
P = Punctuation at the end
S= Check spelling

©themeasuredmom.com

Connected Text (8-10 m)

Today you will read this passage about a boy who is stuck in the house on a cold, blustery day. Let's read the title together. (Have students whisper read the passage. Then read it chorally. Conclude with questions about the passage. Students can answer the questions independently.)

Name	ow (as in snow)

Snowing and Blowing

It has been snowing since I got up, and the wind is blowing. The snow on the driveway is so thick that I know I can't get a ride to my friend's house. Even grown-ups are not supposed to travel.

"I know you're feeling low," Mom says, "but we can still have a fun day." Mom gets a bowl of snacks. We play the game of Risk on the rug next to the glow of the lamp. The slow day begins to speed up. Mom has always won Risk, but now that I am ten, I think I can beat her.

When the game ends, Mom groans. "I wanted to defeat you, but I should have known that you'd win! Now that you've grown, I don't stand a chance. Come on. Let's go out and build a snowman."

Why am I feeling bored and glum?

_____

What do Mom and I do to pass the time?

_____

Mom has always won. Why do I win this time?

_____

©themeasuredmomplus.com

The Debate Between Print-to-Speech and Speech-to-Print

One of the current areas of debate among science of reading advocates is whether a print-to-speech or speech-to-print approach to teaching phonics is superior. This gets confusing because, in addition to describing two different types of phonics instruction, *print-to-speech* also refers to skills needed for decoding, and *speech-to-print* also refers to skills needed for encoding (spelling). To avoid confusion, I prefer the terms *traditional phonics instruction* (print-to-speech) and *linguistic phonics* (speech-to-print).

The traditional approach is the most common way of teaching phonics. Most commercial programs, including those that are based on the Orton-Gillingham approach, fall under this umbrella. Linguistic phonics programs include Reading Simplified, Evidence-Based Literacy Instruction (EBLI), Phono-Graphix, Sounds-Write, SPELL-Links, and others. The traditional and linguistic phonics approaches are both based on the science of reading; however, they *apply* the science differently.

SO WHAT'S THE DIFFERENCE?

In traditional phonics instruction, letters and sounds are taught together in isolation. "This is a *g*. G spells /g/." With linguistic phonics, sounds are taught in the context of words. Students break a word into its phonemes, spell each sound, and read back the word they've spelled. Letter names are not a focus during initial reading instruction; when word building, teachers might say, "Move the /m/" instead of "Move the letter *m*."

In some traditional programs, irregular words (sometimes called "red words") are taught by letter names and memorization. Students might arm tap a word by saying its name and spelling it while tapping down the arm. "S-A-I-D spells SAID." With linguistic phonics, the focus is on the phoneme. Instead of reciting the letters, students say the *sound* of each grapheme as they write it. Another important distinction is that traditional phonics instruction typically teaches one spelling at a time to mastery. But linguistic phonics approaches teach multiple spellings for a single sound at one time, with constant review and application. For example, instead of just teaching that o-consonant-e spells the long o sound, students might also be taught O, OA, OW, and OE at the same time.

The traditional approach often aims for mastery before moving on; linguistic phonics is about mastery over time, which allows students to move at a faster pace. This lets students move out of decodable books sooner than students using a traditional program.

Many traditional phonics programs organize instruction by focusing on rules, exceptions, syllable types, and/or syllable division. Linguistic phonics approaches focus on patterns without relying on rules. They teach a flexible strategy for reading longer words instead of teaching elaborate syllable division strategies. They also lack keywords, flashcards, and the multisensory material (such as sandpaper or shaving cream) common in some traditional phonics programs.

IS ONE APPROACH SUPERIOR?

Traditional phonics instruction and linguistic phonics have a lot in common, but they are also quite different. We need more research that compares the two approaches before we can confidently claim that one is superior.

The bottom line? Be open to learning as much as you can about each approach so you can find what works best for your students.

 Key Things to Remember

- Students do better at both word recognition and reading comprehension when their initial reading instruction emphasizes systematic, explicit phonics.
- When compared to other types of phonics instruction, synthetic phonics has the strongest research support.
- Children benefit from direct teaching of letter names and sounds through paired-associate learning.
- Teachers should explicitly teach blending routines.
- Word building and word chaining are effective ways to integrate phonemic awareness and phonics.

- ◆ Regularly spelled high-frequency words are best taught alongside the corresponding phonics skill. We can teach irregular high-frequency words by examining the regular and irregular parts of the word.
- ◆ Effective phonics instruction includes practice with decodable texts, but decodable texts should not be used indefinitely.
- ◆ We should teach children a strategy for decoding multisyllabic words and give many opportunities for practice.
- ◆ Spelling should be integrated with phonics instruction in the early grades.

Free Resources
- ◆ Alphabet charts
- ◆ Phonics scope and sequence
- ◆ Mini sound wall
- ◆ Word chain lists
- ◆ Cover, Copy, Compare worksheet
- ◆ Editable blending lines template
- ◆ Phonics lesson template

www.themeasuredmom.com/bookresources/

Learn More
- ◆ Read *A Fresh Look at Phonics* by Wiley Blevins.
- ◆ Read *Making Sense of Phonics* by Isabel Beck and Mark Beck.
- ◆ Watch Wiley Blevins' workshop "Choosing and Using Decodable Text," www.youtube.com/watch?v=M7bm06Wd43k.
- ◆ Watch Dr. Katie Pace Miles' workshop, "High Frequency Words: What, Why, and How it Pertains to the Science of Reading," www.youtube.com/watch?v=M7bm06Wd43k.
- ◆ Watch Dr. Devin Kearns' workshop, "Syllables or Morphemes: When to Teach and Why," www.youtube.com/watch?v=M7bm06Wd43k.

Notes

1. Chall, J. S. (1996). *Learning to read: The great debate*. Harcourt Brace & Company, xix.
2. Blevins, W. (2021). *Meaningful phonics and word study*. Benchmark Education.
3. Adams, M. J. (1998). The three-cueing system. In Osborn, J., & Lehr, F., (Eds.), *Literacy for all: Issues in teaching and learning* (73–99). The Guilford Press.
4. Stanovich, K. E. (2000). *Progress in understanding reading: Scientific foundations and new frontiers*. Guilford Press, 6.
5. Gillis, M. B., & Eberhardt, N. C. (2018). *Phonemic awareness and phonics: Knowledge to practice*. Literacy How Professional Learning Series.
6. Chall, J. S. (1996).
7. National Reading Panel (U.S.) & National Institute of Child Health and Human Development (U.S.). (2000). *Report of the National Reading Panel: Teaching children to read: An evidence-based assessment of the scientific research literature on reading and its implications for reading instruction*. U.S. Dept. of Health and Human Services, Public Health Service, National Institutes of Health, National Institute of Child Health and Human Development.
8. O'Connor, R. E. (2014). *Teaching word recognition*. The Guilford Press.
9. Castles, A., Rastle, K., & Nation, K. (2018). Ending the reading wars: Reading acquisition from novice to expert. *Psychological Science in the Public Interest, 19*(1), 5–51.
10. Connor, C. M., Morrison, F. J., & Underwood, P. S. (2007). A second chance in second grade: The independent and cumulative impact of first- and second-grade reading instruction and students' letter-word reading skill growth. *Scientific Studies of Reading, 11*(3), 199–233.
11. National Reading Panel (U.S.) & National Institute of Child Health and Human Development (U.S.). (2000).
12. Ehri, L. C. (2003, March 17). *Systematic phonics instruction: Findings of the National Reading Panel*. [Paper presentation]. Seminar organized by the Standards and Effectiveness Unit, Department for Education and Skills, British Government, London, England, 16.
13. Johnston, R. S., & Watson, J. E. (2004). Accelerating the development of reading, spelling, and phonemic awareness skills in initial readers. *Reading and Writing: An Interdisciplinary Journal, 17*(4), 327–357.
14. Christensen, C. A., & Bowey, J. A. (2005). The efficacy of orthographic rime, grapheme-phoneme correspondence, and implicit phonics approaches to teaching decoding skills. *Scientific Studies of Reading, 9*(4), 327–349.
15. Brady, S. (2020). A 2020 perspective on research findings on alphabetics (phoneme awareness and phonics): Implications for instruction. *The Reading League Journal, 1*(3), 20–28.

16. Weisberg, P., & Savard, C. F. (1993). Teaching preschoolers to read: Don't stop between the sounds when segmenting words. *Education and Treatment of Children, 16*(1), 1–18.

17. Carnine, D. W., Silbert, J., Kame'enui, E. J., Tarver, S. G., & Jungjohann, K. (2005). *Teaching struggling and at-risk readers: A direct instruction approach*. Pearson.

18. Fry, E. (2004). Phonics: A large phoneme-grapheme frequency count revised. *Journal of Literacy Research, 36*(1), 85–98.

19. Bond, G. L., & Dykstra, R. (1967). The cooperative research program in first-grade reading instruction. *Reading Research Quarterly, 2*(4), 5–142.

20. Adams, M. J. (1990). *Beginning to read*. MIT Press.

21. Piasta, S. B. & Wagner, R.K. (2010). Learning letter names and sounds: Effects of instruction, letter type, and phonological processing skill. *Journal of Experimental Psychology*, 105(4), 324–344.
    McBride-Chang, C. (1999). The ABCs of the ABCs: The development of letter-name and letter-sound knowledge. *Merrill-Palmer Quarterly, 45*(2), 285–308.

22. Allen, K. A., & Neuhaus, G. F. (2018). Alphabet knowledge. In Birsh, J. R., & Carreker, S., (Eds.), *Multisensory teaching of basic language skills* (171–203). Paul H. Brookes Publishing Co., p. 177.

23. Piasta, S. B., Purpura, D. J., & Wagner, R. K. (2010). Fostering alphabet knowledge development: A comparison of two instructional approaches. *Reading and Writing, 23*, 607–626.

24. Piasta, S. B. (2023). The science of early alphabet instruction: What we do and do not know. In Cabell, S. Q., Neuman, S. B., & Terry, N. P., (Eds.), *Handbook on the science of early literacy* (p. 83–94). The Guilford Press.

25. Geiger, A. (Host). (2023, March 27). What does the research say about teaching the alphabet? with Dr. Shayne Piasta (No. 117) [Audio Podcast Episode]. In *Triple R Teaching*. Anna Geiger. https://www.themeasuredmom.com/research-alphabet-shayne-piasta/.

26. Justice, L. M., & Ezell, H. K. (2002). Use of storybook reading to increase print awareness in at-risk children. *American Journal of Speech Language Pathology*, 11(1), 17–29.

27. Roberts, T. A., Vadasy, P. F., & Sanders, E. A. (2020). Preschool instruction in letter names and sounds: Does contextualized or decontextualized instruction matter? *Reading Research Quarterly, 55*(4), 573–600.

28. Piasta, S. B. (2023).

29. Ibid.

30. Jones, C. D., & Reutzel, D. R. (2012). Enhanced alphabet knowledge instruction: Exploring a change of frequency, focus, and distributed cycles of review. *Reading Psychology, 33*(5), 448–464.

31. Vadasy, P. F., & Sanders, E. A. (2021). Introducing grapheme-phoneme correspondences (GPCs): Exploring rate and complexity in phonics instruction for kindergartners with limited literacy skills. *Reading and Writing, 34*(1), 109–138.

32. Sunde, K., Furnes, B., & Lundetrae, K. (2020). Does introducing the letters faster boost the development of children's letter knowledge, word reading and spelling in the first year of school? *Scientific Studies of Reading, 24*(2), 141–158.

33. Moats. L. C., & Tolman, C. A. (2019). *LETRS Volume 1*. Voyager Sopris Learning.

34. Piasta, S. B. (2023).

35. Boyer, N., & Ehri, L. C. (2011). Contribution of phonemic segmentation instruction with letters and articulation pictures to word reading and spelling in beginners. *Scientific Studies of Reading, 15*(5), 440–470.

36. Roberts, T. A., Vasady, P. F., & Sanders, E. A. (2019). Preschoolers' alphabet learning: Cognitive, teaching sequence, and English proficiency influences. *Reading Research Quarterly, 54*(3), 413–437.

37. Ehri, L. C., Deffner, N. D., and Wilce, L. S. (1984). Pictorial mnemonics for phonics. *Journal of Educational Psychology, 76*(5), 880–893.

38. Roberts, T. A., Vasady, P. F., & Sanders, E. A. (2019).

39. Beck, I. L., & Beck, M. E. (2013). *Making sense of phonics*. The Guilford Press.

40. O'Connor, R. E., & Padeliadu, S. (2000). Blending versus whole word approaches in first grade remedial reading: Short-term and delayed effects on reading and spelling words. *Reading and Writing, 13*, 159–182.

41. Blevins, W. (2023). *Phonics from a to z*. Scholastic.

42. Blevins, W. (2016). *A fresh look at phonics*. Corwin Literacy.

43. Seamer, J. (2021, February 18). *Moving on from sounding out*. Jocelyn Seamer Education. https://www.jocelynseamereducation.com/blog/46933-moving-on-from-sounding-out.

44. McCandliss, B., Beck., I. L., Sandak, R., & Perfetti, C. (2003). Focusing attention on decoding for children with poor reading skills: Design and preliminary tests of the word building intervention. *Scientific Studies of Reading, 7*(1), 75–104.

45. Farrell, L., Osenga, T., & Hunter. M. (2013). *Comparing the Dolch and Fry high frequency word lists*. Readsters. https://www.readsters.com/wp-content/uploads/2013/03/ComparingDolchAndFryLists.pdf.

46. Joseph, L. M., Konrad, M., Cates, G., Vajcner, T., Eveleigh, E., & Fishley, K. M. A meta-analytic review of the cover-copy-compare and variations of this self-management procedure. *Psychology in the Schools, 49*(2), 122–136.

47. Stollar, S. (N.D). *Reading science academy*. Stephanie Stollar Consulting. https://www.readingscienceacademy.com/.

48. O'Connor, R. E. (2014).

49. Foorman, B., Beyler, N., Borradaile, K., Coyne, M., Denton, C. A., Dimino, J., ... & Wissel, S. (2016). *Foundational skills to support reading for understanding in kindergarten through 3rd grade.* Educator's Practice Guide. NCEE 2016-4008. What Works Clearinghouse.

50. Castles, A., Rastle, K., & Nation, K. (2018).

51. Farrell, L., Hunter, M., & Osenga, T. (2013). A new model for teaching high frequency words. *Readsters reader, 3*(1), 1–7.

52. Adams, M. J. (2009). Decodable text: Why, when, and how? In Hiebert, E. H., & Sailors, M. (Eds.), *Finding the right texts: What works for beginning and struggling readers* (23–46). Guilford Press.

53. Seamer, J. (2021). The role of decodable texts in learning to read. *LDA Bulletin, 53*(2), 23.

54. Fountas, I. C., & Pinnell, G. S. (1999). *Matching books to readers: Using leveled books in guided reading, K-3.* Heinemann.

55. Blevins, W. (2021), p. 41.

56. Juel, C., & Roper-Schneider, D. (1985). The influence of basal readers on first-grade reading. *Reading Research Quarterly, 20*(2), 151.

57. Goldberg, M. (2019, November 13). *The drudgery (and beauty) of decodable texts.* The Right to Read Project. https://righttoreadproject.com/2019/11/13/the-drudgery-and-beauty-of-decodable-texts/.

58. Juel, C., & Roper-Schneider, D. (1985).

59. Compton, D. L., Appleton, A. C., & Hosp, M. K. (2004). Exploring the relationship between text-leveling systems and reading accuracy and fluency in second-grade students who are average and poor decoders. *Learning Disabilities Research & Practice, 19*(3), 176–184.

60. Jenkins, J. R., Peyton, J. A., Sanders, E. A., & Vadasy, P. F. (2004). Effects of reading decodable texts in supplemental first-grade tutoring. *Scientific Studies of Reading, 8*(1), 53–85.

61. Shanahan, T. (2018, August 25). *Should we teach with decodable text?* Shanahan on Literacy. https://www.shanahanonliteracy.com/blog/should-we-teach-with-decodable-text.

62. Blevins, W. (2021). *Choosing and using decodable texts.* Scholastic.

63. Mesmer, H. A. (2005). Text decodability and the first-grade reader. *Reading & Writing Quarterly, 21*(1), 61–86.

64. Blevins, W. (2021).

65. Hiebert, E. H., & Fisher, C. W. (2007). Critical word factor in texts for beginning readers. *The Journal of Educational Research, 101*(1), 3–11.

66. Cheatham, J. P., & Allor, J. H. (2012). The influence of decodability in early reading text on reading achievement: A review of the evidence. *Reading and writing, 25*, 2223–2246.

67. Moats, L. C. (1998). Teaching decoding. *American Educator, 22*(1), 42–49.

68. Geiger, A. (Host). (2023, March 20). What is set for variability? A conversation with Dr. Marnie Ginsberg (No. 116) [Audio Podcast Episode]. In Triple R Teaching. Anna Geiger. https://www.themeasuredmom.com/what-is-set-for-variability-a-conversation-with-dr-marnie-ginsberg/.

69. Share, D. L. (1999). Phonological recoding and orthographic learning: A direct test of the self-teaching hypothesis. *Journal of Experimental Child Psychology, 72*(2), 95–129.

70. Mesmer, H. A. (2020, September 24). Fear not the decodable: Why? When? How? *Heinemann Blog.* https://blog.heinemann.com/fear-not-the-decodable-why-when-how.

71. Farrell, L. (2022, August 26). *How and when to use decodable readers for maximum effectiveness.* [Video]. YouTube. https://www.youtube.com/watch?v=e5UTzPZPcdk.

72. Seamer, J. (2021).

73. Kearns, D. M., & Whaley, V. M. (2019). Helping students with dyslexia read long words: Using syllables and morphemes. *Teaching Exceptional Children, 51*(3), 212–225.

74. White, T. G., Sowell, J., & Yanagihara, A. (1989). Teaching elementary students to use word-part clues. *The Reading Teacher, 42*(4), 302–308.

75. Blevins, W. (2016).

76. Archer, A. L., Gleason, M. M., & Vachon, V. L. (2003). Decoding and fluency: Foundation skills for struggling older readers. *Learning Disability Quarterly, 26*(2), 90.

77. Beck, I. L., & Beck, M. E. (2013).

78. O'Connor, R. E. (2014).

79. Kearns, D. M. (2020). Does English have useful syllable division patterns? *Reading Research Quarterly, 55*, S145–S160.

80. O'Connor, R. E., Beach, K. D., Sanchez, V. M., Bocian, K. M., & Flynn, L. J. (2015). Building BRIDGES: A design experiment to improve reading and United States history knowledge of poor readers in eighth grade. *Exceptional Children, 81*(4), 399–425.

81. O'Connor, R. E. (2014).

82. *Beck, I. L., & Beck, M. E. (2013).*

83. Archer, A. L., Gleason, M. M., & Vachon, V. L. (2003).

84. Kearns, D. M., Lyon, C. P., & Kelley, S. L. (2021). Structured literacy interventions for reading long words. In Spear-Swerling, L. (Ed.), *Structured literacy interventions*. Guilford Press.

85. Carreker, S. (2011). Teaching spelling. In Birsh, J. R., & Carreker, S., (Eds.), *Multisensory teaching of basic skills*. Paul H. Brookes Publishing Co.

86. Moats. L. C., & Tolman, C. A. (2019).

87. Adams, M. J. (1990).

88. Ehri, L. C., & Rosenthal, J. (2007). Spellings of words: A neglected facilitator of vocabulary learning. *Journal of Literacy Research*, *39*(4), 389–409.

89. Blevins, W. (2016).

90. Grace, K. E. S. (2007). *Phonics and spelling through phoneme-grapheme mapping*. Sopris West Educational Services.

91. Blevins, W. (2016).

CHAPTER 6

Fluency

According to Jan Hasbrouck, "First, foremost, and forever, accuracy is the foundation of fluency." Hasbrouck and Deb Glaser define **fluency** as "reasonably accurate reading, at an appropriate rate, with suitable expression, that leads to accurate and deep comprehension and motivation to read."[1] Remember Scarborough's Reading Rope? The tightly woven part at the end, where all the strands come together, represents fluent reading.

The Components of Fluency

The three components of fluency are accuracy, rate, and prosody.

1. **Accuracy** refers to reading words correctly. According to research, students' accuracy rates should be at least 95 percent.[2] Below that, comprehension deteriorates. For younger emergent readers, accuracy rates should be 97–98 percent.[3] Hasbrouck reminds us that "first, foremost, and forever, accuracy is the foundation of fluency."[4]

2. **Rate** refers to the speed of reading and is measured in words correct per minute (WCPM). Your goal should always be to have your students read at an *appropriate* rate, not a lightning fast one. When students read too fast, comprehension suffers.

   If you're wondering how many words per minute your students should read, refer to the oral reading fluency norms compiled by Hasbrouck and Tindal (see

Table 6.1). A good benchmark goal is to have students read at the 50th percentile for their grade and time of year. There is no evidence that pushing students beyond the 50th–75th percentile range results in long-term benefits.[5]

3. **Prosody** refers to reading with expression. When students read with prosody, they know when to speed up or slow down, when to emphasize particular words, and how to read with phrasing. We are still unsure whether prosody leads to comprehension or is a result of it, but it appears that the extent to which students read with prosody is an indicator of how well they understand the text.[6]

Table 6.1 Oral Reading Fluency Norms

Grade	Percentile	Fall WCPM	Winter WCPM	Spring WCPM	Average weekly improvement
1	90	–	97	116	1.2
	75	–	59	91	2.0
	50	–	**29**	**60**	**1.9**
	25	–	16	34	1.1
	10	–	9	18	0.5
2	90	111	131	148	1.2
	75	84	109	124	1.3
	50	**50**	**84**	**100**	**1.6**
	25	36	59	72	1.1
	10	23	35	43	0.6
3	90	134	161	166	1.0
	75	104	137	139	1.1
	50	**83**	**97**	**112**	**0.9**
	25	59	79	91	1.0
	10	40	62	63	0.7
4	90	153	168	184	1.0
	75	125	143	160	1.1
	50	**94**	**120**	**133**	**1.2**
	25	75	95	105	0.9
	10	60	71	83	0.7
5	90	179	183	195	0.5
	75	153	160	169	0.5
	50	**121**	**133**	**146**	**0.8**
	25	87	109	119	1.0
	10	64	84	102	1.9
6	90	185	195	204	0.6
	75	159	166	173	0.4
	50	**132**	**145**	**146**	**0.3**
	25	112	116	122	0.3
	10	89	91	91	0.1

Source: Hasbrouck, J. & Tindal, G. (2017). An update to compiled ORF norms (Technical Report No. 1702). Eugene, OR, *Behavioral Research and Teaching*, University of Oregon.

Automaticity theory says that when students are not automatic at word recognition, they must use their cognitive energy to decode. As a result, they pay less attention to understanding what they read.[7] Automaticity is a prerequisite for good reading comprehension.[8] This is similar to the role of automaticity in other skills. After

Automaticity is a prerequisite for good reading comprehension.

taking piano lessons for four years, I had a new teacher, Ms. Harris. When Ms. Harris saw that I was still writing the names of the notes in my music, she was appalled. "You won't be doing *that* anymore!" I gulped and realized I had to commit note names to memory once and for all. After I accomplished this, playing piano became much easier. I finally had extra mental energy to focus on rhythm, dynamics, and technique. Something similar happens when children learn to be fluent readers.

Fluency and Comprehension

Fluency is often called the bridge between word recognition and comprehension.[9] While we don't fully understand the complex relationship between fluency and comprehension, we know that the fluency both contributes to comprehension and is an outcome of it.[10]

When students first learn to sound out words, they lack automaticity. As a result, their reading is anything but fluent. Speech pathologist Alison Clarke describes it this way: "They grunt and groan and sweat through the words. Most of their cognitive horsepower gets used up just extracting words from the page, and they don't understand much of what they've read. It's certainly not fluent. It looks and sounds more like a hard slog than fun."[11] This stilted, word-by-word reading can be painful to listen to; ask any kindergarten or first grade teacher! However, Clarke reminds us that it's essential that students work through this stage as they create new circuits in the brain.

It's tempting to have students "read" predictable, leveled books instead of the more challenging decodable texts. When students memorize the pattern and use the pictures to identify words, they sound fluent from the beginning. Ahhh . . . it's so much easier to listen to! And students "read" so quickly that they can actually tell us about the text. Unfortunately, this fluency is fake.

Try as we might, we can't fast forward our way to fluency. Children must build their reading brains by decoding words until they've orthographically mapped them.

Try as we might, we can't fast forward our way to fluency.

Developing Automaticity at the Letter and Word Level

If I pointed out a "No Parking" sign to you and asked you not to read it, you would read it in spite of yourself, without conscious attention. You would read it *automatically.*

Our students will develop automaticity only when they recognize words instantly. How do students become automatic? Practice!

The type of practice our students need depends on where they are in their reading development. Before becoming fluent with connected text, they must first become automatic at naming letters,[12] knowing letter-sound correspondences,[13] and word reading.[14]

HOW TO ACHIEVE AUTOMATICITY WITH LETTER NAMES

For students who are learning to be automatic with letter names, an alphabet arc (see Figure 6.1) can help. Provide each student with an arc and a set of plastic letters.

1. Have students match the plastic letters to the letters on the arc, saying the letter names as they do so.
2. The teacher should then name letters and have students pull those letters down from the arc.
3. Next, the teacher should point to letters and have students name them.
4. Eventually, teachers can provide an arc with only the anchor letters A, M, N, and Z (see Figure 6.2). How quickly can students name the letters as they put them in order? For a final challenge, teachers can provide a curved line only.
5. Have students use the alphabet arc to help them name the missing letter on a set of cards (see Figure 6.3).

With alphabet fluency grids (see Figure 6.4), students roll a die and name the letters in the corresponding row as quickly as possible. If you want to make fluency grids a whole class or small group activity, have one student roll the die. That student should name the letters loudly while the rest of the students name them in a whisper.

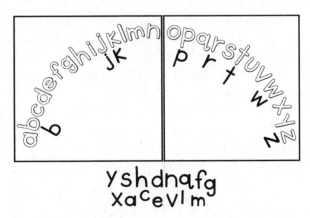

Figure 6.1   The alphabet arc.

Image by Rocio Zapata

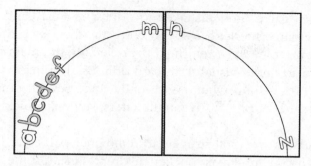

Figure 6.2 Alphabet arc with anchor letters only.
Image by Rocio Zapata

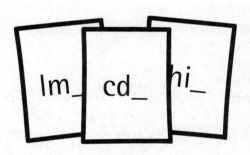

Figure 6.3 Missing letter cards.
Image by Rocio Zapata

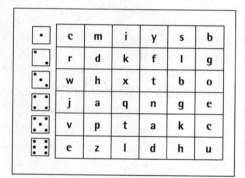

Figure 6.4 Fluency grid.

HOW TO ACHIEVE AUTOMATICITY WITH LETTER SOUNDS

You can easily repurpose alphabet arcs and fluency grids to focus on letter sounds instead of letter names. You could also play a game like *SLAP*. For this game, two students divide a deck of letter cards in two. They place the cards face down and take turns flipping a card over, placing it face up between them, and saying the letter's sound. Each round, a particular card is the "SLAP" card. When it's flipped, students should try to be the first one to slap the card as they say its sound; they will then gain all the cards that have accumulated so far. When the decks run out, or after a certain time has elapsed, whoever has the most cards wins.

BANG! is a similar game. Students take turns drawing a card and naming the sound of the letter. If they name the letter's sound correctly, they keep the card, but if they draw the "BANG" card, they must return all their cards to the main pile.

Many teachers also find a visual flash card drill, used in many Orton-Gillingham–based programs, to be helpful when consistently done several times a week. As the teacher flashes the cards of previously taught letters, students quickly say the sound of each letter.

If you have students who still struggle to remember particular letters and sounds, try O'Connor's technique known as "pocket children." First, test these students to learn which letter-sound relationships are solid and which ones they don't yet know. Then write four of the solid letters on small cards and one tenuous letter on a separate card; these should fit in the teacher's pocket. At one-minute breaks throughout the day, pull aside the child and have them say the sound on each card. If any are missed, model the correct sound. Then have the student say it with you and then repeat it on their own. When the student is solid on all five cards, remove one and add a new one from the shaky set. Some teachers can manage up to four pocket children.[15]

HOW TO ACHIEVE AUTOMATICITY WITH WORD READING

Phonics instruction does not guarantee automaticity in word reading. Lots of decoding practice is key! After each phonics lesson, have students read a word list with the featured pattern as well as review words. Blending lines (see Chapter 5) are another useful tool. After students have been taught to decode using synthetic phonics, you can use word family activities to build automaticity with common spelling patterns.

Developing Fluency at the Text Level

When children are in kindergarten and early first grade, we should focus on accuracy at the letter and word level. By the middle of first grade, however, when students are reading connected text with reasonable accuracy, it's time to focus on text-level fluency. We start with assessment.

ASSESSING FLUENCY

An excellent assessment tool is called oral reading fluency (ORF). Despite its name, ORF is not a complete measure of fluency. Rather, it measures accuracy and rate. These measures combined help teachers know how their students are doing when it comes to automaticity.[16]

To conduct an ORF assessment, the teacher listens for one minute to a student read aloud from an unpracticed, grade-level passage. The teacher follows along with a copy of the passage and marks any errors. At the end of one minute, the teacher determines the student's ORF score by subtracting the number of errors from the total number of words read. The score is expressed as words correct per minute (WCPM). Afterward, the student is given one minute to retell the passage. The teacher should follow this procedure with three passages per student. You can use an assessment tool like Acadience or Dibels 8 to get beginning, middle, and end of the year passages for each grade level, beginning in the middle of first grade.

Almost 40 years of research have shown that the WCPM scores predict reading comprehension better than any other tool we have; the correlation is in the range of 0.7–0.9.[17] And a full ORF assessment takes under seven minutes per student!

Just as a thermometer lets you know there's a fever but doesn't tell you the reason for it, a low WCPM score indicates a problem but not its cause. If a student scores more than 10 WCPM below the 50th percentile, they are at risk for reading difficulty. Diagnostic assessments can help pin down the issue. (For more about assessment, see Chapter 10.)

Here's what's key: If students' accuracy rate is poor, they need more work on decoding. If their accuracy rate is good, but their WCPM is below benchmark, they need fluency-building instruction. To say this another way, *do not* use a typical fluency intervention if a student struggles to sound out words. Fluency instruction will not repair deficits in foundational skills. All that said, we don't know exactly how fluent decoding skills must be before students will benefit from fluency instruction.[18]

FLUENCY INTERVENTIONS

The following fluency interventions are ideal for one-on-one tutoring sessions.

Timed Repeated Reading

S. Jay Samuels published his Repeated Reading technique in 1979.[19] Decades of research confirm that repeated reading leads to improvements in reading rate, accuracy, and comprehension.[20]

Use the following intervention 3–5 times a week, for 10–15 minutes a session, with students who are accurate but slow readers. Do not use it with students who are inaccurate readers; they need more decoding instruction. Do not use it with students who are already reading fluently; it will bore them.

Timed Repeated Reading Procedure

1. Choose a short passage (50–200 words) that is at or slightly above the student's instructional level.[21]
2. Have the student read the passage aloud for one minute while you time the reading and record errors on a graph. Errors include words that the student does not read within three seconds.
3. Compute a WCPM score, review the errors with the student, and ask at least one comprehension question so that the focus isn't only on rate. Together, set a WCPM goal for the next reading.
4. The student reads the same text again while you time the reading and record errors. Again, give feedback and ask a comprehension question.
5. Repeat this procedure until the student reads with 95 percent accuracy in 75 percent of the time it took for the first reading. Usually this takes 3–4 readings.[22]

Paired Reading

With paired reading, the student and adult sit side-by-side holding a shared text. They read the text together, with the adult adjusting their pace so the student can keep up. The student should track the text with a finger or ruler while reading. If the student feels confident enough to read solo, they nudge the tutor as a signal. The adult backs off, reading softly or not at all until the student needs assistance. This procedure continues for 10–15 minutes. The adult need not be a teacher; one researcher found that paired reading done regularly with parents led to improvements in fluency and comprehension.[23]

Phrase-Cued Text

Phrase-cued texts are useful for students who lack prosody in their reading. Because prosody and comprehension are related, they may also be useful for students who struggle to remember or understand what they read.

In a phrase-cued text (see Figure 6.5), phrase boundaries are marked with lines or slash marks, cueing the reader to pause at each mark. A 1983 study found that comprehension improved when children in grades 1 through 3 read phrase-cued text.[24] Rasinski found evidence that phrase-cued reading positively affects reading proficiency.[25]

Helping Sell Hot Dogs

Ross|is selling hot dogs|at a hot dog stand.|It is a big day,|so six men|are helping Ross.|But Ross sees|that the men are chatting,|not helping.|Plus,|the men|keep grabbing hot dogs.|They are snacking on the hot dogs|and are not|paying for them.|

Ross|is thinking|of firing the men.|They are not good help.|He tells them,|"You are robbing me.|You must help|and not chat.|You must pay|for the hot dogs you take."|

The men|are hoping to keep the job.|"We are sorry.|Here|is what we must pay you.|Also,|we will stop chatting|and begin helping."|

The men|begin helping so well|that people|begin tipping them.|More and more people|are coming|to the hot dog stand.|Ross is glad|to have such good help!

Figure 6.5 Phrase-cued text.

Phrase–Cued Text Procedure

1. Choose a text in which the reader is at least 95 percent accurate.
2. Mark the text by putting a slash after each phrase. (There's nothing scientific about this; mark the text in a way that makes sense to you.)
3. Introduce the activity by explaining why phrasing is important. Model proper and improper phrasing. Then draw attention to the phrase marks in the passage and read it aloud as a model.
4. Have the student read the text with proper phrasing, rereading as needed. Give feedback after each reading.
5. Finally, have the student read the text again, this time without the phrase marks.

Phrase-cued reading can also be done with the whole class; pass out the text to each student and model as they follow along. Then have students read the text together as a class, or put them in pairs as they take turns reading the cued text.

WHOLE-CLASS FLUENCY INSTRUCTION

You can use the following activities to build fluency in a whole-class setting.

Echo Reading

Echo reading is when the teacher reads a portion of the text aloud and the students follow by reading the text in unison.

Echo reading makes the most sense when you are introducing more complex texts. The scaffolding will make these texts more accessible. Just make sure that each section you read aloud is long enough that students cannot memorize it; they are to *read* the text, not simply parrot you.

Echo Reading Procedure

1. Choose a text that will challenge your students. Make a copy for everyone.
2. Check that all students are paying attention. Then read a short portion of the text.
3. Circulate the room while students chorally read the portion of text that you just read aloud. Their goal should be to match your expression and pacing.
4. Gradually increase the amount of text you read before having students echo. A good long-term goal is for your students to echo read several paragraphs.[26]

Choral Reading

With **choral reading**, the teacher first reads the passage aloud. Next, the students join in as the teacher fades their voice. Students should read as quickly as possible as a group without speed reading.

Choral reading provides less support than echo reading; it's especially useful as a follow-up to echo reading of challenging texts. Even if students are reading the text accurately, choral reading can help improve pacing and expression.[27]

Partner Reading

Partner reading is an excellent way to get your students reading *more*, and it's also a way to have stronger readers support weaker ones since you can't be everywhere at once.

Tips for success with partner reading:

◆ Pair more proficient readers with less proficient ones. An easy way to do this is to privately order your students from most to least proficient reader. Then tear your list in half and line up the halves. In a class of 24 students, pair student 1 with student 13, student 2 with student 14, and so on.

- Make sure that the text is not higher than the instructional level of the lower reader. To test this, have the weaker reader read part of the text. If they miss more than 1 out of 10 words, the text is too hard.
- Have the stronger reader begin by reading for several minutes or by reading a portion of the text (a sentence, paragraph, or page). This provides a strong model for the weaker reader. When listening, students should always follow along with a finger or ruler.
- When the timer beeps or the first reader has read the agreed-upon portion, have the weaker reader read the same text that the first student read.
- Teach your students a procedure for helping a partner who misreads a word.
  - Point to the word. "You misread that word. What is it?"
  - If the student reads it correctly, say, "Good. Now read the whole sentence again."
  - If the student is incorrect, or says nothing after four seconds, say the correct word. "The word is *bridge*. Now read the sentence again."
- Teach your students how to get help if neither of them can read a word. They might write it on a mini dry erase board. As you circulate the room, you can stop and help.
- Build in a comprehension procedure such as paragraph shrinking. After a student finishes a paragraph, their partner should give the following prompts.[28]
  - Name the most important who or what.
  - Tell the most important thing about the who or what.
  - Say the main idea in 10 words or fewer. (Students can count on their fingers as they summarize the paragraph. They may need to restart a few times!)

Reader's Theater

Reader's Theater is when students practice reading from a script and perform it for an audience at the end of the week. While we lack a lot of research on the effectiveness of Reader's Theater in the primary grades, it gives struggling readers a model of fluent reading, offers many opportunities for rereading, and includes feedback from the peers and teacher—all of which have research support.[29] Perhaps best of all for busy teachers— Reader's Theater is acting with the voice, so no costumes or props are necessary!

Chase Young recommends this weekly procedure for Reader's Theater, spending no more than 5–10 minutes per day, Monday through Thursday, with a longer time slot reserved for Fluency Friday.[30]

Monday: Read each of the possible scripts aloud to the class. Students take a copy of the script they'd like to participate in. (Make sure that you provide no more scripts than the number of parts in a particular play; otherwise, too many children may choose the same script.) They take the script home and consider their first, second, and third choices for the role they'd like to play.

Tuesday: Students bring back their scripts (be prepared to replace scripts left at home) and choose their parts. (Also be prepared for crying when students don't get their first choice!) Then students form groups and take turns reading their parts. Tuesday's focus is decoding and accuracy. If students come to a difficult word, they highlight it. As you circulate the room, stop to help students decode the highlighted words. All groups should read and reread their scripts until the timer beeps. Students take their scripts home to practice.

Wednesday: Students practice their scripts in groups again. Circulate as you identify any problems with meaning, word recognition, and expression. Students bring their scripts home to practice.

Thursday: Students practice performing the script in small groups; circulate as you listen for any difficulties.

Fluency Friday: The students perform the script for school staff, parents, or other visitors. They might even travel to a different classroom and perform for their peers.

A caveat: Remember that fluency improves when students do a *lot* of reading. A script in which a struggling reader has only a few short lines is not likely to improve fluency. Instead of assigning parts, you might consider having students sit side by side in a particular order; each student can read the next line rather than a particular part.

Reader's Theater is so much fun that it can take over the literacy block. Let it be a side dish, not the main entrée.

The Fluency Development Lesson (FDL)
The fluency development lesson (FDL) is an efficient way to build fluency practice into a classroom routine and has been shown to increase reading rate.[31]

The FDL Procedure

1. Choose a 50–200-word poem or selection that will challenge your students.
2. Read the text aloud 2–3 times, while students follow along in their own copies.
3. Discuss the meaning of the text and tricky vocabulary words.
4. Students should read the text chorally.

5. Divide your students into pairs. One student should read the text 2–3 times, with feedback from a partner. Then the partners should switch roles so the other student can do repeated reading with feedback.

6. If desired, students may perform the text for their peers.

7. If time allows, choose words from the text for word study.

8. Students should take the text home and read it to an adult.

9. The following day, students can read the text to a peer before the teacher begins again with a new selection.

Wide Fluency-Oriented Reading Instruction (FORI)

Wide fluency-oriented reading instruction (FORI) combines repeated oral reading with assisted and independent silent reading. This technique is particularly useful for scaffolding grade-level text so all students can be successful with it.

Wide FORI Procedure

Choose three grade level texts of considerable length; students will need to read for 20–30 minutes daily.

- **Monday:** Read the first text aloud to the class and lead a discussion about vocabulary and meaning. At home, students read any text of their choice for 20–30 minutes.
- **Tuesday:** Echo read the first selection with your students. Again, lead a short discussion of the text. Students read the text at home to a family member.
- **Wednesday:** Students complete extension activities related to the text. These may include writing a summary or completing a graphic organizer. All students should read 20–30 minutes at home, whether that's the text read in class or one of their choice.
- **Thursday:** Together, echo read the second selection. Lead a discussion after the reading. If time allows, students partner-read the text. At home, students reread the day's text or read one of their choice for 20–30 minutes.
- **Friday:** Repeat Thursday's procedure with a third text.[32]

What About Sustained Silent Reading?

The National Reading Panel published a review of studies that examined the role of sustained silent reading (SSR). To many teachers' shock and disappointment, the panel did not find evidence supporting sustained silent reading as a way to increase reading achievement.[33] While it's true that students who read more are stronger readers, we don't know whether they read more because it's easy for them or because reading practice actually leads to reading achievement. There is simply not evidence to recommend sustained silent reading as an instructional practice.

The question is not whether students should practice reading connected text. All students need to practice decoding so they can orthographically map more words, leading to automaticity and paving the way for fluency. But early and struggling readers need support as they read—whether at the small group table, with a peer, or as they read along with a taped recording.

As they get into second and third grade, SSR is useful for skilled readers. The more reading that skilled readers do, the more vocabulary they learn and the more background knowledge they gain. This will make the next text they read easier to understand, while they continue to learn more vocabulary and background knowledge. But for students who struggle, SSR is essentially a waste of time. They may choose books that are too difficult, fake their reading to save face among their peers, or simply repeat errors because they are not receiving immediate feedback.

If you do implement a short period of SSR in your classroom, do not sit at your desk reading or grading papers. Instead, meet with a small group of children who need extra help with decoding or fluency. For the children who are reading independently, monitor their book choices. Build in accountability by asking questions about their books and occasionally requiring a written response.

 Key Things to Remember

- ◆ Fluency's components are accuracy, rate, and prosody.
- ◆ Students must become automatic at word recognition so they are able to focus on comprehension.
- ◆ Children need to be reasonably accurate at word recognition before receiving fluency instruction at the text level.

◆ Teachers can learn which students are at risk for reading difficulties by administering the ORF assessment. Students who are accurate but slow readers need fluency intervention.
◆ A variety of fluency-building procedures can be used with the whole class.

Free Resources
◆ Printable alphabet arcs
◆ Missing letter cards
◆ Fluency grids
◆ Fluency poems

www.themeasuredmom.com/bookresources/

Learn More
◆ Read *Reading Fluency* by Jan Hasbrouck and Deb Glaser.
◆ Watch PaTTAN's workshop with Lindsay Kemeny to learn more about a class-wide reading intervention for building fluency: www.youtube.com/watch?v=-Q3iO_NUCPI&t=1870s.
◆ Search "fluency Jan Hasbrouck" on YouTube and watch one or more of Dr. Hasbrouck's workshops.

Notes
1. Hasbrouck, J., & Glaser, D. (2019). *Reading fluency*. Benchmark Education Company, 10.
2. Rasinski, T. V., Reutzel, D. R., Chard, D., & Linan-Thompson, S. (2011). Reading fluency. In M. L. Kamil, M. L., Pearson, P.D., Moje, E. B., and Afflerbach, P. P. (Eds.), *Handbook of reading research* (Vol. IV), (286–319). Routledge.
3. Foorman, B. R., Francis, D. J., Shaywitz, S. E., Shaywitz, B. A., & Fletcher, J. M. (1997). The case for early reading intervention. In Blackman, B. (Ed.), *Foundations of reading acquisition and dyslexia: Implications for early intervention* (243–264). Paul H. Brookes.

4. Hasbrouck, J. [The Reading League Wisconsin]. (2023, April 4). *Fluency; Key to comprehension* [Video]. YouTube. https://www.youtube.com/watch?v=zCnQ9VTswKo.

5. Hasbrouck, J., & Glaser, D. (2019).

6. Hudson, R. F., Lane, H. B., & Pullen, P. C. (2005). Reading fluency assessment and instruction: What, why, and how? *The Reading Teacher, 58*(8), 702–714.

7. LaBerge, D., & Samuels, S. J. (1974). Toward a theory of automatic information processing in reading. *Cognitive Psychology, 6*(2), 293–323.

8. Aaron, P. G., Joshi, R. M., & Quatroche, D. (2008). *Becoming a professional reading teacher*. Paul H. Brookes Co.

9. Pikulski, J. J., & Chard, D. J. (2005). Fluency: Bridge between decoding and reading comprehension. *The Reading Teacher, 58*(6), 510–519.

10. Hasbrouck, J. [The Reading League Wisconsin]. (2023, April 4).

11. Clarke, Alison. (N.D.) *The sweaty sounding-out stage builds reading muscle*. Spelfabet. https://www.spelfabet.com.au/2021/09/the-sweaty-sounding-out-stage-builds-reading-muscle/.

12. Adams, M. J. (1990). *Beginning to read*. MIT Press.

13. Hudson, R. F., Pullen, P. C., Lane, H. B., & Torgesen, J. K. (2008). The complex nature of reading fluency: A multidimensional view. *Reading & Writing Quarterly, 25*(1), 4–32.

14. Ehri, L. C., & McCormick, S. (1998). Phases of word learning: Implications for instruction with delayed and disabled readers. *Reading & Writing Quarterly: Overcoming Learning Difficulties, 14*(2), 135–163.

15. O'Connor, R. E. (2014). *Teaching word recognition*. The Guilford Press.

16. Geiger, A. (Host). (2022, October 24). What to do after administering the ORF: A conversation with Dr. Jan Hasbrouck (No. 98) [Audio Podcast Episode]. In *Triple R Teaching*. Anna Geiger. https://www.themeasuredmom.com/what-to-do-after-administering-the-orf-a-conversation-with-dr-jan-hasbrouck/.

17. Ibid.

18. Hudson, R. F., Pullen, P. C., Lane, H. B., & Torgesen, J. K. (2008).

19. Samuels, S. J. (1979). The method of repeated readings. *The Reading Teacher, 32*(4), 403–408.

20. Stevens, E. A., Walker, M. A., & Vaughn, S. (2017). The effects of reading fluency interventions on the reading fluency and reading comprehension performance of elementary students with learning disabilities: A synthesis of the research from 2001 to 2014. *Journal of Learning Disabilities, 50*(5), 576–590.

21. Hasbrouck, J., & Glaser, D. (2019).

22. O'Connor, R. E. (2014).

23. Topping, K. (1987). Paired reading: A powerful technique for parent use. *The Reading Teacher, 40*(7), 608–614.

24. O'Shea, L. J., & Sindelar, P. T. (1983). The effects of segmenting written discourse on the reading comprehension of low- and high-performance readers. *Reading & Writing Quarterly, 18,* 458–465.

25. Rasinski, T. V. (1990). *The effects of cued phrase boundaries on reading performance: A review.* Bloomington, IN: ERIC Clearinghouse on Reading and Communication Skills. (ED 313–689)

26. Kuhn, M. R., & Levy, L. (2015). *Developing fluent readers.* The Guilford Press.

27. Ibid.

28. Kemeny, L. [PaTTAN]. (2022, August 26). *A Classwide Reading Intervention that Works* [Video]. YouTube. https://www.youtube.com/watch?v=-Q3iO_NUCPI.

29. Hudson, R. (2011). Fluency problems: When, why, and how to intervene. In O'Connor, R. E. & Vadasy, P. F. (Eds). *Handbook of reading interventions* (169–197). The Guilford Press.

30. Geiger, A. (Host). (2022, November 14). How to implement Reader's Theater: With Chase Young (No. 101) [Audio Podcast]. In *Triple R Teaching.* Anna Geiger. https://www.themeasuredmom.com/implement-readers-theater/.

31. Rasinski, T. V., Padak. N., Linek, W., & Sturtevant, E. (1994) Effects of fluency development on urban second-grade readers. *The Journal of Educational Research. 87* (3), 158–165.

32. Kuhn, M. R., & Levy, L. (2015).

33. National Reading Panel (U.S.) & National Institute of Child Health and Human Development (U.S.). (2000). *Report of the National Reading Panel: Teaching children to read: An evidence-based assessment of the scientific research literature on reading and its implications for reading instruction.* U.S. Dept. of Health and Human Services, Public Health Service, National Institutes of Health, National Institute of Child Health and Human Development.

CHAPTER 7

Vocabulary

Vocabulary is the knowledge of words and their meanings. Meaningful vocabulary instruction involves discussions of words, using words in a variety of contexts, and teaching students to learn words on their own.

The task is a big one: Our goal is to help all students develop a vocabulary of about 50,000 words over their school years.[1] This number is far more than we can possibly teach; it's tempting to give up altogether! But we can't leave vocabulary learning to chance.

Stahl and Nagy wrote that "it may overstate the case to say that vocabulary knowledge is central to children's and adult's success in school and in life, but not by much."[2]

What the Research Says

- **Vocabulary knowledge is closely related to reading comprehension throughout the grades.** Cunningham and Stanovich found that first graders' vocabulary knowledge predicted reading comprehension in their junior year of high school![3]
- **Children learn many words without formal instruction,** far more words than they could ever learn in school.[4]

- **It is important to teach students to use context to discern word meanings.**[5] However, having students infer meaning through context, even when that context is designed to be helpful, is less effective than directly teaching the definitions of words.[6]

- **Teaching word meanings through dictionary definitions alone is not adequate.**[7] Students do better when teachers revise the definitions to be student-friendly.[8]

- **Teaching word meanings through shared read-alouds can increase knowledge of specific vocabulary.** Merely drawing attention to the words isn't enough. Coyne et al. found high effect sizes when teachers provided simple definitions, led discussions about the words, and scheduled review and practice.[9]

- **Robust vocabulary instruction,** which includes the direct teaching of words and using them in a variety of ways over an extended period of time, **is effective for learning word meanings and for affecting reading comprehension.**[10]

- **It is important to review vocabulary words over days and weeks.**[11]

- There is some evidence that **teaching morphemes (such as prefixes, suffixes, and roots) can help students infer the meanings of words.**[12]

- **Teaching vocabulary greatly increases the comprehension of texts that contain that vocabulary.**[13]

- **Specific vocabulary instruction has smaller effects on improving general comprehension.**[14] Try not to be discouraged by this; even if general measures of comprehension show little improvement, vocabulary instruction will still improve writing and speaking skills.

- **One of the best ways to promote vocabulary growth is to promote wide, regular reading after students are automatic at word-reading skills.**[15] Wide reading is the independent reading of a variety of fiction and nonfiction text genres.

How to Decide Which Words to Teach: The Three Word Tiers

Choosing words for vocabulary instruction can feel like a monumental task when we think about the number of words to choose from. During their school career, children will encounter about 88,000 word families[16] (a word family could include *wonder, wonderful, wondrous,* etc.). Even if we directly teach our students about 10 words a week over their school career, we'll only teach about 4,500 total words.

The good news is that our students don't need us to teach them *all* the words. Our job is to teach words with a lot of "mileage"[17]—words they are likely to encounter in text but are unlikely to learn on their own.

My favorite way to choose vocabulary words for instruction is to use Beck and McKeown's concept of word tiers.[18] This system will help you identify the most useful words to teach.

> *Our job is to teach words with a lot of "mileage"—words students are likely to encounter in text but are unlikely to learn on their own.*

- ◆ Tier One words are basic words that most children know when they come to school. These are words like *baby, clock, chair,* and *happy.*
- ◆ Tier Two words are common in written language but not as common in conversation. Tier Two words include words like *emerge, discover*, and *avoid.*
- ◆ Tier Three words are rare because they apply to specific domains. Students may encounter these words in social studies, science, or math. They include words like *peninsula* and *mammal.* Tier Three also includes words that are so rare even an avid reader may never encounter them.

The sweet spot for direct vocabulary instruction is Tier Two. The best Tier Two words are those that represent a concept that students already understand. For example, students understand what it means to keep away from something, but they may not know the word *avoid.* It's also best to choose Tier Two words that can be applied in many different contexts. When riding a bike, you *avoid* potholes in the road. If your friends have said mean things to you, you might *avoid* them at recess.

When teaching Tier Two words, introduce your students to other words in the same family (*avoided, avoidance*, and *unavoidable*).

If you're hoping for a master list of Tier Two words, I'm sorry to say that there isn't one. Nor is there research about which words students should know at each grade level. You need to use your best judgment when choosing Tier Two words for instruction, but the following questions can help.

Questions to ask when choosing Tier Two vocabulary words:

- ◆ Is this a word that many of my students probably don't know?
- ◆ Is this a word that they are unlikely to learn on their own?
- ◆ Is this a word that students are likely to encounter in text (whether they read it or it's read to them)?
- ◆ Is this a word for which my students understand the general concept?
- ◆ Is this a word that can be applied in many different contexts?
- ◆ Can I teach other words in the same family?

Teaching Individual Tier Two Words

Select vocabulary words from the texts you're reading to or with your students. If you can't find good Tier Two words within the text, choose words that are related to the story or concept.

If I'm reading aloud the book Cynthia DeFelice's *One Potato, Two Potato* to kindergartners, I might choose the following words from the text for direct instruction: *discuss, dismay, trembling,* and *scold.* Since I'd like a total of five words for this book, I'll also teach *astonished,* even though it doesn't appear in the story. (Mr. and Mrs. O'Grady are *astonished* when they discover that their pot is magic.)

Beck et al. recommend teaching three to five words in a single lesson and introducing the rest later in the day or in the next day's lesson. This yields a total of about 10 words per week.[19]

The following procedure is based on Beck, McKeown, and Kucan's approach—one they've dubbed "robust vocabulary instruction."[20]

STEP 1: READ AND PRONOUNCE THE WORD

Before or after reading the book aloud, teach each of the vocabulary words. Begin by posting the first word so all students can see it. "This word is *discuss.* Let's say the word together: discuss. What's the word?"

STEP 2: PRESENT THE WORD IN CONTEXT

Next, read the sentence in which the word appears.

1. "Mr. O'Grady longed for a friend, someone with whom he could *discuss* potato weevils and root rot."
2. "Mr. O'Grady was digging in the garden. To his *dismay,* he saw that he had come to the very last potato in the very last row of his garden."
3. "Mrs. O'Grady held up the two potatoes. 'Husband,' she *scolded,* 'you oughtn't joke about such things!'"
4. Mr. and Mrs. O'Grady were *astonished* when they saw that every single item they put in the pot came out as two.
5. "Mrs. O'Grady went over to the mattress and, with *trembling* fingers, took out the gold coin. 'Husband,' she said, 'do you suppose the pot's magic will work on this?'"

STEP 3: PROVIDE A KID-FRIENDLY DEFINITION

I love using *Collins COBUILD Learner's Dictionary*, which provides simple definitions students actually understand.

1. If you *discuss* something, you talk about it with someone.

2. If you feel *dismay,* you have a strong feeling of fear, worry, or sadness.

3. If you *scold* someone, you speak angrily because they've done something wrong.

4. If you are *astonished,* you are shocked or amazed that something happened.

5. If something is *trembling,* it's slightly shaking.

Resist the urge to ask, "Who can tell me what *discuss* means?" What typically happens is that students guess the meaning. "Incorrect guesses pile up as the teacher calls on more students, trying to ferret out knowledge."[21] This wastes time and also runs the risk of students remembering an incorrect definition rather than the true one!

STEP 4: PROVIDE ADDITIONAL CONTEXT FOR THE WORD

When teaching a specific word, it's important to also use it in a context that's different from the one in the story.

1. If you are misbehaving, your mom might sit down with you to *discuss* the problem.

2. I wanted to get tickets to Disney World. To my *dismay,* they were sold out!

3. I *scold* my puppy when he barks too loudly.

4. If my son grew five inches in one summer, I would be *astonished.*

5. If my teeth are chattering from the cold, I might also be *trembling.*

STEP 5: PROVIDE MORE OPPORTUNITIES FOR STUDENTS TO PROCESS THE WORD'S MEANING

Your students need many encounters with each new word in order to make it their own. Many of the following activities are based on those shared by Beck, McKeown, and Kucan in their books *Robust Vocabulary Instruction* and *Bringing Words to Life.* Choose some of these activities to use over the course of a week.

Example/Nonexample

If I say something that would *astonish* you, say "astonish!" If not, say nothing.

◆ An elephant walks into our classroom.

◆ I bring each of you a giant box of donuts.

◆ When you turn on the faucet, water comes out.

Picture Example/Nonexample

If the picture shows a reason you might *scold* your pet dog, say "scold!" If not, say nothing.

- A dog is playing fetch with a little girl.
- A dog is chewing a shoe.
- A dog has chewed up a couch cushion.

Word Associations

- Which word goes with *sadness?* (dismay)
- Which word goes with *surprise?* (astonished)
- Which word goes with *shaking?* (trembling)

More Word Associations

Work with your partner to decide which of our five words goes with the sentence.

- Our family went to our favorite ice cream shop to celebrate, but it was closed! (dismay)
- The ground shook after the earthquake. (trembling)
- We had a snowstorm in the summer! (astonished)

Fill in the Blank

- I felt _____ when I realized that I left my math worksheet at home. (dismay)
- I was afraid my teacher would _____ me because I forgot my homework. (scold)
- I'm _____ because my teacher smiled and told me that everyone makes mistakes! (astonished)

Generate Context

- With your small group, list three things that would *astonish* you.
- Give two reasons why someone's hands might be *trembling*.
- What are three common reasons that a person might *scold* their pet dog?

Finish the Sentence

Work with your partner to finish each sentence. After a couple of minutes, I'll call on one of you to say your whole sentence.

- I felt *dismay* when . . .
- My mom *scolded* me because . . .
- I was *trembling* because . . .

Word Charades

I'm going to act out each of this week's words. When you know the word, whisper it to your partner. (Eventually students can do the acting!)

◆ Sit at a table and pretend to talk animatedly, using your hands as you do so. Take a moment to pretend you're listening to the other person speak. (discuss)
◆ Pretend to be scolding a puppy as you shake your finger. (scold)
◆ Drop your jaw and stare at something with your eyes open wide. (astonished)

STEP 6: REVIEW THE WORDS OVER TIME

Don't let your students forget about the words after the initial week! Write each word on an index card with a kid-friendly definition. File the words in alphabetical order in an index card box. Each day, when you have a couple of minutes to fill, pull out a word or two to review. Choose from the following activities.

◆ Have students use the word in a sentence.
◆ Begin a sentence using the word, and have students finish it.
◆ Help students list as many words as they can that belong in the word's family.
◆ Create a sentence using the word either correctly or incorrectly. Students should give a thumbs up or down and explain their answer to a partner.
◆ State the word's definition. Can students name the word?

Teaching Tier Three Words

Your main focus should be Tier Two words, but you'll want to teach Tier Three words as well. I suggest developing text sets for each social studies or science topic you teach your students. A text set is a set of books on the same topic that you read aloud to your students. Each set should contain a mix of fiction and nonfiction books appropriate for your grade level. Page through the books and choose a set of Tier Three words to teach over the course of the unit. Since the books are on the same topic, students are likely to hear each word multiple times, making the words more likely to stick.

The following guidelines are based on Neuman and Wright's recommendations in their book, *All About Words*.[22]

◆ Choose books that include challenging vocabulary related to important concepts.
◆ Choose books from a variety of genres.
◆ Make sure that the information about your topic is accurate and likely to expand children's knowledge.
◆ Choose books that have some overlap in vocabulary and concepts.
◆ Most of the time, choose books that are a grade level or two above your students' current grade level.

A SAMPLE TEXT SET

If you are reading about insects to kindergartners, for example, you might select this text set:

- *Hey, Little Ant* by Phillip and Hannah Hoose (fiction)
- *From Caterpillar to Butterfly* by Deborah Heiligman (nonfiction)
- *Bob and Otto* by Robert Bruel (fiction)
- *Tiny Workers: Ants in Your Backyard* by Nancy Loewen (nonfiction)
- *It's a Good Thing There Are Insects* by Allan Fowler (nonfiction)

Possible Tier Three words for this text set include insect, colony, larva, pupa, cocoon, chrysalis, metamorphosis, life cycle, molt, and antennae.

ACTIVITIES FOR TIER THREE WORDS

Most of the activities for Tier Two words will also work with Tier Three words. Here are a few more to try.

Semantic Mapping

Semantic mapping[23] is an excellent way to introduce a nonfiction unit because it activates background knowledge and promotes rich discussion.

1. At the beginning of the unit, guide your students as they brainstorm a list of words related to the topic.
2. Come up with several categories that the words could fit under, and draw a semantic map on the board. Together, assign each of the listed words to an appropriate category. (See Figure 7.1.)
3. Read a related text to or with your students.
4. Discuss what students learned from the book. Modify the map to reflect what was learned.

Categorizing

Categorizing[24] is an activity that's best for the middle or end of a unit. Provide a list of words related to the topic. Provide categories or ask students to generate them. Sort the words together. For example, you might present your students with these words:

abdomen	butterfly	larva	sting
antennae	camouflage	mimicry	wasp
bee	egg	pupa	wings

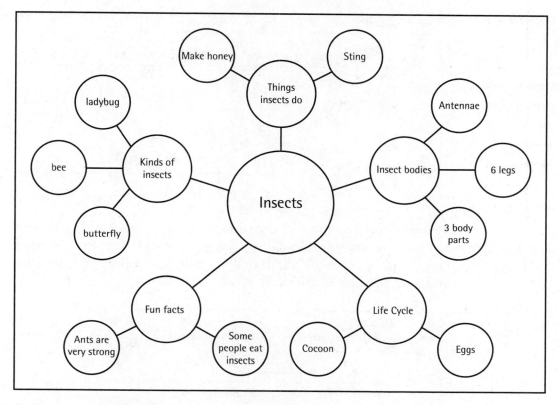

Figure 7.1 A semantic map.

The final result could look like this:

Kinds of Insects	Body Parts	Life Cycle	Defenses
bee	abdomen	egg	camouflage
butterfly	antennae	larva	mimicry
wasp	wings	pupa	sting

Semantic Feature Analysis

Semantic feature analysis[25] uses a grid to help children see how sets of things are related to each other. It's a little more complicated, but this powerful activity can be used in the primary grades with teacher support. On the left side of the grid, write names of members of the group. Across the top, write words or phrases that indicate how the group members could be similar or different. Work as a class or in small groups to use + or − to indicate whether each member has a particular feature. A +/− can be used if some members of the group have the feature, while others do not. See Table 7.1.

Table 7.1 A Semantic Feature Analysis

	Can fly	Has 6 legs	Lays eggs	Has spots	Can camouflage	Can sting	Uses mimicry
Butterfly	+	+	+	+	+	−	+
Ladybug	+/−	+	+	+	−	−	−
Ant	+/−	+	+	−	+	+/−	−
Honeybee	+	+	+	−	+	+	−
Stick bug	+	+	+	−	+	−	+

The Frayer Model

You can create a Frayer Model[26] with your class or have students in second grade and above complete the model in small groups. Give students the vocabulary word to write in the center of the graphic organizer. Then have them write the definition, characteristics, examples, and nonexamples (Figure 7.2).

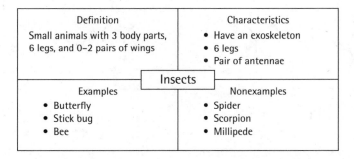

Figure 7.2 A Frayer Model.

Teaching Word–Learning Strategies

Time limits the number of words we can teach in depth, so we also need to teach strategies that will help students figure out word meanings on their own.

USING CONTEXT CLUES

Context clues are the words, phrases, and sentences surrounding a word. Baumann et al. identified five types of context clues that are useful for students to know. While their work was with middle school students,[27] you can informally teach the use of context clues in kindergarten through second grade and begin more formal instruction in third grade.[28] See Table 7.2.

Table 7.2 Types of Context Clues

Context Clue Type	Example
Definition: The definition is provided right in the sentence.	*Dolphins* are marine mammals that breathe with lungs and give birth to live babies.
Synonym: The author uses another word that means the same thing.	Some dolphin *species,* or types, can live over 60 years.
Antonym: The author uses another word that is about the opposite of the unfamiliar word.	The most *widespread* species are the common dolphin and the bottlenose dolphin. One of the rarest species is called the hourglass dolphin.
Example: The author provides one or more examples.	Dolphins live in *aquatic* environments, such as oceans, bays, gulfs, and estuaries.
General: The author gives clues to the word's meaning through other words or sentences.	A dolphin breathes through the *blowhole* on the top of its head.

It's important that your students know that context clues aren't always helpful. After teaching context clue types, share sentences that include an unfamiliar word or nonsense word. Make sure that some sentences provide a clue as to the word's meaning while others do not. Help your students differentiate between the two.

USING WORD PARTS

We need to teach word parts because students can often discern the meanings of words from the meaning of their parts.[29] Word parts are also called **morphemes**.

Morphemes are the smallest units of meaning in words. Every word has at least one morpheme. **Free morphemes** can exist as words all on their own. They are also called *root words.* **Bound morphemes** cannot stand alone. When they take the form of a Latin or Greek root, they may also be called *roots.* The word *cats* has two morphemes: cat + s. It has both a free morpheme (cat) and a bound morpheme (s). The word *distraction* consists of three bound morphemes: dis + tract + ion.

Morpheme may feel like a strange and unfamiliar word, but students learn morphemes as they learn to speak. I remember when my youngest bounced into the room to tell me, "I hunged my wet swimsuit on the rack." I gently corrected him, "You *hung* it on the rack?" "Yes!" he said joyfully. "It's hunging!" While he didn't yet know the irregular form of the verb, he knew how to use the morphemes *-ed* and *-ing*.

Morphology is the study of morphemes. When students have **morphological awareness**, they are aware of both spoken and written morphemes. They understand what prefixes and suffixes look like and how to attach them to base elements.[30]

Is It Really Necessary to Teach Morphology?

Yes! Research has shown morphological awareness to positively impact word reading,[31] reading comprehension,[32] and spelling.[33]

A basic understanding of morphology is important for even our youngest learners because English is a **morphophonemic** language. It's a code that represents *both* sound and meaning. *Jumped* is not spelled *jumpt* because the "ed" is needed to communicate that the action happened in the past. The word *pleasant* is not spelled *plezzant* because it's related to the word *please*. The word *sign* has a silent g because it's related to the words *signal* and *signature*, in which the g is pronounced. *Musician* is spelled as it is because it's related to the word *music*. In the word *pterodactyl*, "pt" is not a spelling for /t/. Rather, the word includes the Greek root *ptero*, for "wing" or "winglike."

How to Begin

Start by examining basic compound words that your students can read. Help them see that the two parts can help us define the word. A *cupcake* is a cake in the shape of a cup. A *fishbowl* is a bowl for a fish.

Continue with the most basic morphemes: plurals, past tense, and present tense (*-s, -es, -ed* and *-ing*). When doing dictation with these inflectional endings, have students write each one in its own box to emphasize that these are units of meaning.

$$\underline{m} \quad \underline{i} \quad \underline{ss} \quad \boxed{ed}$$

$$\underline{m} \quad \underline{i} \quad \underline{ss} \quad \boxed{ing}$$

Continue with the most common prefixes and suffixes (see Chapter 5). Teach students how to break words apart into their morphemes in order to understand their meaning. For example, when teaching the prefix *pre-*, students might complete the following chart.

Word	Morphemes	Meaning
preheat	pre + heat	to heat before
preview		
presell		
presoak		

Have students keep a little notebook to record the morphemes that they learn. On each page they should write a morpheme, its meaning (or purpose), and words that include the morpheme.

Greek and Latin Roots

Teaching the general meaning of common Greek and Latin roots can help students discern the meaning of unfamiliar words. It also helps clarify spelling, because the root's spelling stays the same even when pronunciation changes. For example, the words *nature, native, natural,* and *nativity* all contain the Latin root *nate* which means *born* or *birth*. Each word retains the *nat* spelling, even though the pronunciation of that element changes.

A Final Word About Morphology

The more I learn about morphology, the more I appreciate its importance, even in the primary grades. In her eye-opening book, *Beneath the Surface of Words*, Sue Scibetta Hegland writes that "morphology is not an advanced topic; it's the foundation of the entire spelling system."[34] I recommend reading Hegland's book and exploring the resources in the appendix. You will look at words in an entirely new way!

USING THE DICTIONARY

Your students are ready to learn to use a dictionary if they understand alphabetical order and have the word recognition skills to read a dictionary definition. This may not be until second or third grade.

Don't ask your students to look up vocabulary words and copy their definitions. Instead, teach them to use dictionaries the way adults do—to find the meaning of an unfamiliar word they encounter in their reading.

PUTTING THE WORD-LEARNING STRATEGIES TOGETHER

Context clues, morphology, and the dictionary are best used in tandem. Here's a useful procedure for students to use when they encounter an unfamiliar word in their reading. Model this procedure and practice it many times together before expecting students to use it on their own.

1. Reread the sentence. Does the context help you figure out the meaning of the word?
2. Do the parts of the word help you with its meaning?
3. If you're still stuck, check a dictionary. Read all the definitions.
4. Which definition makes the most sense in the sentence you read?
5. If you're still unsure, ask someone for help.

Key Things to Remember

- Vocabulary is closely related to reading comprehension.
- Focus primarily on Tier Two words as you give robust vocabulary instruction.
- Give students opportunities to hear their words in different contexts.
- Review vocabulary words over time.
- Teach word learning strategies like context clues, morphology, and dictionary skills.

Free resources

- Graphic organizers
- Morphology resources

www.themeasuredmom.com/bookresources/

Learn More

- Read *Beneath the Surface of Words* by Sue Scibetta Hegland.
- Read *Bringing Words to Life* by Isabel Beck, Linda Kucan, and Margaret McKeown.
- Read *Creating Robust Vocabulary* by Isabel Beck, Margaret McKeown, and Linda Kucan.
- Watch Anita Archer's videos about teaching vocabulary in elementary school at https://explicitinstruction.org/video-elementary/.

Notes

1. Graves, M. F. (2016). *The vocabulary book.* Teachers College Press.
2. Stahl, S. A., & Nagy, W.E. (2005). *Teaching word meanings.* Routledge, 4.
3. Cunningham, A. E., & Stanovich, K. E. (1997). Early reading acquisition and its relation to reading experience and ability 10 years later. *Developmental Psychology, 33*(6), 934.
4. Nagy, W. E., Anderson, R. C., & Herman, P. A. (1987). Learning word meanings from context during normal reading. *American Educational Research Journal, 24*(2), 237–270.

5. Fukkink, R. G., & de Glopper, K. (1998). Effects of instruction in deriving word meaning from context: A meta-analysis. *Review of Educational Research, 68*(4), 450–469.

6. Pany, D., Jenkins, J. R., & Schreck, J. (1982). Vocabulary instruction: Effects on word knowledge and reading comprehension. *Learning Disability Quarterly, 5*(3), 202–215.

7. Miller, G. A., & Gildea, P. M. (1987). How children learn words. *Scientific American, 257*(3), 94–99.

8. McKeown, M. G. (1993). Creating effective definitions for young word learners. *Reading Research Quarterly, 28*(1), 17–31.

9. Coyne, M. D., Simmons, D. C., Kame'enui, E. J., & Stoolmiller, M. (2004). Teaching vocabulary during shared storybook readings: An examination of differential effects. *Exceptionality, 12*(3), 145–162.

10. Beck, I. L., McKeown, M. G., & Kucan, L. (2013). *Bringing words to life*. The Guilford Press.

11. Beck, I.L., & McKeown, M.G. (1991). Conditions of vocabulary acquisition. In R.E. Barr, M.L.E. Kamil, P. Mosenthal, & P. Pearson (Eds.), *Handbook of reading research* (Vol. 2, pp. 789–814). Erlbaum.

12. Carlisle, J.F. (2007). Fostering morphological processing, vocabulary development, and reading comprehension. In Wagner, R.K., Muse, A.E., & Tannenbaum, K.R. (Eds.), *Vocabulary Acquisition*. The Guilford Press.

13. National Reading Panel (U.S.) & National Institute of Child Health and Human Development (U.S.). (2000). *Report of the National Reading Panel: Teaching children to read: An evidence-based assessment of the scientific research literature on reading and its implications for reading instruction*. U.S. Dept. of Health and Human Services, Public Health Service, National Institutes of Health, National Institute of Child Health and Human Development.

14. Stahl, S. A., & Fairbanks, M. M. (1986). The effects of vocabulary instruction: A model-based meta-analysis. *Review of Educational Research, 56*(1), 72–110.

15. Anderson, R. C., & Nagy, W. E. (1992). The vocabulary conundrum. *American educator: The professional journal of the American Federation of Teachers, 16*(4).

16. Nagy, W. E., & Anderson, R. C. (1984). How many words are there in printed school English? *Reading Research Quarterly*, 304–330.

17. Beck, I. L., McKeown, M. G., & Kucan, L. (2008). *Creating robust vocabulary*. The Guilford Press.

18. Beck, I. L., McKeown, M. G., & Omanson, R. C. (1987). The effects and uses of diverse vocabulary instructional techniques. In McKeown, M. G., & Curtis, M. E. (Eds.), *The nature of vocabulary acquisition* (147–163). Lawrence Erlbaum Associates, Inc.

19. Beck, I. L., McKeown, M. G., & Kucan, L. (2013).

20. Beck, I. L., McKeown, M. G., & Kucan, L. (2008).
21. Beck, I. L., McKeown, M. G., & Kucan, L. (2013), p. 42
22. Neuman, S. B., & Wright, T. S. (2013). *All about words*. Teachers College Press.
23. Johnson, D. D., Pittelman, S. D., & Heimlich, J. E. (1986). Semantic mapping. *The Reading Teacher*, *39*(8), 778–783.
24. Sedita, J. (2013). *The key vocabulary routine*. Keys to Literacy.
25. Pittelman, S. D. (1991). *Semantic feature analysis: Classroom applications. Reading aids series*. International Reading Association.
26. Frayer, D., Frederick, W. C., & Klausmeier, H. J. (1969). *A schema for testing the level of cognitive mastery*. Wisconsin Center for Education Research.
27. Baumann, J. F., Edwards, E. C., Font, G., Tereshinski, C. A., Kame'-enui, E. J., & Olejnik, S. (2002). Teaching morphemic and contextual analysis to fifth-grade students. *Reading Research Quarterly*, *37*(2), 150–176.
28. Graves, M. F. (2016).
29. Stahl, S. A., & Nagy, W. E. (2005).
30. Apel, K. (2014). A comprehensive definition of morphological awareness: Implications for assessment. *Topics in Language Disorders*, *34*(3), 197–209.
31. Apel, K., & Diehm, E. (2014). Morphological awareness intervention with kindergarteners and first and second grade students from low SES homes: A small efficacy study. *Journal of Learning Disabilities*, *47*(1), 65–75.
32. Ibid.
33. Bryant, P., & Nunes, T. (2004). Morphology and spelling. In *Handbook of children's literacy* (91–118). Springer Netherlands.
34. Hegland, S.S. (2021). Beneath the Surface of Words. Learning About Spelling, 46.

CHAPTER 8

Comprehension

I'd like to tell you that if you teach decoding, comprehension will follow naturally, but I can't. I'd like to tell you that if you ask questions after students read, comprehension will just happen, but it won't. I'd like to tell you that comprehension is simply a set of skills to be taught, but it's not. Like it or not, comprehension is a complex beast.

The five key factors in learning to read identified by the National Reading Panel (NRP) are sometimes called the five pillars of reading instruction. It's true that these elements should be present in every reading program, but the common five pillars graphic (see Figure 8.1) presents all five areas as if they're fundamentally the same in complexity. It gives the false impression that comprehension can be taught in the same way that we teach phonemic awareness and phonics.[1]

The RAND Reading Study Group presented comprehension as a combination of factors in three categories: the reader, the text, and the activity. Readers bring different knowledge and interests to the reading task. Texts vary in genre, topic, and difficulty. The activity varies depending on one's purpose for reading. According to RAND, these factors interact with each other within a sociocultural context.[2]

What Is Comprehension?

Comprehension is an *outcome*. It is the goal of reading. According to the RAND Reading Study Group, reading **comprehension** is "the process of simultaneously extracting and constructing meaning through interaction and involvement with written language."[3]

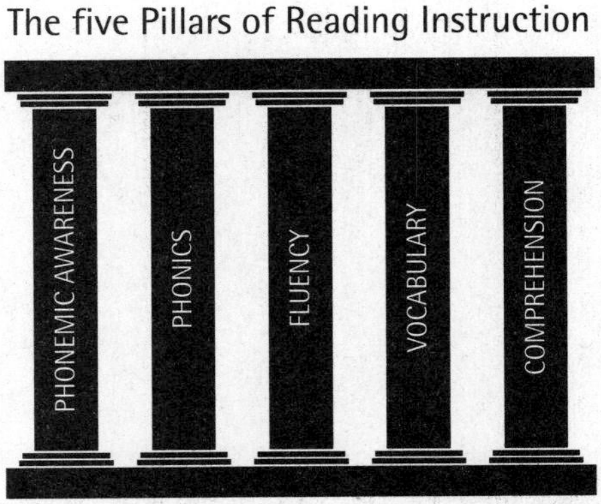

The five Pillars of Reading Instruction

Figure 8.1   This popular graphic has led to misunderstandings about reading comprehension.

This definition highlights something I tend to forget . . . both the text *and* the reader bring something to the table. In other words, comprehension isn't just about understanding the words on the page.

Tim Shanahan writes:

> Readers must be able to combine meaning extraction and meaning construction if they are to grasp an author's message, both stated and implied. Readers do this by using the information in a text and the knowledge that they bring to the text. It is not one or the other. It is both, in combination.[4]

THE MENTAL MODEL

What's a novel that you love so much you've read it multiple times? For me, it's Betty Smith's *A Tree Grows in Brooklyn*. Even though I've read the book many times, I can't tell you the story word for word. But I could tell you the gist (the general essence or meaning) of the book. That's because I have a mental model of the text. A **mental model**[5] (sometimes called a **situation model**[6]) is an overall representation of the meaning of a text. It's what the reader walks away with.

Your ultimate goal for your students is that they create a strong mental model of the text they read. For students in kindergarten through first grade, this will typically be done with texts that you read aloud. As students enter second grade and beyond, continue with whole-class read-alouds, but also challenge them with complex texts that they read with your support.

Background Knowledge

To create a mental model, students must combine the literal representation of the text with their background knowledge. **Background knowledge** refers to all the knowledge a reader brings to the reading task. Higher levels of background knowledge help children better understand text.[7] Teachers can (and should!) build background knowledge before reading. But before we get into the *how,* let's tackle the *why.*

Why Teach Knowledge?

In these days of easy Internet access, you may wonder if teaching knowledge for knowledge's sake is worth your time. Doesn't everyone have an encyclopedia in their pocket? Shouldn't you spend less time teaching information and more time teaching critical thinking?

The most obvious reason to teach knowledge is that it gives students something to think *about.* But there's more to it. Knowledge actually makes learning to read easier.[8]

Background Knowledge Helps With Inferring   One way that knowledge makes learning to read easier is that it helps you make inferences.[9] **Inferences** are conclusions you reach based on the information that you have. You get this information from the text itself *and* from your background knowledge. Inferences help you fill in gaps with information that the author doesn't explicitly state. According to reading expert Hugh Catts, "The richer the knowledge base, the faster and more automatic the inference."[10]

Consider the picture book *Stellaluna,* in which a baby bat is separated from her mother and ends up living with a family of birds. When an owl spies Stellaluna's mother at the beginning of the book, children can use their background knowledge to remember that owls are birds of prey and are thus a danger to bats.

Background Knowledge Gives You a Place to Attach New Information   It's easier to remember new information when you already have some knowledge of the topic.[11] Researcher Marilyn Adams calls prior knowledge "mental Velcro" because it gives the words of the text places to stick.[12]

Background Knowledge Frees Up Space in Working Memory   If everything you're reading is new information, it all takes up space in your working memory. Before long, you'll reach cognitive overload and comprehension will suffer.

Recht and Leslie tested middle school students who were either good or poor readers and who had either a strong or weak understanding of baseball. All the students read a passage about a half-inning of a baseball game and were then asked to use figures to reenact and describe what they'd read. Students who were weak readers, but had a strong understanding of baseball, performed better than strong readers with a weak understanding of baseball.[13] This is because the students who didn't know much about the sport didn't have enough free space in their working memories to keep track of the events of the game; they were overwhelmed by the task of trying to understand how baseball works.[14]

Background Knowledge Opens Up Space for Critical Thinking Because background knowledge frees up working memory, our brains are freed to think more deeply. In other words, "knowledge improves thinking."[15]

How to Decide What Information to Teach

It's important to build background knowledge before your students read or listen to a text. But this activity shouldn't exceed three to five minutes. How can you build background knowledge in a time-efficient manner?

According to Anita Archer, you should ask yourself a set of questions like these:

- ◆ What can I teach that will make it easier for my students to learn new knowledge?
- ◆ What information can I teach that will reduce cognitive overload?
- ◆ What information will be useful for understanding this text *and* for understanding other texts on the same topic?
- ◆ What information will increase motivation so that students are actually interested in reading or listening to this text?[16]

Let's imagine that I'm teaching third grade and I'm about to read aloud the picture book *Henry's Freedom Box*, a true story about a man who mailed himself from Virginia to Philadelphia to free himself from slavery. My students will understand this book better if I give a brief history of slavery in the United States. I can reduce cognitive overload by explaining that the Underground Railroad was a secret network and not a real railroad. I can increase motivation by asking students to think about the steps a man might take to secretly mail himself to another state.

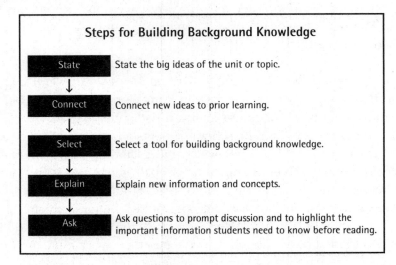

Figure 8.2   Steps for building background knowledge.
Courtesy of Sharon Vaughn

How to Build Background Knowledge

Researcher Sharon Vaughn shares a step-by-step method for building background knowledge (see Figure 8.2).[17] When you're ready to select a tool for building knowledge, consider doing one or more of the following:

◆ Show related images.
◆ Share and discuss a physical object.
◆ Show a quick video related to the topic.
◆ Read a short, simpler text on the same topic.
◆ Simply state the new information.

Building Background Knowledge: Sample Lesson

State	Today I'm going to read *Turtle and Tortoise Are Not Friends*, by Mike Reiss. These two creatures are assigned the same enclosure at the zoo. Turtles and tortoises are a lot alike, but the tortoise says they can't be friends because they're so different.
Connect	Have you ever seen a turtle before? Where did you see it? Finish each of my sentences.

• A turtle is covered with a hard . . . (shell).
• A turtle is not a bird. It is not a fish. A turtle is a . . . (reptile).
• When a turtle is in danger, it might put its head . . . (inside its shell).

Did you know that a tortoise is a kind of turtle? Turtles and tortoises look a lot alike, but they're also different.

Select	We're going to watch this two-minute YouTube video about the differences between turtles and tortoises. Listen for the ways they are alike and different.
Explain	(Watch the video together, pausing to comment as needed.)
Ask	What is one way that turtles and tortoises are the same? Turn and tell your partner. What are two ways that they're different?

A little goes a long way when it comes to building background knowledge. According to Anita Archer, "Even a thin slice of knowledge supports comprehension and learning."[18]

Teaching Sentence Comprehension

It would be nice if the ability to understand spoken language completely carried over to an understanding of written language, but the two are very different. A major reason for this is that the structure of sentences in written language is more formal and complex.

Syntax is the arrangement of words, phrases, and clauses to create well-formed sentences. Understanding syntax in written text can be challenging for students, especially those who struggle with comprehension.[19] As a reading teacher, you have two jobs when it comes to syntax. First, you need to spot sentences with challenging syntax so you can help your students understand them (whether your students are reading or listening to the text). Second, you need to do activities that will build **syntactic awareness**, which is the ability to keep track of the order of and relationship between words while speaking, reading, and writing.

Let's start with identifying tricky sentences. It's easier said than done! Since the text you read aloud (or the complex text your students read) is easy for you, you won't naturally spot the tricky parts. However, a quick review of eighth-grade grammar will prepare you to identify challenging sentences in the text students read or listen to.

PARTS OF SPEECH

Individual words operate as different parts of speech. Students should understand the role that each part of speech has within a sentence (see Table 8.1).

Phrases

A **phrase** is a group of words that can be used to communicate something (see Table 8.2). A phrase cannot stand alone because it's not a complete thought.

Table 8.1   Parts of Speech

Part of Speech	Role Within the Sentence
Noun	Tells who or what
Pronoun	Replaces or refers to a who or what
Verb	Tells what a who or what is doing or feeling
Adjective	Describes a who or what
Adverb	Tells how, when, where, or why
Preposition	Shows the relationship between words
Conjunction	Connects words, phrases, or clauses
Interjection	Expresses emotion

Table 8.2 Types of Phrases

Type of Phrase	Role Within the Sentence	Example
Noun phrase	Tells who or what	*My funny chickens* chase each other around the coop.
Verb phrase	Tells what the who or what is doing or feeling	The chickens *have been laying* eggs for two years.
Adjective phrase	Describes the who or what	The *goofy, loveable* chickens follow me around.
Adverb phrase	Tells when, where, how, or why	The chickens go to sleep *quite easily* when the sun goes down.
Prepositional phrase	Shows how two words are related	Each day, I check for eggs *in their nests*.

Clauses

Unlike a phrase, a **clause** is a complete thought that contains a subject and a verb. It forms a sentence or part of a sentence (see Table 8.3).

Table 8.3 Types of Clauses

Type of Clause	Definition	Example
Independent (or main) clause	A clause that can stand alone and make a complete sentence	*I don't need to go to the farmer's market* because I grow my own vegetables.
Dependent (or subordinate) clause	A clause that begins with a conjunction (such as *although, because,* or *while*) or relative pronoun (such as *who, which,* or *that*); it cannot stand alone	I don't need to go to the farmer's market *because I grow my own vegetables*.

Types of Sentences

Clauses combine to form different types of sentences. See Table 8.4.

Table 8.4 Types of Sentences

Type of Sentence	Definition	Example
Simple	An independent clause	We have a new pet turtle.
Compound	Two independent clauses that are joined by a coordinating conjunction	We have a new pet turtle, but it hasn't come out of its shell.
Complex	An independent clause and at least one dependent clause	When we brought the turtle home, it crawled into the corner of its tank and stayed there.
Compound-complex	Two independent clauses and one or more dependent clauses	We offered the turtle lettuce, so it came out of its shell because it loves vegetables.

Cohesive Ties

Now I'm going to ask you to move beyond eighth-grade English as I share a concept that may be new to you: cohesive ties. **Cohesive ties** are generic words or phrases that link different parts of a sentence or one sentence to another (see Table 8.5).

Table 8.5   Types of Cohesive Ties

Cohesive Tie	Example
Pronoun	Kate visited the African game reserve with her family. *She* spotted an elephant and its calf.
Ellipsis (the omission of a verb or noun phrase to avoid repetition)	Kate couldn't wait to feed the giraffes, and her kids *couldn't*, either. Kate spent so much change paying for giraffe treats that she had *very little* left.
Whole and part	Kate brought *some snacks* for the trip. She enjoyed a *biscuit* while she waited for the shuttle with her family.
Item and container	Ellie asked for some *water*; her mom gave her a *bottle*.
Synonym	Just then, Gus spotted a *lion* through the window. The *big cat* was lounging in the sun.
Connectives	**Connectives that show time** *Before*: Earlier, before, previously *Later*: After, next, afterward, eventually, finally *Simultaneously*: During, while, at the same time **Connectives that show a causal relationship** Because, so that, for this reason, therefore **Connectives that compare** Similarly, in the same way **Connectives that contrast** In contrast, however, although, on the other hand **Connectives that show continuity** And, also, as well as, for example

HOW TO SPOT CHALLENGING SENTENCES

When you're aware of the ways that phrases, clauses, and cohesive ties can make a sentence difficult to comprehend, you're better able to pick out the tricky sentences and provide support.[20]

Challenging sentences may include the following:

◆ Many words and ideas
◆ Multiple phrases and clauses
◆ An embedded dependent clause that splits up the main clause
◆ Challenging conjunctions (although, unless, etc.)
◆ Unusual word order
◆ Passive voice or double negatives
◆ Significant use of punctuation
◆ Use of cohesive ties

Cover the right two columns below. Then read each sentence from *Charlotte's Web* and see if you can identify what makes it challenging. What questions could you ask to help your students make sense of the sentence?

Challenging Sentence	The Tricky Part	Questions You Might Ask to Scaffold the Reading
"Every afternoon, when the school bus stopped in front of her house, she jumped out and ran to the kitchen to fix another bottle for him."	The sentence includes an embedded dependent clause (*when the school bus stopped in front of her house*).	"What did Fern do when the school bus stopped in front of her house?"
"Mr. Arable fixed a small yard especially for Wilbur under an apple tree, and gave him a large wooden box filled with straw, with a doorway cut in it, so he could walk in and out as he pleased."	The sentence is long and includes multiple phrases and clauses.	"What did Mr. Arable put in the yard for Wilbur? What did he fill it with? Why did Mr. Arable cut a doorway into the box?"
"Friendless, dejected, and hungry, he threw himself down in the manure and sobbed."	The adjective phrase at the beginning of the sentence is an example of unusual word order.	"The author uses three words to describe Wilbur in this sentence. What are they?"
"He could hardly believe what he was seeing, and although he detested flies, he was sorry for this one."	The embedded dependent clause includes a challenging conjunction (*although*).	"The author means that *even though* Wilbur didn't like flies, he felt sorry for this one. Why do you think he felt sorry for the fly?"
"Wilbur heard the trill of the tree toad and the occasional slamming of the kitchen door. All of these sounds made him feel comfortable and happy."	"All of these sounds" is a cohesive tie that refers back to the sound of the toad and the slamming of the door.	"Which sounds make Wilbur feel happy? Why do you think so? What are some comfortable sounds we hear in the classroom?"

Quotes from White, E.B. (1952). *Charlotte's Web*. Harper & Brothers.

ACTIVITIES THAT PROMOTE SENTENCE COMPREHENSION

In addition to spotting challenging sentences and helping your students understand them, you can do activities that will build syntactic awareness.

Words Working Together

This activity, inspired by the one in Hennessy's *The Reading Comprehension Blueprint*, helps students see how the words of a sentence work together to communicate meaning.[21] Since this activity takes just a few minutes, you could do it every day.

1. Present a complex sentence that teaches important information. Consider choosing a sentence directly from your social studies or science text.

> Many animals migrate to places where they can hibernate during the winter.

2. Have students chorally read the sentence. (If most of your students are not yet able to decode the words, start with a simpler sentence, such as *Some whales migrate to get food.*)
3. Ask a series of questions that help students see how the words work together. I always start with "what."
    a. Which word answers *what?* (animals)
    b. Which word tells *which* animals? (many)
    c. Which word tells what animals *do?* (migrate)
    d. Which word tells where animals migrate *to?* (places)
    e. Which word tells what animals *do* in those places? (hibernate)
    f. Which phrase tells *when* animals hibernate? (during the winter)

Sentence Anagrams

A **sentence anagram** is a collection of words that can be rearranged to make a complete sentence. To do this activity, write words or phrases on individual slips of paper. Have students work together to construct a complete sentence. Teach them to start with the action, then find the who or what, and finally arrange the rest of the words and phrases. Consider creating anagrams using sentences from your read-alouds.

Anagram example #1 (Easy)

| Fern | Wilbur | with a bottle | fed |

Anagram example #2 (More challenging)

Fern	with a bottle	heated
the milk	and	fed	Wilbur

Reading Comprehension Strategies

A **reading comprehension strategy** is a deliberate mental action to improve reading comprehension.[22] A great deal of research shows that instruction in these strategies improves understanding.[23] Dan Willingham tells us that this instruction should be explicit and brief, since the strategies "are quickly learned and require minimal practice."[24]

Many teachers (including yours truly) have gone about strategy instruction backward. I spent weeks on a particular strategy—such as predicting, activating prior knowledge, or visualizing—with the goal of helping my students master the *strategy* rather than learn the content. I should have started with a quality text and *then* chosen one or more strategies (see Table 8.6) to help students understand it.

When teaching a strategy, use what you know about explicit instruction. Identify the strategy, explain what it is, and stress how it will help students take conscious steps to better understand the text. As you read, think aloud by saying what you are thinking while you read. Guide your students in using the strategy; eventually, ask them to apply it on their own.

Table 8.6 Reading Comprehension Strategies

Strategy	Description
Comprehension monitoring	Awareness of whether or not you understand the text and taking steps to clear up misunderstandings
Making connections	Connecting prior knowledge to the text
Creating mental images	Imagining a movie or picture in your mind while reading a text
Recognizing text structure	Identifying and understanding how a text is organized
Asking questions	Asking yourself questions about the text
Answering questions	Using evidence from the text to answer questions
Predicting	Making an educated guess about what will happen next based on prior knowledge and clues in the text
Summarizing	Determining what is most important, condensing it, and putting it into your own words

Always keep in mind the end goal—that students create a mental model of the text. Strategies are only useful insofar as they help students understand and remember what they read.

COMPREHENSION MONITORING

My second son was a good decoder from early on, but he developed the habit of speed reading. During a summer reading challenge at home, I realized that he didn't understand the purpose of reading: to understand it. His only goal was to read the words on the page and be done with it. I asked him to summarize an entire chapter, but it was too much to ask. We had to back up all the way to the paragraph level; after each paragraph he summarized what he read. Eventually he could read a whole chapter without checking in.

My son needed to learn the **comprehension monitoring** strategy, which is being aware of whether or not you understand the text. It's what good readers do as they create a mental model.

Good readers know when they're confused.[25] They ask themselves questions as they read and notice when meaning breaks down. They deal with problems as they come up—whether that's finding the meaning of an unknown word, rereading the previous paragraph, or fixing a word they misread.

To model this strategy, monitor comprehension as you read aloud. Pause to ask yourself questions (see Figure 8.3) and fix up your reading—even if you have to manufacture confusion for the benefit of your students!

MONITORING COMPREHENSION

ASK YOURSELF ...

- Can I picture the story in my mind?
- Can I retell the story?
- Can I remember what I've learned?
- Do I understand the words?

IF YOU'RE STUCK ...

- Sound out the tricky word.
- Read more slowly.
- Reread a section.
- Restate it in your own words.
- Keep reading to see if that helps.

Figure 8.3   Anchor chart for monitoring comprehension.

RECOGNIZING TEXT STRUCTURE

Recently I read an article and couldn't follow it. I knew the vocabulary. I understood each individual sentence. Yet I couldn't track how the sentences were related to each other. The problem was that the text had no meaningful structure. After the reading, I couldn't give a summary of the article because I had no mental model.

Text structure is how an author organizes a text. Research shows that explicit instruction in text structure leads to gains in comprehension.[26] As Moats and Hennessy note, "If readers can anticipate that a text will contain certain types of information, and that information will be presented in a certain way, they'll have an easier time picking out the key ideas and are more likely to remember what they read."[27]

Understanding text structure is important even before students can read. You can begin teaching text structure as early as kindergarten through read-alouds.[28] As students progress, you can teach signal words, nonfiction text features, and the use of graphic organizers.[29]

Nonfiction text features include:

- ◆ Headings
- ◆ Boldface type
- ◆ Graphics
- ◆ Glossary and index
- ◆ Table of contents

The authors of the CORE Reading Sourcebook define a graphic organizer as "a visual representation of knowledge that structures information to develop relationships."[30] Graphic organizers can be used to guide students through a text. They're useful for summarizing what's been read (or listened to) and can also be pre-writing activities that get students ready to write a paragraph or essay.

Narrative Text Structure

Narrative text tells a story or describes a series of events (whether fiction or nonfiction). **Story grammar** represents the basic structure of a narrative text. The basic story elements are described in Table 8.7.

Table 8.7 Story Elements

Story Element	Teacher Prompts
Setting Where and when the story takes place	• Where and when does the story take place? • How do you know? • Name two words that describe the story's setting.
Characters The people, animals, or creatures who are important to the story	• Who is the story about? • Who is the main character? • Describe the character's appearance using one word. • Describe the character's personality using one word. • Do any of the characters change? How?
Problem The main conflict, struggle, or issue that the characters are trying to overcome	• Who has a problem in this story? Describe the problem. • What reason does the character have for resolving the problem?
Plot or action What happened to the main characters or what they did to try to solve the problem	• What happens at the beginning, middle, and end? • What do you think is the most important event in the story?
Solution How the problem is solved	• How does the story end? • How did the character solve the problem?
Theme The central message of a story	• What lesson did the main character learn? • What lesson does the author want you to remember? • What's the big idea of the story?

Procedure for Teaching Story Elements

1. Start with a familiar story or a variation of a popular tale.
2. Before reading, present a series of questions that you'll be pausing to ask as you read aloud the text.[31]
   a. Who is the story about?
   b. What are they trying to do?
   c. What happens when they try to do it?
   d. What happens in the end?
3. Pause to ask each question at an appropriate point in the read-aloud.
4. Together, complete a graphic organizer.
5. Teach your students to retell the story using five fingers as a scaffold (see Figure 8.4) Another option is to use an anchor chart or bookmark with a series of images as prompts (Figure 8.5).[32] In one study, students who received explicit instruction in these types of techniques showed better comprehension than those who did not.[33]

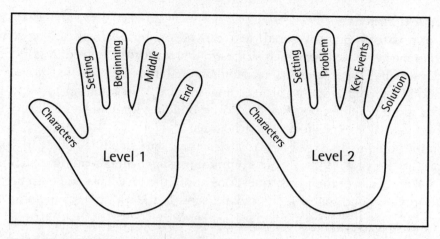

Figure 8.4 Five-finger retelling scaffold.

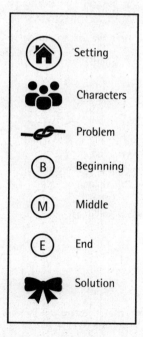

Figure 8.5 Retelling bookmark.

Expository Text Structure

Because **expository** (informational) text can be organized in a variety of ways, it's trickier than narrative text, in which stories follow a reliable pattern. A good goal is to make at least half of your students' reading material informational text, whether you're reading aloud or your students are reading the text.[34] In addition to exposing your students to more complex text, you'll also be building knowledge. Refer to Table 8.8 to find the five major expository text structures.

When introducing an expository text structure, start small. Use a clearly organized paragraph instead of a longer, more complex passage. After reading, teach your students to ask and answer their own questions about the text. This will help them organize the information and rehearse it so that it stays in their long-term memory.[35]

Table 8.8 Expository text structures

Text Structure	Signal Words	Teacher Prompts	Sample Graphic Organizer
Description *The text provides details or characteristics of something.*	• for example • consists of • such as • looks like • sounds like	• Who or what is being described? • What did you learn from the description?	
Sequence *The information is presented as a list of chronological events or steps in a sequence.*	• first • next • later • following • finally	• What happened first? • Then what happened? • What happened after ____? • What happened last?	
Cause & Effect *The author describes an event (cause) and the effects that follow.*	• as a result of • reasons why • was caused by • therefore • effect	• What happened when ___? • Why did ____ happen? • What caused ____ to happen?	

Text Structure	Signal Words	Teacher Prompts	Sample Graphic Organizer
Compare and/or contrast *The author shows how two or more things are alike and different.*	• in common • both • different • similar to • unlike	• What things are being compared? • How are they alike? • How are they different?	
Problem and solution *The author introduces a problem and tells how it could be solved.*	• because • in order to • the problem is • so that • result	• Describe the problem. • What is being done to solve the problem? • What are possible solutions?	

Sample Text Structure Lesson

1. Name and describe the text structure.

   Teacher Today you're going to read a descriptive paragraph. It provides details about something.

2. Have your students read the paragraph alone or with a partner.

   Teacher Read the paragraph until the timer beeps. If you finish before time is up, read it again.

3. Read the paragraph chorally.

   An echidna is a small, spiny creature that lives only in Australia and New Guinea. Echidnas are monotremes, mammals that lay eggs. Echidnas are sometimes called spiny anteaters because ants are some of their favorite foods. They also eat other tiny creatures, such as worms, insect larvae, and termites. Echidnas look

a bit like hedgehogs because they are covered with fur and spines. To get away from
predators, they will burrow into the ground so only their spines stick out. Echidnas
are good at many things, such as swimming, climbing trees, digging, and slurping.
But they are best at being unique!

4. Identify signal words. Invite your students to highlight them.

> *Teacher*   I see a few signal words that help me know that I'm reading a description. Let's find and highlight them. "Such as . . . look a bit like . . . such as." Do you see any other signal words that help you know that this is a descriptive paragraph?

5. Ask students questions about the paragraph.

> *Teacher*   As I'm looking at this paragraph, I could ask this question: "Where do echidnas live?" Ones, find the answer and tell it to your partner.
>
> Another question I could ask is, "Why are echidnas called spiny anteaters?" Twos, find the answer and tell it to your partner.

6. Have students each form a question to ask a partner. Then have them ask and answer their own questions.

> *Teacher*   Your turn! Think of a question you could ask your partner. . . . Ask your question.
>
> Now here's a trick . . . find a question you can ask *yourself*. Then turn over the paragraph and answer it from memory. For example, I could ask myself, "How do echidnas get away from predators?" Then I can turn the paper over and answer it: "They burrow into the ground so their spines stick out." If I can't remember the answer, I can peek, but I must turn the paper over when answering my question.

7. Complete a graphic organizer together.

> *Teacher*   You have a graphic organizer in front of you. Let's fill it out together. What is this paragraph about? Write the word "echidnas" in the center circle. Now we need to add information that describes the echidna. Read the first sentence with me. What did we learn? Write "live in Australia and New Guinea" in one circle. (Keep going until the organizer is complete.)

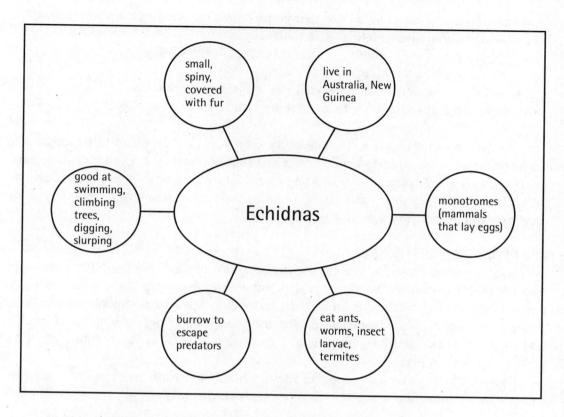

8. Together, write a paragraph using the graphic organizer.

Teacher   Turn over your paragraph. Let's use the notes from the graphic organizer to write a paragraph. What could our topic sentence be? (Write the new paragraph together.)

SUMMARIZING

Summarizing (giving a brief statement of the main points) goes hand-in-hand with comprehension monitoring and is a powerful strategy for improving comprehension.[36] Students should start with oral summaries and gradually progress to written summaries, because students' comprehension is increased when they write about what they read.[37]

I have found a variation on the paragraph-shrinking strategy[38] to be the simplest way to teach summarizing. It works as follows:

- Name the who or what.
- Tell the most important information about the who or what.
- Shrink the information into a summary that is 10 words or less.

You can model this quick strategy every time you read aloud. Wait to summarize until you've read the whole story. If you're reading nonfiction, stop after each section.

Eventually, teach your students to pause and follow this procedure when they read independently. When they pause to summarize the major points of a text, they're on their way to constructing a mental model.

MULTIPLE-STRATEGY TEACHING

Spending weeks on a single strategy isn't a good use of time. But the NRP found support for multiple-strategy teaching, in which the reader uses multiple strategies while interacting with the teacher. Each of these approaches requires explicit modeling by the teacher, lots of guided practice during the We Do It phase (in which the teacher and students work together), and finally a gradual release as students follow the procedure in small groups.

If you teach students in second grade or above, it's worth looking into multiple-strategy procedures and using one or more with your students.

Question–Answer Relationships

Exploring question-answer relationships[39] improves comprehension by helping students understand the different types of questions.

1. Explain that there are four types of questions that students may answer about a test:
   a. Right-there questions have answers found directly in the text.
   b. Think-and-search questions require readers to combine information from different parts of the text.
   c. Author-and-me questions require that the reader read the text and relate it to their own experience.
   d. On-my-own questions require students to rely on their background knowledge.
2. Read a passage aloud.
3. Ask questions related to the passage. Help students classify each question and find its answer.

4. After a lot of guided practice, have students create their own questions after reading a passage. Challenge them to create at least one question for each of the four types.

ReQuest

ReQuest[40] is a questioning technique that has been shown to help students focus on text and pay attention to detail.

1. Have students read an assigned text (a few sentences or a few paragraphs).
2. The teacher closes the book, and students ask as many questions as possible. The teacher answers the questions and provides feedback about the quality of the questions.
3. The students close their books, and the teacher asks *them* questions, making sure to ask a variety of question types.
4. The teacher and students repeat the sequence for the rest of the text.
5. When appropriate, the teacher pauses the process and asks students to make and verify predictions.

Collaborative Strategic Reading

Collaborative Strategic Reading (CSR)[41] teaches students to use comprehension strategies in small groups and is especially powerful for monitoring comprehension.

1. **Preview:** Students preview the passage by looking at headings and other text features. They discuss what they know about the topic and predict what they will learn.
2. **Click & Clunk:** Students read until they reach a clunk—something they don't understand. They use "fix-up" strategies to repair comprehension.
3. **Get the Gist:** For each paragraph, students should identify the most important who or what and the most important idea about the who or what. They should summarize the gist in as few words as possible.
4. **Wrap Up:** Students should generate questions about the passage they've read as if they're the teacher. They should then answer their own questions.

Putting It All Together

Tim Shanahan reminds us that "comprehension instruction should introduce students to the idea that understanding and remembering are choices that one makes, and that there are ways of thinking about texts and operating on them that increases the chances of understanding and remembering."[42]

I recommend using a planning guide for each comprehension lesson, whether you're reading the text aloud or your students are reading it with you. This planning guide can help.

Comprehension Planning Guide

What **big ideas** or understandings do you want
your students to have after reading or
listening to the text?

What **text challenges** do you need to address?   (Tricky sentences, cohesive ties, inferences, text structure)

-
-
-
-

What **vocabulary** words will you teach?

What **background knowledge** would be helpful   (Share images, video, a simpler text, etc.)
for your students? How will you teach it?

What will be the **purpose** for reading?

Will you model and teach any **comprehension**   (QAR, ReQuest, CSR, monitoring comprehension,
strategies or use a specific **process** to help   summarizing, etc.)
students understand the text?

Where will you stop to analyze text structure,   •
ask questions, etc.?   •
-
-
-
-

After reading, what questions will you ask, how   (Graphic organizer, retell, oral summary, written
will you review vocabulary, and what guided   summary, etc.)
and/or independent work will students do?

Key Things to Remember

- The ultimate goal of reading is comprehension.
- Background knowledge increases students' comprehension of text.
- Teachers should use their understanding of syntax to spot challenging sentences and teach students to understand them.
- Reading comprehension strategies are deliberate mental actions that improve reading comprehension.
- Rather than spending weeks on a particular comprehension strategy, teachers should first choose a quality text and then teach the strategies that would best support understanding of it.
- Students should be taught to monitor their comprehension.
- Summarizing is a powerful strategy for improving comprehension.
- Research supports multiple-strategy teaching, in which the reader uses multiple strategies while interacting with the teacher.

Learn More

- Read *The Comprehension Blueprint* by Nancy Hennessey.
- Watch Dr. Sharon Vaughn's IDA presentation, "The Science of Reading Comprehension." www.youtube.com/watch?v=s1LHkGXfRdw&t=2s.

Free Resources

- Words Working Together activities
- Graphic organizers
- Comprehension planning guide

www.themeasuredmom.com/bookresources/

Notes

1. Catts, H. W. (2022). Rethinking how to promote reading comprehension. *American Educator, 45*(4), 26.
2. Snow, C., & RAND Reading Study Group. (2002). *A research agenda for improving reading comprehension*. RAND Corporation.
3. Ibid.
4. Shanahan, T. (2019). *Improving reading comprehension in the primary grades*. NCCA, 2.
5. Johnson-Laird, P. N. (1983). *Mental models: Towards a cognitive science of language, inference, and consciousness* (No. 6). Harvard University Press.
6. Kintsch, W. (1998). *Comprehension: A paradigm for cognition*. Cambridge University Press.
7. Smith, R., Snow, P., Serry, T., & Hammond, L. (2021). The role of background knowledge in reading comprehension: A critical review. *Reading Psychology, 42*(3), 214–240.
8. Willingham, D. T. (2006). How knowledge helps. *American educator, 30*(1), 30–37.
9. Adams, B. C., Bell, L. C., & Perfetti, C. A. (1995). A trading relationship between reading skill and domain knowledge in children's text comprehension. *Discourse Processes, 20*(3), 307–323.
10. Catts, H. (2023, March 13). *Rethinking reading comprehension*. [Symposium session]. AIM Institute 2023 Symposium. https://institute.aimpa.org/programs-research/research-to-practice-symposium/2023-symposium/2023-symposium-recordings
11. Schneider, W., Körkel, J., & Weinert, F. E. (1989). Domain-specific knowledge and memory performance: A comparison of high-and low-aptitude children. *Journal of Educational Psychology, 81*(3), 306.
12. Adams, M. J. (2014). Knowledge for literacy. *American Federation of Teachers*.
13. Recht, D. R., & Leslie, L. (1988). Effect of prior knowledge on good and poor readers' memory of text. *Journal of Educational Psychology, 80*(1), 16.
14. Willingham, D.T. (2006).
15. Moats, L. C., & Hennessy, N. (2010). *Digging for meaning: Teaching text comprehension*. Sopris West Educational Services.
16. OregonRTIi. (2022, May 4). *Anita Archer—Background knowledge: Key to learning & reading comprehension* [Video]. YouTube. https://www.youtube.com/watch?v=eU_IWCmz-2M.
17. International Dyslexia Association Georgia. (2023, February 9). *The science of reading comprehension: Effective reading comprehension instruction* [Video]. YouTube. https://www.youtube.com/watch?v=s1LHkGXfRdw&t=2s.
18. OregonRTIi. (2022, May 4).

19. Oakhill, J., Cain, K., & Elbro, C. (2015). *Understanding and teaching reading comprehension*. Routledge.

20. Scott, C. (2004). Syntactic contributions to literacy learning. In Stone, C. A., Silliman, E. R., Ehren, B. J., & Wallach, G. P. (Eds.), *Handbook of language and literacy: Development & disorders* (pp. 340–362). Guilford Press.

21. Hennessy, N. L. (2021). *The reading comprehension blueprint*. Paul H. Brookes Publishing Co.

22. Shanahan, T., Callison, K., Carriere, C., Duke, N. K., Pearson, P. D., Schatschneider, C., & Torgesen, J. (2010). Improving Reading Comprehension in Kindergarten through 3rd Grade: IES Practice Guide. NCEE 2010–4038. *What works clearinghouse*.

23. National Reading Panel (U.S.) & National Institute of Child Health and Human Development (U.S.). (2000). *Report of the National Reading Panel: Teaching children to read: An evidence-based assessment of the scientific research literature on reading and its implications for reading instruction*. U.S. Dept. of Health and Human Services, Public Health Service, National Institutes of Health, National Institute of Child Health and Human Development.

24. Willingham, D. T., & Lovette, G. (2014). Can reading comprehension be taught? *Teachers College Record, 116*, 1.

25. Baker, L., and Brown, A. L. (1984). Metacognitive skills and reading. In Pearson, P. D., Barr, R., Kamil, M. L., & Mosenthal, P. (Eds.), *Handbook of reading research*, Vol. 1. (pp. 353–394). Longman.

26. Williams, J. P. (2005). Instruction in reading comprehension for primary-grade students: A focus on text structure. *The Journal of Special Education, 39*(1), 6–18.

27. Moats, L. C., & Hennessy, N. (2010).

28. Oakhill, J., Cain, K., & Elbro, C. (2015).

29. Coté, N., & Goldman, S. R. (1999). Building representations of informational text: Evidence from children's think-aloud protocols. *The construction of mental representations during reading*, 169–193.

30. Honig, B., Diamond, L. & Gutlohn, L. (2018). *Teaching reading sourcebook*. Arena Press.

31. Baker, L., and Brown, A. L. (1984).

32. VandenBerge, N. (2013, March 9). Retelling rope. First Grade Wow. http://firstgradewow.blogspot.com/2013/03/retelling-rope.html.

33. Paris, A. H., & Paris, S. G. (2007). Teaching narrative comprehension strategies to first graders. *Cognition and Instruction, 25*(1), 1–2.

34. Duke, N. K. (2013). Starting out: Practices to use in K-3. *Educational Leadership, 71*(3), 40–44.

35. Shanahan, T. (2019).

36. National Reading Panel (U.S.) & National Institute of Child Health and Human Development (U.S.). (2000).

37. Graham, S., & Hebert, M. (2011). Writing to read: A meta-analysis of the impact of writing and writing instruction on reading. *Harvard Educational Review*, *81*(4), 710–744.

38. Fuchs, D., & Fuchs, L. S. (2005). Peer-assisted learning strategies: Promoting word recognition, fluency, and reading comprehension in young children. *The Journal of Special Education*, *39*(1), 34–44.

39. Raphael, T. E., & Au, K. H. (2005). QAR: Enhancing comprehension and test taking across grades and content areas. *The Reading Teacher, 59*(3), 206–221.

40. Manzo, A. V. (1969). The request procedure. *Journal of reading*, *13*(2), 123–126.

41. Klingner, J. K., & Vaughn, S. (1998). Using collaborative strategic reading. *Teaching Exceptional Children, 30*(6), 32–37

42. Shanahan, T. (2019). *Improving reading comprehension in the primary grades.* NCCA, 21.

CHAPTER 9

Linking Reading and Writing

One of the most powerful ways to improve reading comprehension is to have students write about what they read.[1] In order to write well, students need to be automatic at handwriting, spelling, and punctuation so they can focus most of their working memory on higher-level skills like generating ideas, organization, and word choice.[2]

This chapter touches on what research says about teaching writing and shares tips for teaching handwriting and spelling. I also describe ways to teach your students to write sentences and paragraphs so they're prepared to write about the text they read or listen to.

What the Research Says

◆ **Writing about content material increases student learning** in social studies, science, math, and language arts.[3]
◆ **Students comprehend text better when they write about it.**[4]
◆ **Teaching spelling improves word-reading and comprehension.**[5]
◆ **The quality of student writing improves when students write in pairs**, provided that the teacher has taught specific guidelines and procedures for writing with a partner.[6]

- ◆ **Students benefit from explicit instruction in how to plan their writing.** This may include teaching students to brainstorm or use graphic organizers.[7]
- ◆ **When students have to devote mental energy to handwriting and spelling, they have less mental energy to focus on higher level skills.**[8] Teaching these skills in the primary grades positively impacts student writing.[9]
- ◆ **Teaching sentence construction improves the quality of what students write.**[10]
- ◆ **Students benefit from instruction in paragraph writing.**[11]
- ◆ **Student writing improves when teachers provide specific feedback** that explains problems and offers suggestions for improvement.[12]

Teach Handwriting

Handwriting is often perceived as a trivial, low-level skill that's not worth teaching. However, children need to develop fluent handwriting so that their working memory can focus on higher-level writing skills as they write about what they read.[13]

Researchers recommend that students receive 50–100 minutes of explicit handwriting instruction each week in kindergarten through third grade.[14] This investment of 10–20 minutes a day yields big dividends; when students become proficient at handwriting, both the legibility *and* the quality of their writing improve.[15]

TIPS FOR TEACHING HANDWRITING

- ◆ **Teach letter formation in the context of phonics lessons** in kindergarten and first grade. As you teach each new sound-spelling, have students practice writing the letter or letters that spell it.
- ◆ **Teach proper pencil grip.** The easiest way to teach this is to use the *pinch-and-flip* method. Students should set the pencil in front of them with the tip pointing toward their body. They should pinch near the tip of the pencil using the thumb and index finger. Then they should flip the pencil up and over until it rests securely in the tripod grasp, in which the thumb and index finger pinch the pencil as it rests on the middle finger. (See Figure 9.1.)
- ◆ **Teach your students to sit properly and tilt their paper.** Students should anchor their feet on the floor or a stool. When printing, students should tilt the paper slightly up and away from their dominant hand. When writing cursive, students should slant their paper a full 45 degrees.[16]

Figure 9.1 The pinch-and-flip method for achieving the perfect pencil grip.
Image by Rocio Zapata

◆ **Use the *trace, copy, cover, closed* technique** from Diana King's handwriting curriculum.[17]
  ● Trace: Students should trace each letter, saying its name or sound while tracing.
  ● Copy: Underneath the tracing model, students should copy the letter and again say its name or sound while writing it.
  ● Cover: Students should cover all the written examples and write from memory.
  ● Closed: Students should close their eyes and write the letter using motor memory.

Teach Spelling

Students' writing benefits when their spelling is automatic; if they have to think too hard about spelling, it overloads their working memory and leaves little mental energy for writing about their reading. Unfortunately, traditional spelling instruction has often missed the mark.

The common belief that English spelling is illogical can lead to practices that focus on memorization, like copying words or memorizing a sequence of letters. But English isn't as irregular as many think. Nearly 50 percent of English spellings are predictable based on sound-spellings that can be taught. An additional 34 percent of words are predictable except for one sound. When word origin and word meaning are considered, only 4 percent of English words are truly irregular.[18] The bottom line? Spelling can and should be taught!

TIPS FOR TEACHING SPELLING

- ◆ **Teach spelling alongside phonics instruction** in kindergarten and first grade (see Chapter 5). Follow your phonics scope and sequence as you progress from simple to more complex spelling patterns.
- ◆ **Give students many opportunities to practice writing words with the featured sound-spelling.** Sound mapping, word chains, and dictation are all effective practice methods (see Chapter 5).
- ◆ **Avoid practice that involves mindless repetition and copying.** It's time to let go of the age-old practice of writing spelling words five times each.
- ◆ **Teach your students that correct spelling is about both phonology and morphology.** In other words, teach your students that spelling is more than matching a sound to one or more letters. It's also about the preservation of roots, prefixes, and suffixes.

   Example #1: Rather than teach that the short e sound is spelled with *ea* in *dealt*, teach your students that *dealt* is related to *deal*, in which the /ĕ/ sound is spelled with *ea*.

   Example #2: Rather than teach that *bt* spells the /t/ sound in debt, explain that the word includes a silent b because it comes from the Latin word *debitum*, meaning "thing owed."

- ◆ **Use the etymology of words to unpack surprising spellings.** For example, the word *knee* is of Anglo-Saxon origin. The *k* used to be pronounced. Over time the pronunciation changed, but the spelling didn't.
- ◆ **Teach spelling patterns and generalizations**. See Table 9.1 for a list of common spelling patterns.

Table 9.1   Spelling Patterns and Generalizations

FLOSS Rule	When a one-syllable short vowel word ends with the /f/, /l/, /s/ or /z/ sound, double the final letter.	stuff, will, dress, fuzz Exceptions: bus, gas, pal, us, if, this
C/K Spelling Rule	When spelling /k/, use c before the vowels *a, o,* and *u.* Use *k* before the vowels *e* and *i.*	cat, cot, cup keep, kite
Final /k/ Rule	When a one-syllable short vowel word ends with /k/, use *ck.* Use *k* after a consonant or long vowel.	stick, duck milk, rake
The V Rule	English words do not end with plain *v.* When /v/ occurs at the end of a word, it is followed by a silent e.	give, have, live
TCH	When a one-syllable word ends with a short vowel and /ch/, spell /ch/ with *tch.*	switch, latch Exceptions: much, such, rich, which

DGE	When a one-syllable word ends with a short vowel and /j/, spell /j/ with *dge*.	bridge, badge
VCE Rule	When a word has the vowel-consonant-e pattern, the final *e* typically makes the preceding vowel spell its name.	cake, gate
Doubling Rule	If a one-syllable word ends with a short vowel and single consonant, double the final consonant before adding a vowel suffix. Do not double when adding a consonant suffix.	sad + er = sadder sad + ly = sadly
Drop It Rule	Words ending with silent *e* drop the *e* before adding a vowel suffix. They keep the *e* when adding a consonant suffix.	hope + ed = hoped hope + ful = hopeful
Change It Rule	When a word ends with a consonant and *y*, change the *y* to *i* when adding a suffix that does not already begin with *i*.	tidy + er = tidier tidy + ing = tidying
Plurals	Add *-es* to words ending with *s, ss, sh, ch,* or *x.* Change *f* or *fe* to *v* and add *-es.*	bus + es = buses match +es = matches knife + es = knives
Prefix Rule	Never double a consonant when adding a prefix. If the prefix's final consonant and the root word's initial consonant are the same, keep them both.	mis + spell = misspell un + necessary = unnecessary
AI/AY Pattern	When spelling with *ai* or *ay, ai* is generally used at the beginning or middle of a syllable. *Ay* is generally used at the end.	
OI/OY Pattern	When spelling /oi/, *oi* is generally used at the beginning or middle of a syllable. *Oy* is generally used at the end.	oil boy
OU/OW Pattern	When spelling /ou/, *ou* is generally used at the beginning or middle of a syllable. *Ow* is generally used at the end.	pound cow
Consonant-le Doubling Rule	If a word ends with a short vowel and consonant-le, double the consonant.	bubble giggle

◆ **If you assign a weekly spelling list, make sure that the words' spellings are related.** This means avoiding word lists that are based on a particular topic and choosing words that are related phonetically or morphologically.

For example: *Mammal, fish, reptile, bird,* and *amphibian* are related by topic but not in spelling. This is a vocabulary list, not a spelling list. In contrast, *groan, cloak, foam, toast,* and *coach* all contain the OA vowel team and could be part of the same spelling list. A more advanced list could include words that share the same root: *tractor, subtract, distract, contract,* and *attractive.*

Invented Spelling

While students are still learning letter-sound correspondences, teachers should hold them accountable for what they've been taught but also allow invented spelling. **Invented spelling** (sometimes called *temporary or estimated spelling*) is when students represent sounds based on their limited letter-sound knowledge (such as *motrsikl* for *motorcycle*). Permitting students to use invented spelling for sound-spellings that have not yet been taught does not prevent students from learning conventional spellings; it actually facilitates learning to read and spell.[19]

Some students are uncomfortable with invented spelling and want to know that they've spelled every word correctly. Encourage these students to do their best spelling but to lightly circle questionable words. You can provide the conventional spelling at an appropriate time later in the school day.

Teach Students to Write About What They Read

When students write about what they read, they have to revisit the text, put the information into their own words, and organize it. It's no wonder that writing about reading improves comprehension!

After reading a text to or with your students, teach them to write sentences and paragraphs in response. At first, your students' participation will be mostly oral as you model the writing. Over time, give your students more responsibility for the writing task.

Teach That Sentences Contain a "Who" and a "Do"

Teach your students that sentences contain a "who" and a "do." After reading aloud, refer to a picture from the book as you model how to create and write a complete sentence.

Writing a sentence: sample lesson

Teacher   Today you listened to me read *Ladybugs* by Gail Gibbons. I'm going to show you how to write a sentence about ladybugs. A sentence is a group of words that tell a complete thought. A complete sentence has a "who" and a "do."

On this page, I see a "who," a ladybug. The ladybug is doing something. What is the ladybug doing in this picture? Everyone?

Students	Eating.
Teacher	So *ladybug* is the "who" and *eating* is the "do." I can put these two parts together to make a sentence. *The ladybug is eating.* Say that with me.
All	The ladybug is eating.
Teacher	Watch me write this sentence. First I'll count the words—*the ladybug is eating.* How many words?
Students	Four.
Teacher	Correct. I'll draw four blanks. Then I'll point to each blank so I remember what I was going to write. Say the sentence with me.
All	The ladybug is eating.
Teacher	The first word is *the*. I'll start with a capital letter because this is the beginning of the sentence. *The . . . ladybug.* /l/ /l/ ladybug. What is the first letter of *ladybug?* Everyone?
Students	L.
Teacher	Yes, *ladybug* starts with *l*. *Ladybug* is spelled l-a-d-y-b-u-g. *The ladybug IS.* You know how to spell IS. Everyone?
Students	I-S.
Teacher	Correct. *The ladybug is eating. Eating* is spelled e-a-t-i-n-g. I end my sentence with a period because this is a telling sentence. Let's read the sentence together as I point to the words.
All	The ladybug is eating.

Teach Students to Expand Simple Sentences

Sentence expanding helps students write strong, detailed sentences. To teach this skill, present a simple sentence connected to text you have read to or with your students. Then ask questions that lead your students to expand the sentence by adding a word or phrase.

- ◆ What kind?
- ◆ How many?
- ◆ Where?
- ◆ Why?
- ◆ How?

Expanding a Sentence: Sample Lesson

Teacher   Let's read this sentence together.

> The ladybug flew.

This is a complete sentence. It has a "who," *ladybug*, and a "do," *flew*. But it doesn't give us much information. Today we're going to expand the sentence. That means we're going to make it bigger by adding details.

I'll start by answering a series of questions and recording their answers. My first question is, *what kind* of ladybug is it? This is a *spotted* ladybug.

> spotted

My next question is, *where* did the ladybug fly? Turn to your partner and tell them where the ladybug flew.

The ladybug flew *to the leaf*.

> to the leaf

My next question is, *why* did the ladybug fly to the leaf? Think about why the ladybug flew. Now turn to your partner and tell why the ladybug flew.

The ladybug flew to the leaf because *it wanted to eat aphids*.

> It wanted to eat aphids.

The last question is, *how* did the ladybug fly? The ladybug flew *swiftly*.

> swiftly

Now I need to rewrite *The ladybug flew* to include all this extra information. Let's start with *spotted*. Instead of saying *the ladybug flew*, I can say *the spotted ladybug flew*.

> The spotted ladybug flew.

Now I need to explain where the ladybug flew. How can we combine *ladybug flew* with *to the leaf?* Think for a moment. Then turn and tell your partner the new sentence.

> The spotted ladybug flew to the leaf.

The ladybug *wanted to eat aphids*. Add that information by using the word *because*.

> The spotted ladybug flew to the leaf because it wanted to eat aphids.

We have just one piece of information left to add. We want to explain that the ladybug flew swiftly. Listen to me add that word in different places in the sentence. Think about what sounds best to you.

The spotted ladybug *swiftly* flew to the leaf because it wanted to eat aphids.

The spotted ladybug flew *swiftly* to the leaf because it wanted to eat aphids.

The spotted ladybug flew to the leaf *swiftly* because it wanted to eat aphids.

Which sentence do you like best? Why? Any of these will work. I'm going to write the sentence this way. Read it with me.

> The spotted ladybug flew swiftly to the leaf because it wanted to eat aphids.

Teach Students to Combine Sentences

After reading text to or with your students, present multiple sentences that could be combined to make a single sentence. Ask a series of questions that will help students combine the sentences. As you make each adjustment, state whether you are changing, adding, rearranging, or deleting words.

Sentence Combining: Sample Lesson

Teacher   Today we're going to combine sentences so that they sound better to the reader. Let's read all the sentences together.

> The ladybug lays eggs.
> The eggs are yellow.
> The eggs hatch in 2–10 days.

What new information does the second sentence add?

Students   That the eggs are yellow.

Teacher   I can add just the word *yellow* to the first sentence. *The ladybug lays yellow eggs.* To combine those first two sentences, I added a word to the first sentence and deleted words from the second sentence. Which words did I delete?

Students   The eggs are.

Teacher   What new information do we get from the last sentence?

Students   That the eggs hatch in 2–10 days.

Teacher   I can add that information to the end of the sentence by adding a connective.
The ladybug lays yellow eggs, which hatch in 2–10 days.

Teach Students to Connect Sentences

Present a pair of sentences and possible connectives that are related to the text you've read aloud. Together, discuss what would be the best connective to link their meanings.

Connecting sentences: sample lesson

Teacher   Let's read the two sentences that describe this picture on page 4.

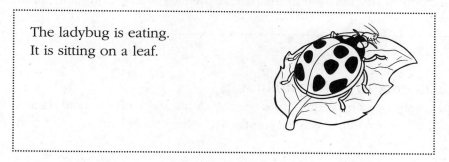

The ladybug is eating.
It is sitting on a leaf.

Teacher   Our possible connectives are *or, but,* or *and*.

or

but

and

Let's try connecting with the word *or*. Say the new sentence.

Students   The ladybug is eating, or it is sitting on a leaf.

Teacher   When you use the word *or*, it means that only one of the statements is true. Either the ladybug is eating, OR it is sitting. What do you see in the picture?

Students   It's doing both.

Teacher   Right. So *or* isn't the best connecting word.
Let's try using the word *but*.

Students   The ladybug is eating, but it is sitting on a leaf.

Teacher   When you use the word *but*, it means that the two ideas are very different or opposite. Eating and sitting don't feel like opposites. You can do both at the same time. Let's try *and*.

Students   The ladybug is eating, and it is sitting on a leaf.

Teacher	When you use the word *and*, you are giving additional information. It means that both things are true. Is this a good connective?
Students	Yes, because in the picture the ladybug is eating and sitting on a leaf.

Teach Students to Write Paragraphs

Model paragraph writing even before your students are ready to write paragraphs independently. It's an excellent way to summarize information learned from text.

Modeling Paragraph Writing: Sample Lesson

Teacher	Now that you've finished listening to *Ladybugs* by Gail Gibbons, I'm going to show you how to write a paragraph about the ways that ladybugs protect themselves from predators.
	My first sentence will introduce the topic. I'm going to write, "Ladybugs have many ways to defend themselves from their enemies."
	Help me write notes about the details. What are different ways that ladybugs protect themselves from their enemies? Think for a moment. Ones, tell your partner one way. Then Twos, tell your partner another way.

> **Topic sentence:**
> Ladybugs have many ways to defend themselves from their enemies.
>
> > ***Details:***
> > ◆ Bright color is a warning
> > ◆ Legs ooze smelly liquid
> > ◆ Pretend to be dead
>
> **Closing sentence:**
> Ladybugs have many ways to stay safe.

(Call on individual students to share ways that ladybugs defend themselves.)

On my chart, I'm going to record the ways that ladybugs defend themselves. These will not be complete sentences; they're just notes in my outline.

Now I need to think of a closing sentence to summarize what I've written. It needs to be different than my first sentence. I'll write, "Ladybugs have many ways to stay safe."

The last step is to combine all this together into a paragraph. I can copy my topic sentence. Now I need to put each of these details into a complete sentence. The first detail is "bright color is a warning." Think about how to state that information in a complete sentence. Tell your partner.

Our first detail sentence will be, "They use their bright colors as a warning to predators."

Now I need to add information about their legs oozing a smelly liquid. This is additional information, so I'm going to include the word *also* in my sentence. Think for a moment. Ones, tell your partners a sentence about the smelly liquid using the word *also*. Twos, tell your partner if you think something about the sentence needs to be changed.

Our next sentence will be, "Ladybugs also ooze a green smelly liquid that makes their enemies run away."

Now we need one more sentence. This one will be about how ladybugs play dead. This will be our last sentence. Use the word *finally* in your sentence. Twos, think of a sentence and tell it to your partner. Ones, give feedback to your partner.

Our last detail sentence will be, "Finally, ladybugs pretend to be dead so their enemies leave them alone."

Almost there! I can copy my closing sentence from my outline. Let's read the whole paragraph together.

Ladybugs have many ways to defend themselves from their enemies. They use their bright colors as a warning to predators. Ladybugs also ooze a green smelly liquid that makes their enemies run away. Finally, ladybugs pretend to play dead so their enemies leave them alone. Ladybugs have many ways to stay safe.

Other Ways for Students to Respond to Text in Writing

At first, your students will participate orally while you do most of the writing. Over time, you can teach them to do the following with you and/or independently as they respond to text:

- Complete a sentence stem when responding to decodable text. "Sam was sad when _____."
- Write a retelling of a decodable story.
- Extend a decodable story by writing additional sentences.
- Write a paragraph that summarizes the main events in a decodable text.
- Write a summary of a nonfiction text using paragraph shrinking (see Chapter 8).
- Compare two characters using a Venn diagram. Use the diagram to write a paragraph comparing and contrasting the characters.
- Complete a graphic organizer that lists details from the beginning, middle, and end of a text. Use that information to write a paragraph.

 ## Key Things to Remember

- Writing about text improves reading comprehension.
- Students need to become automatic at handwriting and spelling so that their working memories are free to focus on composition.
- Teach students to write sentences and paragraphs in response to the text you read to and with them.

Free Resources

- Handwriting practice worksheets
- Spelling games
- Graphic organizers

Learn More

◆ Watch *The Writing Revolution: An Overview of the Hochman Method* on the IDA's YouTube channel. www.youtube.com/watch?v=kO4lRU9LPvc.

◆ Read *The Writing Revolution*, by Judith Hochman and Natalie Wexler.

Notes

1. Fitzgerald, J., & Shanahan, T. (2000). Reading and writing relations and their development. *Educational Psychologist, 35*(1), 39–50.

2. Moats, L. C. (2005). How spelling supports reading. *American Educator, 6* (12–22), 42.

3. Bangert-Drowns, R. L., Hurley, M. M., & Wilkinson, B. (2004). The effects of school-based writing-to-learn interventions on academic achievement: A meta-analysis. *Review of Educational Research, 74*(1), 29–58.

4. Graham, S., & Hebert, M. (2010). *Writing to read: Evidence for how writing can improve reading*. Carnegie Corporation of New York. https://www.carnegie.org/publications/writing-to-read-evidence-for-how-writing-can-improve-reading/.

5. Ibid.

6. Graham, S., MacArthur, C.A., & Hebert, M. (2018). *Best practices in writing instruction*. The Guilford Press.

7. Graham. S. (2006). Writing. In Alexander, P. A., & Winne, P. H. (Eds.), *Handbook of educational psychology* (457–478). Routledge.

8. Scardamalia, M., & Bereiter, C. (1986). Written composition. In Wittrock, M. (Ed.), *Handbook of research on teaching* (778–803). Macmillan.

9. Graham, S., Harris, K. R., & Santangelo, T. (2015). Research-based writing practices and the common core: Meta-analysis and meta-synthesis. *The Elementary School Journal, 115*(4), 498–522.

10. Ibid.

11. Rogers, L. A., & Graham, S. (2008). A meta-analysis of single subject design writing intervention research. *Journal of Educational Psychology, 100*(4), 879–906.

12. Beach, R., & Friedrich, T. (2006). Response to writing. In MacArthur, C. A., Graham, S., & Fitzgerald, J. (Eds.), *Handbook of writing research* (222–234). Guilford Press.

13. Van Cleave, W. (n.d.) *Handwriting in a modern world: Why it matters and what to do about it*. W. V. C. ED. https://www.wvced.com/wp-content/uploads/2023/08/2022-Handwriting-Modern-World.pdf.

14. Graham, S., & Miller, L. (1980). Handwriting research and practice: A unified approach. *Focus on Exceptional Children, 13*(2).

15. Graham, S., Harris, K. R., & Fink, B. (2000). Is handwriting causally related to learning to write? Treatment of handwriting problems in beginning writers. *Journal of Educational Psychology, 92*(4), 620.

16. Van Cleave, W. (n.d.)

17. King, D. H., & Leopold, K. K. (2016). *Learning print* (Student workbook). W. V. C. ED.

18. Hanna, P. R. (1966). *Phoneme-grapheme correspondences as cues to spelling improvement*. Stanford University School of Education.

19. Ouellette, G., & Sénéchal, M. (2017). Invented spelling in kindergarten as a predictor of reading and spelling in Grade 1: A new pathway to literacy, or just the same road, less known? *Developmental Psychology, 53*(1), 77–88.

CHAPTER 10

Dyslexia

As a classroom teacher, I had heard of dyslexia, but I didn't know much about it. I assumed that this specific learning disability was rare, too difficult for me to understand, and something I couldn't do anything about anyway. I was wrong on all three counts.

What Is Dyslexia?

According to the International Dyslexia Association (IDA):

> **Dyslexia** is a specific learning disability that is neurobiological in origin. It is characterized by difficulties with accurate and/or fluent word recognition and by poor spelling and decoding abilities. These difficulties typically result from a deficit in the phonological component of language that is often unexpected in relation to other cognitive abilities and the provision of effective classroom instruction. Secondary consequences may include problems in reading comprehension and reduced reading experience that can impede growth of vocabulary and background knowledge.[1]

The key thing to remember is that students with dyslexia have difficulty recognizing words.[2]

DYSLEXIA MYTHS

To better understand what dyslexia is, it's helpful to debunk common myths. Here is the truth behind seven common misconceptions.

> **Myth:** People with dyslexia see words backward.
> **Fact:** Dyslexia is not a vision problem.

One myth is that people with dyslexia read words backward. But dyslexia isn't a problem with the eyes; it's *neurobiological*. People with dyslexia have different brain activation patterns when reading.[3] (Spoiler alert! Reading intervention can change these patterns for the better.)

Since dyslexia is not a vision problem, research does not support the need for "dyslexia-friendly fonts"[4] or using colored overlays to improve reading rate or comprehension.[5]

> **Myth:** Dyslexia is so rare that regular classroom teachers don't need to understand it.
> **Fact:** Dyslexia is the most common learning disability.

Dyslexia is a spectrum disorder, which means that it can be mild, moderate, or severe. As for how prevalent dyslexia is in the general population, estimates vary; some are as high as 20 percent.[6] Because it's so common, all teachers should know how to recognize the characteristics and signs of dyslexia.

> **Myth:** Dyslexia can't be identified until third grade.
> **Fact:** Early screening is important.

It upsets me when a parent shares concerns about their child's reading delays, only to hear from a well-meaning friend that they should "just let him play! They all catch up by third grade anyway." This is precisely the wrong thing to say because it's *completely untrue*. The longer we wait to intervene, the harder it is for the student to catch up.[7]

Early screening is critical for two reasons. First, the sooner we identify a problem, the sooner we can connect students with reading interventions that can help them overcome their reading challenges. Second, the longer we wait to intervene, the more likely dyslexic children are to develop a negative self-worth and lose interest in reading.[8]

We should begin screening all children for reading difficulties at the start of kindergarten (see Chapter 11).

> **Myth:** All people with dyslexia have special gifts or talents.
> **Fact:** Being dyslexic does not guarantee a particular set of strengths.

Lyn Stone, a teacher, author, and mother of a daughter with dyslexia, writes, "To say that dyslexics are 'out of the box thinkers,' 'more creative,' 'good at design,' etc. is to place dangerous expectations on people already suffering. There is also no evidence whatsoever that this is true."[9]

> **Myth:** Students with dyslexia are lazy. They just need to work harder.
> **Fact:** Children with dyslexia are already working very hard.

One study found that children with dyslexia use nearly five times the brain area as their peers when performing a simple language task.[10]

> **Myth:** Children will outgrow dyslexia.
> **Fact:** Dyslexia never goes away.

Dyslexia is persistent and chronic. While intervention can and does help people with dyslexia learn to read and spell, anyone promoting a "cure" for dyslexia should not be trusted.

> **Myth:** Children with dyslexia will always be behind in reading and writing.
> **Fact:** When given proper instruction, many children with dyslexia succeed in school.

Hasbrouck writes that "we cannot cure dyslexia, but when we provide students with effective literacy learning environments and powerful instruction beginning in PreK, we can greatly influence their ability to read and write on grade level."[11]

Possible Signs of Dyslexia

Preschool
- Trouble learning common nursery rhymes
- Lack of interest in rhyming and other word play
- Trouble learning the letters of the alphabet, numbers, colors, and so on
- Mispronouncing familiar words (persistent baby talk)
- Failure to know the letters in one's name

Kindergarten and First Grade
- Inability to break words apart into syllables or phonemes
- Inability to remember letter-sound associations
- Reading errors that show no connection to the sounds of the letters
- Inability to sound out even simple CVC words
- Complaints about how hard reading is
- Has trouble with spelling
- Has difficulty recognizing common words
- History of reading problems in parents or siblings

Second Grade and Up
- Mispronunciation of long, unfamiliar, or complicated words
- General reluctance to read or write
- Persistent letter and number reversals
- Pausing or hesitating often when speaking
- Using imprecise language ("stuff" or "things" instead of the name of the object)
- Not being able to find the exact word, such as confusing words that sound alike (such as saying *tornado* instead of *volcano*)
- Trouble reading unknown words that must be sounded out
- Inability to read small function words (*that, in, of*)
- Omitting parts of words when reading
- Oral reading full of substitutions, omissions, and mispronunciations
- Reads very slowly with little expression
- Better able to understand words in context than in isolation
- Inability to finish tests on time
- Very poor spelling
- Difficulty remembering spoken instructions

- ◆ Messy handwriting
- ◆ Extreme difficulty learning foreign languages
- ◆ Lack of enjoyment in reading
- ◆ History of reading, spelling, and foreign-language learning problems among family members

Sources: Shaywitz, S. (2020). *Overcoming dyslexia*. Vintage Books. Hasbrouck, J. (2020). *Conquering dyslexia*. Benchmark Education.

WHEN TO SUSPECT DYSLEXIA

If a student has multiple, persistent signs of dyslexia and struggles with decoding and spelling despite effective reading instruction, it's time to suspect dyslexia.[12]

It's important to note that while the core problem with dyslexia is usually a phonological deficit, children with dyslexia often end up reading less than their peers. This leads to a lack of growth in vocabulary and background knowledge, which eventually hurts comprehension.[13]

If you suspect dyslexia, don't wait! Students in the bottom 20 percent in basic reading skills are likely to stay there unless something is done to help.

WHAT TO DO NEXT

While you can't diagnose dyslexia as a classroom teacher, you can use screening procedures to identify children who are at risk for reading failure. A screener is useful when it measures those skills that accurately predict whether a child is at risk for reading failure. According to research, a kindergarten screener should assess letter naming fluency, phonological awareness, and rapid naming or nonword repetition.[14] A first-grade screener should assess letter sound identification, phoneme segmentation, sound repetition, vocabulary, and word identification fluency.[15]

When a screener raises red flags, you can give more specific assessments to find out exactly what kind of help the child needs (I get into this more in Chapter 11).

If you suspect that a student has dyslexia, work with the students' parents to request a complete educational evaluation through the school district. If the parents are reluctant, let them know that the free evaluation will give you more information about their child's learning needs and help you better support them in the classroom.

Though the school evaluation will not diagnose dyslexia, it will provide a picture of the child's learning needs. After the evaluation is completed, a meeting will be held that might include the psychologist, a speech-language pathologist, a special education teacher, and a school counselor. Together, this team will discuss the next steps. Be forewarned: The evaluation process is slow. Work with your school and the child's parents to get the ball rolling as soon as possible.

Some parents may pursue an official diagnosis with a neuropsychologist or other professional at their own expense. School districts are required to consider such diagnoses and reports but are not required to accept them. Because diagnosing dyslexia is so complex, multiple assessments are needed. Some people are concerned that an early diagnosis will "label" a child and do more harm than good. In fact, early diagnosis is important because it allows interventions to begin as soon as possible.

Help for Dyslexia

Ready for some good news? Stone writes that "Dyslexic or not, the path to reading follows the same trajectory from human to human. The stages on that path are complex and vary in length, but their order is the same."[16] In other words, when you understand the science of reading, you're on the right path.

You know that oral language is the foundation for literacy. You know how to give explicit instruction in phonemic awareness, phonics, and spelling. You know strategies for developing fluency, vocabulary, and comprehension. You know how to give explicit, systematic, and cumulative instruction. You know the importance of scaffolding, repetition, and review.

The bottom line? *You have the knowledge you need.*

High-quality instruction will be enough to help the majority of your students reach or exceed grade-level benchmarks. However, even when master teachers provide quality instruction using an evidence-based curriculum, some students will still struggle. In addition to Tier 1 instruction (the instruction that you provide to all students), some students also need Tier 2 or Tier 3 intervention (see Chapter 11).

Whether or not intervention is provided at school, parents may choose to hire an outside tutor. No matter what intervention is given, it's essential that educators frequently monitor the child's progress so that adjustments can be made as needed (see Chapter 11).

ACCOMMODATIONS FOR STUDENTS WITH DYSLEXIA

According to the IDA, "accommodations are adjustments made to allow a student to demonstrate knowledge, skills, and abilities without lowering learning or performance expectations and without changing what is being measured."[17]

People with dyslexia will need accommodations throughout their school career.

People with dyslexia will need accommodations throughout their school career. If you have a student with dyslexia (or merely suspect it), consider implementing one or more of these accommodations.

- Post visual schedules.
- Seat the student close to you.
- Provide instructional aids such as an alphabet chart or spelling folder.
- Repeat directions as needed. Have the student repeat them back.
- Provide audio recordings of reading assignments.
- Teach the student to break assignments into smaller steps.
- Provide more opportunities for practice.
- Provide visual cues on assignments (such as arrows or highlighted instructions).
- Allow more time for reading, writing, and test-taking.
- Reduce distractions during independent work time.
- Provide opportunities for the student to talk about their learning.
- Teach your student how to use a graphic organizer to take notes.
- Emphasize daily review.

Key Things to Remember

- People with dyslexia have difficulty reading and spelling words.
- Early screening is important so that at-risk students receive intervention as soon as possible.
- Students with dyslexia need the same science of reading-based instruction as the rest of your students, but they may require more scaffolding, more repetition, and greater intensity of instruction.

Learn More

- Read *Conquering Dyslexia,* by Jan Hasbrouck.
- Print and read the IDA fact sheets. https://dyslexiaida.org/fact-sheets/.
- Watch "What is dyslexia?" a YouTube video by Kelli Sandman-Hurley. www.youtube.com/watch?v=zafiGBrFkRM.

Notes

1. International Dyslexia Association. (2022, November 12). *Definition of dyslexia*. https://dyslexiaida.org/definition-of-dyslexia/.
2. Kearns, D. M., Hancock, R., Hoeft, F., Pugh, K. R., & Frost, S. J. (2019). The neurobiology of dyslexia. *Teaching Exceptional Children*, *51*(3), 175–188.
3. Ibid.
4. Kuster, S. M., van Weerdenburg, M., Gompel, M., & Bosman, A. M. (2018). Dyslexie font does not benefit reading in children with or without dyslexia. *Annals of Dyslexia*, *68*, 25–42.
5. Henderson, L. M., Tsogka, N., & Snowling, M. J. (2013). Questioning the benefits that coloured overlays can have for reading in students with and without dyslexia. *Journal of Research in Special Educational Needs*, *13*(1), 57–65.
6. Hasbrouck, J. (2020). *Conquering dyslexia*. Benchmark Education.
7. O'Connor, R. E. (2014). *Teaching word recognition*. The Guilford Press.
8. Shaywitz, S. (2020). *Overcoming dyslexia*. Vintage Books.
9. Stone, L. (2019). *Reading for life*. Routledge, 133.
10. Schwarz, J. (1999, October 4). *Dyslexic children use nearly five times the brain area*. University of Washington. https://www.washington.edu/news/1999/10/04/dyslexic-children-use-nearly-five-times-the-brain-area/.
11. Hasbrouck, J. (2020), 27.
12. Ibid.
13. Moats, L. C., & Dakin, K. E. (2008). *Basic facts about dyslexia & other reading problems*. The International Dyslexia Association.
14. Catts, H. W., Nielsen, D. C., Bridges, M. S., Liu, Y. S., & Bontempo, D. E. (2015). Early identification of reading disabilities within an RTI framework. *Journal of Reading Disabilities*, *48*(3), 281–297.
15. Jenkins, J. R., & Johnson, E. (2008). *Universal screening for reading problems: Why and how should we do this*. RTI action network. http://www.rtinetwork.org/essential/assessment/screening/readingproblems.
16. Stone, L. (2019), 134.
17. International Dyslexia Association. (2020). *Accommodations for students with dyslexia*. https://dyslexiaida.org/accommodations-for-students-with-dyslexia/.

CHAPTER 11

Using MTSS to Reach All Readers

You know the science. You have the tools to apply it. You need just one thing more: a *system* that will help you determine what to teach, to whom, and when.

Many schools use the multi-tiered systems of support (MTSS) framework to find out what works to help all students learn. This chapter shows you how your school can use MTSS to prevent reading problems, minimize the need for intervention, and make sure that all your students have the instruction they need to succeed.

Multi-tiered Systems of Support (MTSS)

MTSS is an evidence-based framework for delivering high-quality, research-based instruction to all students. Successful implementation of MTSS requires three things:[1]

1. A collaborative problem-solving model
2. An assessment system
3. Tiers of instruction

A COLLABORATIVE PROBLEM-SOLVING MODEL

I admit that as a classroom teacher, I viewed myself as an island. I did my own thing, and the other teachers did theirs. While I often asked advice from the teacher next door, my problems were mine to solve.

With the collaborative problem-solving model (see Figure 11.1), teachers do not need to solve problems on their own. Instead, they work together with other teachers and staff to solve a problem that concerns an individual student, a class, a grade level, or even the whole school or district.

For example, a team could include the three second-grade teachers, the school psychologist, the Title 1 teacher, and the reading interventionist. They might meet to discuss what can be done to help a particular student who is still a nonreader in second grade. They might meet to plan how to help a second grade class in which 75 percent of students struggle with fluency. They might convene to discuss the grade's low performance on a yearly achievement test.

Collaborative problem-solving meetings should do the following:

- **Identify:** What's the problem?
- **Analyze:** Why is this problem happening?
- **Implement:** What should we do about it using the resources that we have?
- **Evaluate:** Is our plan working? (If not, we need to cycle back through the steps.)[2]

AN ASSESSMENT SYSTEM

MTSS utilizes a system of assessments.[3] Each type of assessment answers a different question (see Figure 11.2).

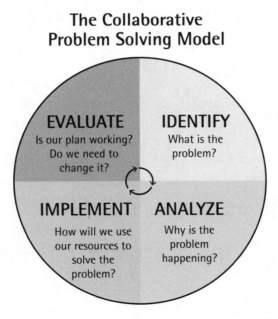

Figure 11.1   The collaborative problem-solving model.

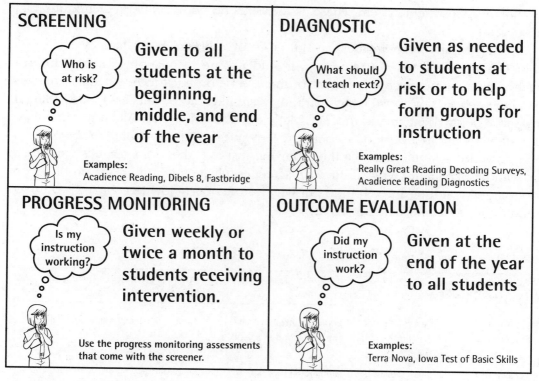

Figure 11.2 Four types of assessment.

Screening Assessments

Screening assessments (also called **universal screeners**) should be given to all students at the beginning, middle, and end of the school year. They should be brief (taking fewer than 10 minutes per student). A universal screener is predictive because it answers the questions, "Which students are on track to become adequate readers in the future? Which students are at risk for reading difficulty?"

Universal screeners should be standardized, reliable, and valid. A **standardized** assessment is given and scored the same way every time it is administered. An assessment is **reliable** if a student would achieve a similar score if they took a different version of the same test at a different time. A test is **valid** if it measures what it claims to measure.

The good news is that you can download universal screening materials for free. Examples of high-quality universal screeners include Acadience, Dibels 8, and FastBridge. Avoid assessments like running records and the Fountas & Pinnell

Benchmark Assessment system. These assessments do not reliably predict future reading success.

The universal screener assesses indicators of essential early literacy skills (see Table 11.1) and will tell you where your students are in relation to a **benchmark**, which is the minimum score required for them to be on track to be adequate readers. If students score at or above benchmark, they are likely to be successful at reading. If they score below benchmark, they are likely to have difficulties. When teachers have this data, they are in a position to both prevent and remediate reading problems.

A universal screener is like a thermometer. Just as a thermometer tells you you're sick without explaining why, a universal screener tells you that there's a problem, but it doesn't tell you the cause. To find out why a student is below benchmark, you need to administer a diagnostic assessment.

Table 11.1   Acadience Reading Universal Screening Measures

Measure	Essential Early Literacy Skills	When to Administer During the School Year
First Sound Fluency (FSF)	FSF assesses students' phonemic awareness by having them name the first sound in a spoken word.	Kindergarten: beginning, middle, end
Letter Name Fluency (LNF)	LNF assesses students' alphabet knowledge by seeing how accurately they can identify upper and lowercase letters in one minute.	Kindergarten: beginning, middle, end First Grade: beginning
Phoneme Segmentation Fluency (PSF)	PSF assesses students' phonemic awareness by having them name the phonemes in spoken words.	Kindergarten: middle, end First Grade: beginning
Nonsense Word Fluency (NWF)	NWF tests students' understanding of the alphabetic principle and basic phonics by having them sound out nonsense consonant-vowel-consonant (CVC) words.	Kindergarten: middle, end First Grade: beginning, middle, end Second Grade: beginning
Oral Reading Fluency (ORF)	ORF measures advanced phonics skills, fluency, and comprehension by having students read three grade-level passages for one minute each. After each reading, students have one minute to retell the passage.	First Grade: middle, end Second Grade: beginning, middle, end Third Grade: beginning, middle, end Fourth Grade: beginning, middle, end Fifth Grade: beginning, middle, end Sixth Grade: beginning, middle, end
Maze	Maze assesses reading comprehension by having students read a passage with missing words. Students choose from three options for each missing word.	Third Grade: beginning, middle, end Fourth Grade: beginning, middle, end Fifth Grade: beginning, middle, end Sixth Grade: beginning, middle, end

Diagnostic Assessments

Diagnostic assessments let you drill down to figure out what's causing a low score on the screener. They answer the questions, "Why is this particular student at risk? What do I need to teach next?" For example, if your student scores below benchmark on the universal screener's Nonsense Word Fluency (NWF) measure, they have difficulty with letter sounds and blending. You give the student a phonics diagnostic assessment (see Figure 11.3) to figure out the specific problem. From the diagnostic assessment you learn that this student knows consonant sounds but mixes up short vowel sounds. The focus of your instruction will be short vowel sounds and blending consonant-vowel-consonant (CVC) words.

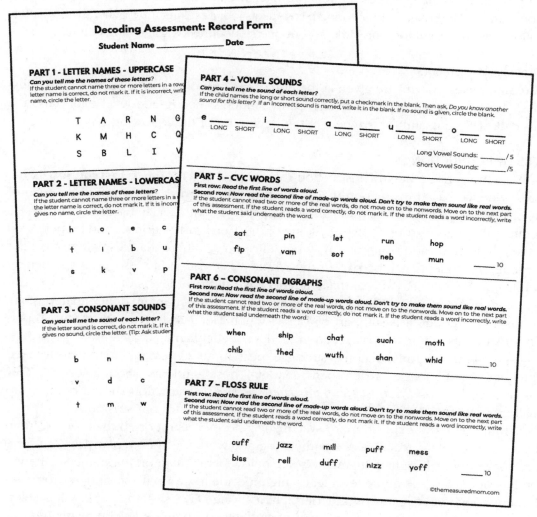

Figure 11.3 An example of a phonics diagnostic assessment.

Progress Monitoring Assessments

After you begin instruction (based on the results of the screener and diagnostic assessments), you should start to administer **progress monitoring assessments** for students receiving interventions. Use the progress monitoring assessments that come with your universal screener.

The purpose of doing progress monitoring is to answer the question, "Is my instruction working?" For example, imagine that a group of kindergartners scores well below benchmark on Phoneme Segmentation Fluency (PSF). To bring them up to benchmark, the intervention teacher meets with these students three times a week to do oral segmenting with CVC words. Each week, the teacher quickly administers a PSF assessment for each student and plots each student's scores on a graph. After five weeks, one student is not showing improvement. The progress monitoring has done its job; it's telling the teacher that this intervention was successful for four students, but one student needs something different.

Outcome Assessments

Outcome assessments are given at the end of the school year. They answer the questions, "Was my instruction effective? Did my students meet grade level expectations?" This data will be useful for teachers at the beginning of the following school year.

TIERS OF INSTRUCTION

MTSS includes three tiers of instruction (see Figure 11.4). **Tier 1 instruction** is the core, evidence-based instruction that is given to all students. This should be a total of 90–120 minutes daily. A common misconception is that Tier 1 instruction is always taught to the whole group; however, some of the Tier 1 instruction should be delivered to the whole class, and some of it may be delivered to differentiated small groups. For example, *all* students will be part of the whole class read-aloud lesson. But screening and diagnostic data may reveal that students have different levels of phonemic awareness and phonics skills. They might receive this instruction in differentiated small groups, even though it is still part of Tier 1. When Tier 1 instruction is strong, 80 percent of students will reach or exceed grade level benchmarks.

Even when Tier 1 instruction is strong, expect about 20 percent of students to need additional instruction to reach benchmarks. These students should receive **Tier 2 instruction** *in addition to Tier 1 instruction*. Tier 2 instruction should be given to small groups of students, 3–5 days a week, for 30–45 minutes per session. The instruction should be more explicit, more systematic, and more supported than Tier 1. In an ideal situation, all the teachers of a particular grade work together to plan Tier 2 instruction. For example, if eight first graders score below benchmark on Phoneme Segmentation Fluency (PSF), the grade level team might decide to group these students for extra phonemic awareness instruction in Tier 2. In a strong MTSS system, Tier 2 will accelerate learning and catch about 15 percent of students up to grade level benchmarks.

Three Tiers of Instruction

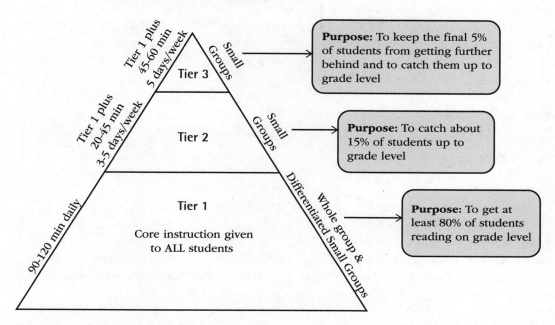

Figure 11.4 Three tiers of instruction.

For a small number of students (about 5 percent), even Tier 2 will not be enough. These students should continue to receive Tier 1 instruction, but teachers should replace Tier 2 instruction with Tier 3 instruction. **Tier 3 instruction** is even more intensive than Tier 2. It should be given daily to groups of 1–3 students for 45–60 minutes per session.

If you're looking at Figure 11.4 and wondering where on Earth you'll find all that instruction time, know that Tier 2 and Tier 3 interventions are usually given by other staff—often a reading interventionist or special education teacher. Work together with that teacher to determine the best time for these students to leave your classroom, but make sure they continue to receive Tier 1 reading instruction.

If you lack support staff, try to schedule a 20-minute block every day to provide Tier 2 instruction to those who need it. The rest of the class may work at centers or read independently while you meet with the students who need extra instruction.

Delivering Tier 1 Instruction

Establishing and implementing MTSS within a school takes time. The perfect place to start is to *get Tier 1 instruction right* so that your school reduces the number of students who need Tier 2 or Tier 3 instruction. Think of Tier 1 instruction as the primary way to prevent reading failure.[4] Quality Tier 1 instruction is given to all students for

90–120 minutes each day using an evidence-based core program. Teachers differentiate instruction based on universal screening data.

Use the chart in Table 11.2 to evaluate your current Tier 1 program and alternatives. If you find that portions of your required program do not align with the science of reading, take heart! You now have the knowledge and skills to make adjustments to meet the needs of your students.

Table 11.2   Program Evaluation Chart

Look for	Avoid
Explicit instruction in phonemic awareness	A focus on larger units (rhyming and syllables) in kindergarten rather than an immediate focus on phonemic awareness
Cumulative review built into the program	Lack of attention to review
Explicit instruction in phonics following a systematic scope and sequence	Phonics skills taught in mini-lessons without a scope and sequence
Letter-sound correspondences taught in sets so that students can start decoding CVC words early in kindergarten	A letter-of-the-week approach that doesn't allow children to start decoding until late in the kindergarten year
Spelling instruction aligned with newly taught phonics skills in the early grades	Lack of attention to spelling or spelling words that are not phonetically related
Decodable texts that align with phonics skills that have been taught	Predictable, leveled texts that require beginners to use pictures and context to identify words
Irregular high-frequency words taught with an emphasis on regular and irregular sound-spellings within the words	Memorization of "sight words" as whole words
A focus on automaticity with letter names and sounds before building text-level fluency	A focus on shared reading of predictable text as the initial fluency-building strategy
Fluency building which includes modeling, oral and repeated reading, and feedback	Fluency building that is focused more on rate than automaticity and accuracy
Fiction and nonfiction interactive read-alouds through which students build oral language, vocabulary, and knowledge	Read-alouds that are primarily simple stories which do not challenge students or build knowledge
Teacher scaffolding of complex, knowledge-building text so all students have access to grade-level material	Small group instruction in which students read text at their instructional level and long periods of silent reading in which students read text at their independent level
A text-first approach in which texts are chosen based on their merits, and teachers use strategies to help students understand and remember the information	A strategies-first approach in which different texts are chosen to help students practice specific comprehension strategies
Assessments that help teachers differentiate instruction and monitor progress	Lack of meaningful assessments

DIFFERENTIATING IN TIER 1

As a balanced literacy teacher, I believed that the best way to differentiate was to make a 60-minute guided reading block the heart of my instruction. Guided reading is small-group instruction in which children read a teacher-selected text at their instructional reading level. According to Fountas and Pinnell, "in guided reading, you meet students where they are and lead them forward with intention and precision."[5] As nice as it sounds, this approach is not backed by research.

While grouping students by *skill* is powerful, grouping students by *level* is not. As I mentioned before, the problem with the guided reading levels is that they rest on the theory of three-cueing, which is unsupported by research. (The books at the early levels *require* students to use three-cueing to "read" them!) Furthermore, readers don't all fall into a single level. What they can read is influenced by their interests and background knowledge.[6] Finally, perhaps the worst feature of guided reading levels is that they don't give us any useful information. I knew I wanted my students at level E to move to level F, but what would it take to get them there? I had no idea.

This is a hard pill to swallow, but there is no evidence that students learn better when grouped at their instructional levels. On the other hand, *skills-based* small group instruction is powerful and effective when done right!

Many curricula expect teachers to teach a whole class phonemic awareness and phonics lesson and *then* differentiate. But in my opinion, there's a problem with this model when your data shows that students have different needs. As Linda Diamond points out, "differentiated instruction happens only *after* students who still need additional time and intensity have already experienced failure or *after* students who previously mastered the specific decoding skills taught to the whole class experience boredom."[7] Avoid these pitfalls by differentiating with small groups right from the start. Students who are below benchmark in foundational skills will get targeted instruction in Tier 1 *and* an extra dose in Tier 2; when given the right kind and amount of instruction, it's more likely that students will reach or exceed grade-level benchmarks.

WHY DIFFERENTIATE TIER 1 INSTRUCTION IN FOUNDATIONAL SKILLS?

There are four primary reasons why it's important to differentiate Tier 1 instruction in foundational skills. The benefits of teaching small groups include:

1. **Focus on mastery:** Grouping students for instruction in word recognition allows teachers to focus on mastery of new concepts before moving on.[8] This is simply not possible when teaching a new sound-spelling to a whole class because students require different amounts of repetition and practice to achieve mastery.
2. **Immediate and individual feedback:** Effective feedback is an important influence on student learning,[9] and the small group approach allows teachers to provide immediate corrective feedback to individual students.

3. **Improved phonemic awareness and phonics skills:** Students with reading difficulties learn phonemic awareness and phonics best when they are taught in small groups.[10]

4. **Personalized instruction:** When teaching small groups, teachers can more easily tailor their instruction to the students in front of them. They may offer more repetitions, adjust their pacing, and provide encouragement to individual students more easily than they can when teaching the whole group.[11]

Targeted small group instruction is important. But for every moment that students are *not* meeting with you during small groups, they are missing out on direct and explicit instruction. For that reason, you will want to minimize the time that students do not spend with an instructor. You can make the most of your time by working with other teachers and staff using the Walk to Read model.

With the Walk to Read model, all the teachers in a particular grade level work to use screening and diagnostic data to group students *across classrooms*. They meet with the reading interventionist, Title 1 teacher, or other support staff to plan differentiated small groups. Then students walk to a different classroom for small group instruction in foundational skills. The goal is to have students spend 30 minutes or fewer in centers.

Walk to Read: Example #1

In this example, the school has three first-grade teachers. They use screener and diagnostic data to group their first graders into eight groups based on their needs. The classroom teachers, reading interventionist, and Title 1 teacher work together to teach all students during Tier 1 instruction.

	Reading Interventionist	Title 1 Teacher	First-Grade Teacher A	First-Grade Teacher B	First-Grade Teacher C
9:00–9:20 AM	Group 1: Phonemic awareness and letter sounds	Group 2: Phonemic awareness and CVC words	Group 3: CVC and CVCC (consonant-vowel-consonant-consonant) words	Group 5: Vowel teams	Group 7: Diphthongs
9:20–9:40 AM			Group 4: CVCE words (consonant-vowel-consonant words that end in a silent e)	Group 6: Advanced vowel teams	Group 8: Multisyllabic words

Walk to Read: Example #2

In this example, a single teacher has used data to group students into four groups. The teacher partners with the Title 1 teacher to teach four small groups during an hour of Tier 1 instruction.

	Title 1 Teacher	First-Grade Teacher
9:00–9:30 AM	Group 1: Phonemic awareness and letter sounds	Group 3: CVCE words
9:30–10:00 AM	Group 2: Phonemic awareness and CVC words	Group 4: Vowel teams

Walk to Read is ideal, but it may be challenging for you if you teach in a small school or have limited staff. If you are on your own, I recommend limiting the number of groups to no more than three or four. Meet with three groups per day for 20 minutes each, always making sure to start by meeting with the lowest-performing students (who will meet with you every day). If possible, enlist a volunteer to oversee students who are working independently so you can give your full attention to students at the small group table. Finally, meet with your administrator to get additional support. Your goal should be to reduce the amount of time students are not meeting with a trained adult.

When students are not meeting with the teacher, they work at centers. When choosing literacy center work, remember these guidelines:

- ◆ Choose activities that will help students practice what they already know (not new content). This will help them become automatic with these skills.
- ◆ When possible, choose activities with a consistent format so that students don't need to learn a new set of directions each time. This will reduce cognitive load so their brains are free to focus on the skill itself.
- ◆ Provide activities that students can complete in pairs so they can keep each other on task.

Use the QR code at the end of this chapter to find specific literacy center ideas on my website.

WHOLE-GROUP PHONICS LESSONS

My personal opinion is that the ideal way to accelerate the growth of all students, including those who are below or above grade level, is to differentiate Tier 1 foundational skills instruction based on diagnostic data and to give additional Tier 2 or Tier 3 instruction to those who need it. However, many teachers believe that all students should get access to grade-level content through a whole-class phonics lesson. Other teachers would like to follow the Walk to Read model, but they lack the personnel to carry it out.

If you choose to give whole-group phonics lessons, make sure you differentiate within each lesson. Students who are below grade level should receive fewer practice activities. In addition, they can listen to an audio recording of the decodable text *before* the lesson. Students who are above level can receive challenge words during blending and dictation, and after reading the new decodable text they can move on to more challenging text.

Unless the entire class is at the same skill level, it is vital that you reserve time to meet with small groups after the whole-group phonics lesson. These fast-paced, targeted lessons should fill gaps for students who are below grade level, help grade-level students whose progress is stalling, and provide those who are above grade level with instruction in skills further along the scope and sequence.

For more about differentiating whole-group phonics lessons, see Wiley Blevins' book *Differentiating Phonics Instruction for Maximum Impact*.

WHEN TO USE WHOLE-GROUP INSTRUCTION

Whether or not you teach a whole-group phonics lesson, I recommend whole-group instruction when building oral language, knowledge, vocabulary, and reading comprehension in Tier 1.

When your students understand the basic code (usually by the beginning of second grade), they are ready to read complex texts with your support. A complex text is one that is at or above grade level. Even if students can't read the text on their own, you can scaffold the reading so that it's accessible to everyone. Students in second grade and above benefit from scaffolding and support when reading challenging texts.[12]

Ways to Scaffold the Reading of a Challenging Text[13]
- Build background knowledge before reading.
- Have students read a simpler text on the same topic before reading the complex text.
- Pre-teach challenging vocabulary.
- Before the group lesson, have students read along with a recording.
- Ask questions after students read short portions of the text.
- Show your students how to break down long and complicated sentences so they understand them.
- Have students read the text in pairs.
- Have less proficient readers read the text with the teacher before meeting with the group.
- Help students use a graphic organizer during or after the reading.
- Teach students to ask and answer questions as they read.

Designing Your Daily Schedule

Use the following sample reading block as a starting point for designing your schedule. Adjust times as needed based on your assessment results.

Sample Reading Block for Kindergarten through Third Grade

Block	Grouping	What It Looks Like	Skills Addressed
Morning Message or Question of the Day 5 minutes *(K–1 only)*	Whole group	The teacher and students discuss and read a pre-written message or answer a question posed to the class.	Oral language, concepts of print, encoding.
Word Work & Literacy Centers 60 minutes	Differentiated small groups (20–30 minutes per group); when possible, teachers group students across the grade level so each teacher teaches no more than 2 groups OR Differentiated whole group (30–40 minutes) followed by small group instruction	Phonics lesson routine • Review • Phonemic awareness • New phonics skill • Handwriting practice • Blending practice • Word chains • High-frequency words • Spelling dictation • Decodable-text reading and response Pre-readers may focus on phonemic awareness and letter sounds. Readers who have mastered basic phonics may have a morphology lesson.	Phonemic awareness, decoding, encoding, high-frequency words, handwriting When not meeting with the teacher, literacy centers allow students to practice previously learned skills to automaticity.
Interactive read-aloud 20–30 minutes	Whole group	The teacher reads a fiction or nonfiction text, stopping to build background knowledge, teach vocabulary, and teach comprehension strategies. Students respond orally and/or in writing.	Comprehension, vocabulary, oral language, writing

(continued)

Block	Grouping	What It Looks Like	Skills Addressed
Partner reading 10–20 minutes	Pairs assigned by the teacher	Students partner read decodable text, shared reading texts, scripts, or other text both readers can read. Partners offer each other feedback while the teacher circulates to offer support. Pre-readers may work on automaticity with letters and sounds.	Fluency, decoding, comprehension
Shared reading of complex text 10–20 minutes	Whole group with scaffolding so all students can access grade-level text	The teacher leads the reading of a grade-level (or above) text. In kindergarten and early first grade, the teacher will do most of the reading. As students move into second and third grade, they will read the text with appropriate scaffolding.	Concepts of print, oral language comprehension, vocabulary, decoding, high-frequency words, reading comprehension
Written response 10–20 minutes	Whole group with scaffolding	The teacher explicitly teaches an aspect of syntax or composition and teaches students to participate according to their stage of development.	Syntax, vocabulary, encoding, comprehension

 ## Key Things to Remember

- MTSS is the framework for delivering high-quality, research-based instruction to all students.
- All students receive Tier 1 instruction. While instruction in oral language, knowledge, vocabulary, and reading comprehension can be delivered to the whole group, differentiated small groups are a powerful and efficient way to teach foundational skills.

◆ Even with high-quality Tier 1 instruction, some students will not reach grade-level benchmarks. They should continue to receive Tier 1 instruction while also receiving Tier 2 instruction. If they still do not make progress, teachers should replace Tier 2 instruction with more intensive Tier 3 instruction.

Free Resources

◆ Assessment flow charts
◆ List of possible interventions
◆ Ideas for science of reading-aligned literacy centers

www.themeasuredmom.com/bookresources/

Learn More

◆ Read Margaret Goldberg's article about a school's success with the Walk to Read model: https://www.readingrockets.org/blogs/right-to-read/differentiation-done-right-how-walk-read-works.
◆ Watch The Reading League's short video about MTSS with Dr. Stephanie Stollar. www.youtube.com/watch?v=oNtXKzcO6bs.
◆ Watch the Reading League Wisconsin's video with Dr. Stephanie Stollar: Tier 1 instruction is risk reduction. www.youtube.com/watch?v=0zmgVT-Tufk&t=2421s.
◆ Read *Differentiating Phonics Instruction for Maximum Impact* by Wiley Blevins.

Notes

1. Stollar, S. (2023). *MTSS: The framework for implementing the science of reading.* [Online course]. Reading Science Academy. https://www.readingscienceacademy.com/mtsssalespage.
2. Ibid.
3. Stollar, S. (2022). *Schoolwide system and four purposes of assessment.* [Course lecture]. Reading Science Academy.

4. The Reading League Wisconsin. (2023, September 12). *Tier 1 instruction is risk reduction: With Dr. Stephanie Stollar.* [Video]. YouTube. https://www.youtube.com/watch?v=0zmgVT-Tufk.

5. Fountas, I., & Pinnell, G. S. (2019, January 8). *What is guided reading?* Fountas and Pinnell Literacy. https://fpblog.fountasandpinnell.com/what-is-guided-reading.

6. Recht, D. R., & Leslie, L. (1988). Effect of prior knowledge on good and poor readers' memory of text. *Journal of Educational Psychology, 80*(1), 16–20.

7. Diamond, L. (2023). *Small-group reading instruction and mastery learning: The missing practices for effective and equitable foundational skills instruction.* Center for the Collaborative Classroom. https://info.collaborativeclassroom.org/small-group-reading-instruction-and-mastery-learning-white-paper.

8. Kulik, C. L. C., Kulik, J. A., & Bangert-Drowns, R. L. (1990). Effectiveness of mastery learning programs: A meta-analysis. *Review of Educational Research, 60*(2), 265–299.

9. Hattie, J., & Timperley, H. (2007). The power of feedback. *Review of Educational Research, 77*(1), 81–112.

10. Foorman, B. R., & Torgesen, J. (2001). Critical elements of classroom and small-group instruction promote reading success in all children. *Learning Disabilities Research & Practice, 16*(4), 203–212.

11. Diamond, L. (2023).

12. Morgan, A., Wilcox, B. R., & Eldredge, J. L. (2000). Effect of difficulty levels on second-grade delayed readers using dyad reading. *The Journal of Educational Research, 94*(2), 113–119.
    Brown, L. T., Mohr, K. A., Wilcox, B. R., & Barrett, T. S. (2018). The effects of dyad reading and text difficulty on third-graders' reading achievement. *The Journal of Educational Research, 111*(5), 541–553.

13. Shanahan, T. (2020, June 27). *Eight ways to help kids read complex text.* Shanahan on literacy. https://www.shanahanonliteracy.com/blog/eight-ways-to-help-kids-read-complex-text.

Conclusion

My hope is that this book has demystified the science of reading and given you a clear path forward. I hope that you will use the "Learn More" resources to deepen your understanding. I pray that the accompanying printables will delight your students and simplify your teaching life.

Most of all, I want to thank you. Thank you for your dedication to the teaching profession. Thank you for the unremitting love you have for your students. Thank you for your commitment to reach all readers. I'm cheering you on!

Glossary

academic vocabulary   words that are traditionally used in academic text and conversation

alliteration   the repetition of the initial sound in two or more words

alphabetic principle   the understanding that written language is a code in which letters and letter combinations represent phonemes

analogy phonics   phonics instruction in which students are taught to use their knowledge of word families to identify unfamiliar words

analytic phonics   phonics instruction in which students are taught to analyze letter-sound relationships in whole words without practicing sounds in isolation

automaticity   a behavior that can be performed with little attention or conscious awareness

background knowledge   all the knowledge a reader brings to the reading task

balanced literacy   an attempt to end the reading wars by taking the best from the whole language and phonics approaches; phonics is typically taught unsystematically

benchmark   the minimum score required for students to be on track to become adequate readers

blending   the stringing of letter sounds together to decode a word

bound morphemes   a morpheme that cannot stand alone but is used to form a family of words

choral reading   a practice in which the teacher reads aloud in unison with the whole class or a small group

clause   a complete thought that contains a subject and a predicate

cognitive load   the amount of information working memory can hold at one time

cohesive tie   a generic word or phrase that links different parts of a sentence or one sentence to another

complex sentence   a sentence with an independent clause and at least one dependent clause

compound sentence   a sentence consisting of two independent clauses that are joined by a coordinating conjunction

compound-complex sentence   a sentence consisting of two independent clauses and one or more dependent clauses

comprehension   the process of extracting and constructing meaning through interaction with written language

comprehension monitoring   a process in which students determine whether or not they understand what they are reading

concepts of print   basic understandings of the function and purpose of print

consonant blend   two or three consonant letters at the beginning or end of a word whose sounds seem to blend together; also called a *consonant cluster*

consonant digraph   a combination of two consonant letters that represent a single phoneme

consonant phoneme   a closed speech sound in which the breath is at least partly obstructed by the lips, teeth, and/or tongue

consonant trigraph   three letters that represent a single consonant phoneme

context clues   words, phrases, and sentences surrounding a word that readers may use to predict words and their meanings

continuant   a speech sound that can be sustained as long as breath lasts

converging evidence   when different and independent sources support a single conclusion

decodable text   a sentence, passage, or book in which a majority of the words can be sounded out based on the sound-spellings the reader has been taught

dependent (subordinate) clause   a clause that begins with a conjunction or relative pronoun and cannot stand alone

derivational suffix   a suffix that changes the meaning of a word and may also change its part of speech

diagnostic assessment   an assessment that is used to identify a child's specific strengths and weaknesses in a particular area

diphthong   a vowel phoneme in which one vowel sound glides into another

dyslexia   a specific learning disability that causes difficulty in recognizing and spelling words

echo reading   when the teacher reads a portion of the text aloud and students follow by reading the text in unison

effect size   a way of measuring the size of the difference between two groups: the students who received the intervention and those who did not

embedded phonics   phonics instruction in which phonics is taught on an as-needed basis without using a scope and sequence

etymology   the study of the history and origin of words

evidence-based practices   teaching methods, based on research, that have been proven to work in a controlled setting

explicit instruction   lesson design and delivery that is direct, engaging, and systematic

expository text   text that gives information

feedback   any response to a student's performance or behavior

fluency   the ability to read a text accurately, at an appropriate rate, and with suitable expression

free morpheme   a base word or root that can exist as a word all on its own

grapheme   a single letter or group of letters that represent a phoneme

high-frequency word   a word that occurs frequently in text

independent clause   a clause with a subject and predicate that can stand alone as a complete sentence

inference   a conclusion the reader reaches based on evidence

inflectional suffix   a suffix that combines with a base word to show tense, number, or mood, without changing the basic meaning of the word

interleaving   when teachers layer the study of related topics, rather than engaging in massed repetition of a single topic

invented spelling   when students represent sounds in writing based on their limited letter-sound knowledge

leveled books   books that are assigned a level based on print features, text structure, content, sentence complexity, word count, word frequency, and other factors

long-term memory   the information that is learned and stored semipermanently for future retrieval

mental model (situation model)   the reader's overall representation of the meaning of a text

meta-analysis   a statistical analysis that combines the results of multiple independent studies

minimal pair   a pair of words that differ by a single phoneme

morpheme   the smallest meaningful unit in a word

morphological awareness   the ability to identify morphemes in words

morphology   the study of morphemes and how they're combined to make words

morphophonemic   a code that represents both sound and meaning

MTSS (multi-tiered systems of support)   an evidence-based framework for delivering high-quality, research-based instruction to all students

narrative text   text that tells a story or describes a series of events

onset   the part of a syllable before the vowel (not all syllables have onsets)

oral language   the complex system through which we use spoken words to communicate

orthographic mapping   the mental process of storing words in memory for future, instant retrieval

orthographic memory   a memory for how sounds are represented in language

outcome assessment   an assessment tool that is used to measure the overall effectiveness of reading instruction

paired-associate learning   when a person is asked to associate one symbol or word with another; refers to an approach in which children are taught the printed letter while saying its name and sound

phoneme   The smallest unit of speech sound within a word that can distinguish one word from another

phoneme blending   combining phonemes to make a word

phoneme isolation   identifying individual phonemes in words

phoneme manipulation   adding, deleting, or substituting phonemes

phoneme segmentation   breaking a word apart into its phonemes

phonemic awareness   The conscious awareness of individual speech sounds in spoken words

phonics   a method of instruction that teaches students the relationships between letters and sounds and how to use those relationships to read and spell words

phonological awareness   the awareness of sound structures in spoken words

phonological sensitivity skills   an awareness of sounds larger than phonemes (syllables, onsets, and rimes)

phonology   the study of how we distinguish, order, and say sounds in words

phrase   a group of words that serves as a grammatical unit but cannot stand alone as a complete sentence

pragmatics   a system of rules and conventions for using language in social settings

prefix   a word part attached to the beginning of a base word or root

print referencing   when an adult directs children's attention to features of written language

progress monitoring assessment   an assessment that is used to determine whether or not students are making adequate progress; may be given weekly or every couple of weeks

r-controlled vowel   a vowel that comes immediately before /r/ so that the /r/ affects its pronunciation

reading comprehension strategy   a deliberate mental action that is taught to students to improve reading comprehension

research-based practices   teaching methods based on what we know from research

retrieval practice   when students practice remembering information

rime   the string of letters in a syllable that begins with the vowel

scaffolding   high levels of guidance and support that are gradually reduced as students learn to perform tasks on their own

schwa   a vowel phoneme that occurs in unstressed syllables and sounds like a short u or short i

science of learning   a body of research related to how students learn and how they should be taught

science of reading   a body of research about reading and issues related to reading and writing

screening assessment (universal screener)   an assessment that is given to all students at the beginning, middle, and end of the year to identify students that may be at risk for reading difficulty

semantics   the study of the meaning of words and phrases

sentence anagram   an activity in which students unscramble words and phrases to build a complete sentence

set for variability   a strategy that a reader uses to correct a pronunciation error to arrive at the proper pronunciation of a word

sight words   words that one recognizes instantly without needing to sound out or guess

simple sentence   a sentence that consists of a single independent clause

sound wall   a visual reference which displays phonemes by manner and/or place of articulation along with the graphemes that spell each one

spacing   engaging in retrieval practice multiple times, over time

statistical significance   when the results of an intervention aren't due to chance alone

stop   a consonant phoneme that cannot be sustained

story grammar   the basic structure of a narrative text (setting, characters, problem, plot, solution, theme)

structured literacy   an approach to teaching reading which provides explicit and systematic instruction in phonology, sound-symbol relationships, syllables, syntax, semantics, and morphology

suffix   a word part attached to the end of a base word or root

syllable   a spoken or written unit that has a single vowel sound

syntactic awareness   the ability to keep track of the order of words and the relationships between them while speaking, reading, and writing

syntax   the system of rules governing word order and how phrases and clauses combine to create well-formed sentences

synthetic phonics   phonics instruction in which students are taught to sound out words from left to right

text structure   how an author organizes a text

three-cueing (also called *MSV*)   a model of reading that says that reading involves gaining meaning from print using context or pictures (meaning), the structure of the sentence (syntax), and the letters on the page (visual); the theory is foundational to whole language and balanced literacy, but is not based on research

unvoiced phoneme   phoneme that does not engage the vocal cords

vocabulary   the knowledge of words and their meanings

voiced phoneme   phoneme that is produced with engaged vocal cords

vowel phoneme   open speech sound which is not a consonant phoneme

vowel team   two or more letters that represent a single vowel phoneme

whole language   a method of teaching reading based on the philosophy that learning to read is as natural as learning to speak; decoding is deemphasized, and children are taught to recognize whole pieces of language

whole word method   a method of teaching reading in which words are taught as individual units based on shape

word awareness   the ability to separate a spoken sentence into words

word building   when students are given a set of grapheme tiles and asked to build particular words using sound-spellings they've been taught; the list of words is called a word chain or word ladder

working memory   the small amount of information that can be held in the mind while working through a problem

Index